Lauren Brill

UNSEAL YOUR SUPERPOWERS

Letters To Inspire The Hero Within You

Copyright © 2023 by Lauren Brill Media All rights reserved.

No part of this publications may be reproduced, distributed, or transmitted in any form or by any means, including photocopying, recording, or other electronic or mechanical methods, without the prior written permission of the author, except as permitted by U.S. copyright law. For permission requests, contact lauren@theunsealed.com.

Book Cover by Marija Džafo

Illustrations and Interior design by Larissa Fleury

Creative Consultant: Saga Foss

Cover Photos Courtesy of Lauren Brill, Daniel Kantrowitz, Luis Moros, Kendra McKool Photography, Haley Jordan, Gabriella Kreuz, Pat Michalik, and Eric LeGrand.

Hard Cover: 979-8-9888582-6-3

Paperback: 979-8-9888582-4-9

E-Book: 979-8-9888582-5-6

www.theunsealed.com

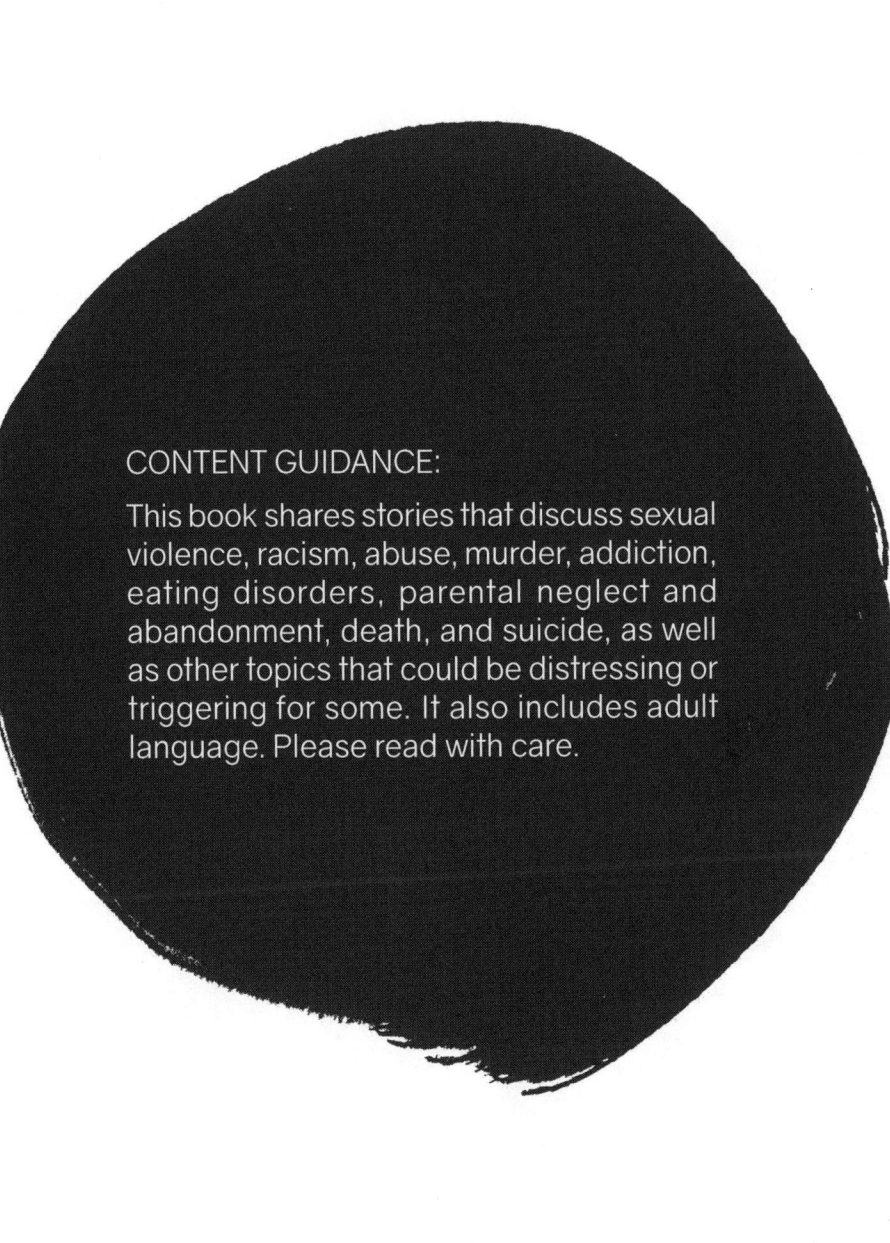

CONTENT GUIDANCE:

This book shares stories that discuss sexual violence, racism, abuse, murder, addiction, eating disorders, parental neglect and abandonment, death, and suicide, as well as other topics that could be distressing or triggering for some. It also includes adult language. Please read with care.

TABLE OF CONTENTS

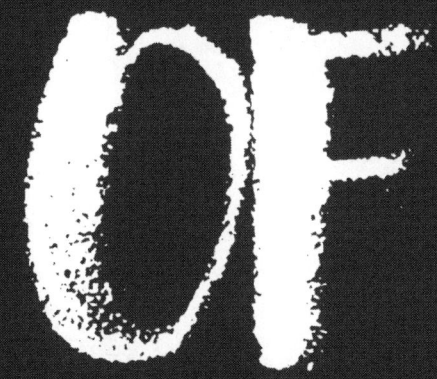

INTRODUCTION - How A Dark Secret Started A Beautiful Journey Lauren Brill 21

OVERCOMING ADVERSITY AND REALIZING YOUR DREAMS 34

Your Mindset Is Everything

What I Learned About Luck From Surviving A Plane Crash Adir Freilich 39

To The Dreamers, Not Everyone Will See Your Vision Trey Moe 43

How Hope Helped Me Survive 16 Years Of Wrongful Imprisonment Jeffrey Deskovic 48

How My Journey Can Teach You How To Unlock Your Dreams Leonard Marshall 55

How One Pitch Changed My Career And One Person Turned It Back Around Mark Wohlers 59

Humble Beginnings

I Was A Homeless And Hungry Child Until These Miracles Came Into My Life Christopher Rivero 66

To Struggling Single Moms, This Is How I Found My Way Angela Dennis 74

If You Listen To This Advice, You Won't Spend Two Decades In Prison Halim Flowers 78

To Young Immigrants, Here Is How I Am Reaching My Goals Luis F. Moros 85

To The Executives Who Didn't See My Talent, This Is What Happened Alex Chisholm 90

Abandoned At Birth, This Is How I Have Been Able To Thrive In Life Angel Thomas 94

How I Made It With The Odds Heavily Stacked Against Me Vaughn McKoy 100

To Students At Ginn Academy, This Is Why It Is So Important That You Listen Xavier Dowdell-Fullbright 101

Lauren's Thoughts - Pursue What You Want Like It's Destined To Be Yours Lauren Brill 114

LOSS 119

Loss Of A Parent

Dear Dear, It's Me Antoine Mason 123

This Is How I Rediscovered My Purpose After I Lost My Dad Tiffany Kay 127

How I Am No Longer Allowing What Hurt Me To Hold Me Back Alaina Coates 131

Mom And Dad, Here Is What I Want You To Know About The Moment You Missed Phil Handy 136

Mom, I Know You Still Believe In Me Hue Jackson 140

How I Found The Courage To Keep My Crown And Pursue My Career Haley Jordan 144

How Two Strangers Helped Me Find My Purpose While I Was In Pain Brittany Mullins 148

Loss Of A Child

To Children Battling Cancer, Your Smile Was My Son's Wish Les Friedman *154*

Loss Of A Partner

How An F-Bomb Changed My Life Chris Cimino *159*

CTE Took Your Mind, But I Still Have Your Heart Alison Epperson *164*

Here Is Where I Found Hope When I Lost My Husband Robin Fiddle Posnack *170*

Other Losses

To All The People I Could Not Save... Pat Michalik *176*

To The Children Of My Fallen Classmates Boyd Melson *181*

Lauren's Thoughts - You Can Find Joy In Life After A Painful Loss Lauren Brill *184*

GENDER, RACE, AND LGBTQ+ *188*

Gender

I Don't Wear Glass Slippers. I Shatter Them Jen Welter *193*

Here Is Why You Need To Stop Being Nice And Start Being Loud Gretchen Carlson *196*

This Is What Happens When You Pitch Like A Girl Marti Sementelli *201*

Why It's Important For Women To Ask For Free Pizza Mikael Austin *204*

To WNBA Players, I Not Only Know Your Name, I See Your Fight Amara Newsom *207*

This Is What I Hope You Learn From A Female Football Coach Alex Hanna *210*

Race

To The Black And White Youth Of America, Let's Get Real About Race
Thomas Q. Jones 216

To White Mothers, This Is How You Can Help Keep My Sons Safe
Angela Dennis 223

I Want You To Feel What The World May Not See
Kanyessa McMahon 227

LGBTQ+

What It Is Like To Be A Trans Woman Of Color In America Gabrielle Inès 232

Here Is Why My Journey To Living Life As An Openly Gay Woman Hasn't Been Easy Robee Berry 236

Lauren's Thoughts - An Open Heart Is The Healer Of Humanity
Lauren Brill 240

COPING WITH HEALTH CHALLENGES, ADDICTION, TRAUMA, OR MENTAL ILLNESS 244

Disabilities

How The Loss Of My Dream Led To The Best Gifts Of My Life Todd Krieg 249

To My Body... Eric LeGrand 253

How Hustle And Heart Helped Me Win Some Prestigious Hardware
Lindsey Zurbrugg 258

This Is How My Team Lifted Me When I Lost My Leg Carrie Owens 262

I Have Autism — Your Doubt Was My Motivation
Anthony Ianni 266

This Is How I Hope You Will Treat My Son As He Enters The Adult World
Ahmad Islam 270

This Is Why My Stutter Won't Stop Me Morgan Shagrin 274

To Parents With Special Needs Children, Here Is My Advice Kathy Cavagnaro 278

To My Little Sister With Down Syndrome — This Is What You Taught Me Adam Dixon 282

How I Learned To Love Myself While Living With Marfan Syndrome Marisa Hart 285

Health

I Was Given Six Months To Live. This Is How My Miracle Revealed My Purpose Dr. James Alberty 289

If Chemo Can't Cure Me, I Believe This Will Kris Sokolowski 295

I Was Excited To Be Pregnant But Scared To Fight Cancer Jordana Beck 302

How Nearly Losing My Life Led Me To My Passion Alexzandria Regan 305

Mental Health

To The Little Girl Who Wants To Be Beautiful Torrie Wilson 310

This Is How Making Mistakes Made Me Happy Josh Copeland 314

Depressed And Stressed, This Is What Helped Me Transition To Life After Football Xavier Cooper 319

Addiction

How I Learned To Live In My Own Light Instead Of My Brother's Shadow Brian Cuban 325

How I Went From A Janitor To The Founder Of A Multimillion-Dollar Business Larry Fagan *330*

I No Longer Need To Be Lucky To Survive Addiction, I Just Need You Alex Neutz *334*

Dad, I Want You To Know This Is How My Life Turned Out After Going To Rehab 38 Years Ago Don Fertman *338*

Trauma

After Spending Five Years In Prison, Here Is Why I Believe In Second Chances Brigitte Harris *345*

How Playing Football At Michigan Led To A Life Filled With Pain And Trauma Jon Vaughn *350*

I Thought It Was love — It Was Abuse Gab Kreuz *356*

Lauren's Thoughts - Your Body Can Only Be As Strong As Your Mind Lauren Brill *362*

TO (OR ABOUT) THE PEOPLE WE LOVE *366*

To One Person Who Changed My Life

Oprah, I Have Written You Many Times, But Here Is Why This Letter Is Different Briana Lee *371*

This Is How Our Friendship Made Me Feel Michael Rickli *375*

From A Follower To A Friend: How One Instagram Message Changed My Life Noah Weber *378*

Here Is What Happens When A Dad Believes In His Daughter Lauren Brill *382*

Here Is What You Did For A Little Boy Who Loved Baseball Terry Francona 386

Why My Dad Is My Hero Jared Simon 391

To My First Boyfriend, After 20 Years, I Want You To Know This Lauren Brill 395

When I Tell You "Good Game," This Is What I Actually Mean Mo Brooks 399

To A Community That Means So Much To Me

Many Of You Don't Even Know Me, But I Would Risk My Life For You Tiara Brown 403

I Could Be On The Path To Make Millions — I Choose To Be Here With You Alex Robertson 406

What Matters Most Are Not The Memories We Are Missing Daniel Kantrowitz 412

Dear Buffalo, This Is How Our "Mafia" Backs More Than Just Our Bills Del Reid 415

To My Students, I Trained In The Ring, But This Is What I Fight For Sonya Lamonakis 418

This Is What I Want To Say To Those Who Helped Me Make It To The Big Leagues Pedro Borbón Jr. 423

Thank You, Astros, By Giving My Dad Baseball In October, You Gave My Dad So Much More Gerald Sanchez 429

Lauren's Thoughts - The Life We Live Is Determined By The Love We Feel Lauren Brill 434

CONCLUSION - It's The Spirit Within You That Unseals Your Superpowers Lauren Brill 440

About The Book

No matter who you are or what your dreams may be, each one of us faces major roadblocks as we pursue our goals. When those challenges hit, we get tired. We may cry. Frustration overwhelms us. But deep within ourselves lies the power to persevere.

Each letter in this book was written by/as told to me, Lauren Brill, the founder of The Unsealed. After interviewing each person, I helped them craft their message in an open letter.

The topics addressed in this book include love, grief, illness, addiction, poverty, discrimination, and more. These letters have already proven to have the power to uplift, encourage, and inspire us.

Jena Boyer from Illinois said, "Reading stories on The Unsealed truly inspires me to share my own story and be proud of it. Learning about people's experiences and seeing how they have persevered through life's challenges make you realize how strong we all are."

New York City Psychotherapist Alyson Cohen, LCSW, explained, "The Unsealed is an invaluable resource for those feeling in search of community and emotional well-being. The stories will have your eyes glued to the page and refill the empty places in your soul — restoring your hope in humanity and healing."

Former NFL Head Coach Hue Jackson said, "The opportunity that Lauren gave me to tell my story to my mom was very empowering for me. I think everybody has a story to tell. And when you're dealing with Lauren, she tells your story the way it needs to be told. I think she has a tremendous gift of taking something that you feel and you think in real time and making it come to life. I think she empowered me to be able to say some things to my mom that I've always wanted to say. That letter will stick with me for the rest of my life."

What Is The Unsealed?

The Unsealed **(theunsealed.com)** is a writing community where people write, share, and respond to personal and inspirational open letters. I write our featured letters (like the ones in this book). Members of our community submit the remainder of the letters and poems on our site.

Also, we hold weekly writing workshops and conversations, inviting interesting guests and community members to discuss their stories. Our platform aims to heal, empower, connect, encourage, and inspire people to persevere through their problems and pain.

If you would like to share your story, head to **theunsealed.com.**

Dedication

Dedication

I am dedicating this book to my parents for their endless love, support, and belief in me and to all the people in this book who trusted me with their stories. It is their truth that will change the world.

We will donate 10% of the profits from this book for the first six months to Lift Our Voices and Team LeGrand of The Christoper and Dana Reeve Foundation.

Team LeGrand is a fundraising arm of The Christopher and Dana Reeve Foundation. The Christopher and Dana Reeve Foundation supports those suffering from spinal cord injuries and invests in discovering new treatments and potential cures.

For more information, check out
christopherreeve.org

Lift Our Voices aims to transform the American workplace by eliminating silencing mechanisms in the workplace (forced arbitration clauses and non-disclosure agreements) that allow the vicious cycle of secrecy surrounding toxic workplace issues to thrive. The nonprofit organizes communities to change laws and policies, advocates for survivors, conducts much-needed research and promotes awareness for a safer and more inclusive workplace environment.

For more information, check out
liftourvoices.org

Enjoy our stories! Within each letter lies a lesson you can apply to your life.

Introduction

INTRODUCTION

How A **Dark Secret** Started A Beautiful Journey

This book, and my life's work, all started with a secret. Not a secret someone shared with me, but something that happened to me — something I buried for years in the darkest corner of my mind — a place in my brain that my consciousness couldn't, or wouldn't, access. Maybe a small part of me was embarrassed. But mainly, I couldn't process the reality of what those boys did to me. I wasn't just hiding what happened from others; it was something I couldn't accept within myself.

It took nearly half my life to turn that secret into my superpower.

In 2002, when I was 16, I woke up in a New York mansion overlooking the Hudson River. As I opened my eyes and looked at this incredible view of the Tappan Zee Bridge, there was a strange moment of calmness after a night of utter confusion.

That moment didn't last very long. I felt very nauseous. As I got up to go to the bathroom to throw up, one of my friends walked into the room crying hysterically.

Through her tears, she asked, "What the fuck happened last night?"

I had the same thought, but I didn't say a word. Besides the churning of my stomach, I felt absolutely nothing. I wasn't upset, and I wasn't angry. Instead, I was completely numb.

As we drove home, my two friends and I were uncustomarily radio silent. Without putting a name to what just happened, I remember gripping the wheel, looking out into the road ahead with a blank stare, and knowing that my life would never be the same.

I thought I'd never be the person I was 24 hours prior. And I knew that night would somehow change the trajectory of my life.

At the time, I tried to move on with my life as I was accepted to one of the best schools in the country, Columbia University. But my secret stayed with me and made me sick — physically and mentally. Within a year of that dreadful day, I lost 30 pounds, becoming emaciated and too weak to play soccer, the sport I loved, at the collegiate level. I developed debilitating anxiety as I constantly feared who lurked around the corner.

Luckily, my ambitions were stronger than my fears, and I still pursued my childhood dream of becoming a sportscaster. I interned at CBS and NBC in their respective sports departments during my sophomore and junior years. By my senior year of college, I was writing for WNBA.com. Shortly after graduating from Columbia at 21, I began writing for NBA.com. I was the youngest writer and the only female journalist in the room. After the NBA, I moved on to work in TV in New York, Buffalo, and Cleveland. At different points in my career, I experienced an overwhelming amount of sexism and sexual harassment, which was both triggering and eye-opening. It made me realize how society facilitates and enables abuse toward women. Even so, I still amassed seven Emmy nominations and one AP Award for Best Sports Reporting.

As a kid, sports were my happy place. My dad used to take me to New York Rangers games, and I loved the aggressive nature of hockey and the time I spent one-on-one with my dad. I garnered a lot of attention in school because I was one of the best female athletes in my class. However, what attracted me most to sportscasting was storytelling. That was my passion, and I specifically enjoyed telling sports stories because I saw sports as a lens to see the human spirit.

Growing up, if I struggled in school, got rejected from a program, or didn't get the playing time I thought I deserved, my dad would tell me stories about athletes to motivate me to persevere through adversity.

When I made varsity soccer as a freshman but, at first, wasn't playing as much as I wanted, my dad told me, "You know when Michael Jordan went to North Carolina, everyone said he would never play over Buzz Peterson."

I responded, "Who is Buzz Peterson?"

My dad smirked as he replied, "That's exactly my point. Just keep working hard."

By the middle of the season, I was starting and scoring goals regularly.

As a sports reporter, I thrived on sharing stories of athletes who had overcome a tremendous amount of adversity to realize their dreams: athletes who were once homeless or hungry as children but still found a way to make it to college or even the NFL, athletes who were blind or deaf but still managed to play Division I baseball or run Ironman triathlons, and athletes who had missing limbs but didn't let that stop them from bicycling across the country or playing tennis.

The more I told stories about other people, the more I began to peel back the layers of my own story. And then, in 2014, I started to write and write and write some more.

I did not know exactly why I was writing. I did not create an outline, mapping out every topic I wanted to discuss or each experience I wanted to share. Instead, I just wrote.

It was almost a stream of consciousness, letting the words roll from my brain to my fingertips as I tapped and typed into emotions I did not know I felt and lessons I did not realize I had learned. Through my writing, I exposed myself to myself, viewing a completely naked and raw version I had not seen before.

Through writing, I found my voice, faced my pain, and realized my courage.

Writing led me to openly talking about what happened to me with my friends and family. Then, while working as a sportscaster in Cleveland, I interviewed a fellow broadcaster, Gab Kreuz. On air, Gab shared her story. She was in a physically and emotionally abusive relationship in college. But after moving on from the relationship, she became an All-American runner, broke six school records, and started a nonprofit organization called Love Doesn't Shove, going to high schools to discuss dating violence.

After her story aired, I asked her why she decided to speak out publicly, and she told me, "It is the silence of victims that allows predators to continue their predatory behavior."

That's when it hit me. I needed to tell my story — not just to my mom and dad, but to everyone. And I knew writing would be the perfect way to do it. A few months later, before the MeToo movement, I wrote an open letter to sexual assault survivors telling them what happened to me when I was 16 years old. At a party thrown by a classmate, kids from another school showed up, and two of them drugged and sexually assaulted me. After falling off the bed and hitting the floor hard, both boys ran out of the room in a panic. They left me on the floor all alone, undressed, barely conscious, and too sedated to walk.

That was the lowest and most confusing moment of my life.

In my letter to survivors, I wanted them to know what hurt me didn't hold me back. I wanted them to know that even though I struggled, I persevered, getting into my top-choice school, Columbia University, gaining back all the weight I initially lost after my assault, and achieving my childhood dream of becoming a sportscaster.

The day I published my letter, I no longer felt like a victim or a survivor; that was the day I officially felt like a fighter.

My letter went viral around the country, becoming the top story on my station's website for several weeks. NBA and NFL players started tweeting my story, showing their support by saying, "We got your back" or "We believe in your mission." And people around the country wrote to me, thanking me for making them feel inspired and less alone.

Fifteen years after my assault, I finally felt unchained from the weight of my secret. And that's when and why I decided to leave my career as a sportscaster in a top-20 market to start my own company called The Unsealed. It is a safe online space where people can share their personal stories through open letters and express themselves through the written word.

While now we allow people to submit their letters, at first, I ghostwrote every single letter on the site. In year one, we reached more than a quarter million people in nearly every country in the world. More importantly, a former foster child told me I made her feel seen for the first time. A father who lost his son to cancer thanked me for caring about his child's legacy. A teenage rape survivor told me that I am the reason she shared her story, and I am the reason she feels hope for her future. Countless people expressed gratitude for listening to them, helping them express themselves, and amplifying their voices.

In this book, I share some of the letters I ghostwrote in The Unsealed's first few years (2019-2023). Irrespective if your life experiences are similar to the ones in this book, each letter shares a message about courage, resilience, and the power of love.

As you read these letters, I hope they remind you that you can find meaning in life from within yourself. I hope you become empowered by the knowledge that you have the strength to navigate your way and joy in life, regardless of your obstacles. I hope you realize it is OK not to be perfect, and it is OK to make mistakes as long as you use them to make you better instead of tearing you down. I hope you learn that sometimes the reason you want to pursue a project, a goal, or anything for that matter, is not nearly as important as your desire to do so. Ultimately, the reason will reveal itself.

Today, there are many days I still think about that 16-year-old girl lying naked on the floor and waking up the next day looking out at the Hudson River — not because I am angry or sad, but because I am so proud that I transformed the worst moment of my life into a beautiful way to help people far and wide.

I am not numb, and I am certainly not silent. Instead, my secret is now my superpower because I am using my truth to inspire you to unseal yours.

Lauren

Unseal Your Superpowers

Here Is My Original Letter:

(Published in April of 2017)

Dear Sexual Violence Survivors:

After years of being too scared to write to all of you, now I am hoping the world will share this letter so it can actually find each and every one of you. The decision to reveal my truth this week on Facebook COO Sheryl Sandberg's site for her new book, "Option B," was not an easy one.

I feared my career would be negatively impacted or that people would judge me unfairly. Even more distressing, I worried I'd torment my parents, as I would no longer be able to shield them from the horror I endured. However, the people I have interviewed throughout my career as a sports reporter gave — and continue to give — me courage, as they've made me understand the value of raw honesty.

> *According to the National Sexual Violence Resource Center one out of every five women will be raped at some point in their lives. The Department of Justice definition of rape includes various forms of sexual penetration without consent. Rape is not exclusive to women, as men and transgender are affected as well.*

Unfortunately, just like you, I've experienced sexual violence. However, today I am officially done being a victim and I am trying to be more than just a survivor. I want to be a fighter and share with you the wisdom I've gained and the support you've needed.

At 16 years old, I couldn't even process the reality that I was drugged and sexually abused by two boys I did not know.

For nine years, I did not tell anyone. It was easier to blame myself for accepting one drink than it was to fault them for drugging and attacking me.

It wasn't only the sexual component of the assault that was so traumatizing but also that for a moment in time my own body didn't belong to me. I was strong and athletic, yet in the most desperate moment of my life, my muscles betrayed me.

I could barely move or speak, as I felt completely powerless. I tried my best to say the words, "No!" and, "Stop!," but my voice was much louder inside my own head where I prayed and pleaded, "Please, God, don't let this be how I lose my virginity." Thankfully, I fell off the bed as one of my attackers attempted, but I believe failed, to advance from violating me with his hands and fingers to his genitals. When I hit the floor, both boys ran out of the room in a panic.

Despite starting off at a healthy weight, I lost 30 pounds in one year, becoming too weak to play soccer, the sport I loved, at the collegiate level. Often I found myself on edge, always worrying about who lurked around the corner. At times, I felt alone in my own anxiety, but I eventually realized I had plenty of company.

Sadly, sexual assault has become practically a dismal rite of passage for women in our society, but according to Rape, Abuse & Incest National Network (RAINN) per the Department of Justice two out of every three sexual assaults go unreported.

I want you to know I am what another survivor looks like. I am what another survivor sounds like.

I was an honor student and a star athlete with two highly involved parents and great friends. But when those boys violated me, my background and my resume were completely irrelevant. My attack was not my fault and you are not to blame for your assault either, as no one is immune to sexual violence or responsible for someone else's predatory behavior.

Today, more than a decade after that fateful night, there is little chance that I will ever find out who hurt me. That is a very tough reality for me to accept, but I've had to move on. I was lucky enough to discover my passion for storytelling, which subconsciously catalyzed my recovery. The stories I have told about others, coupled with writing about my own journey, have given me hope, happiness and healing.

Now, I feel confident and encouraged, which has bestowed upon me an unshakeable sense of responsibility to be a leader for those of you still trapped inside your own silence. I want you to know, you, too, can survive. You can be happy. You can realize all of your dreams. Find a passion that is so strong it forces you to overcome everything that you fear and any trauma symptoms that affect you. When you're ready, express your truth through a means that suits you, whether it be writing, music, art, conventional therapy or any other method that makes sense to you.

I have told so many stories about athletes who have faced incredible challenges and have gone on to achieve unimaginable successes. Through them, I've learned that truth can have many different effects on both the people receiving it and those revealing it. Truth can be freedom. Truth can be change. Truth can be inspiration.

My wish is that sharing my past impacts you in a way that helps heal your spirit, brings some peace to your life and emboldens you to reveal your own experiences. If so, my honesty will serve a purpose that far outweighs my fears, as together our truths will become our power.

With love and hope,

Lauren Brill

- chapter 1

I could walk ew or of but the rs p yoff game when I 5 miles I knew I wanted the a report or female. Ph after n ou asked BC executive in 1995, ing enc fifth grade and ready st career utive at a New school in ockland lea s had not yet begun at was in when it my mother and we ing w months afte tice i vier very v an i a busy i ubu abo es nor rth rdinated th or Ro early in the sch s I ga Rico ought e win ould not y pass a b I pulled nclos ed b an ABC h had t soccer practi h o orkitchen ed n busy sub f she ew v gh the as insi de wanted to S it wa County). As I ion for K reporti nd w, we pa hat n t we led wit When led o ig y and ready w p ook, s "TKR" writ land in our had atiqu om if s flipped thi le to get t other ame T ound TV cable st npany. I thought re se nty Tha got it!" he per ith iasm est of Negr bb phor d it on our is o our little kit becaus ki he stat came h n an o y a gate. I were one. R Cable Comp hy spo here I started or kids. i rson w hat build red tra e e wall nex to c me he movie. I wa didn't yet have ur big ye egment. Si d if they had an call b ck the film er ca hlete, as I to get to or onger, a ducer, who tol id 8 s. T he g and I bo usiasm, Rets. After ve my mother County w I w he erator an ger I was n a !" In tl te who played sport who answe cont 5, I was ing a norm w with a sports s ly, an un to f portunities who I w 3, I w from work R retire out 35 Oceans. When I wit ew Jennifer Tilly, and J bui to ig ean Drive. I knew t called Grillfish nough for d s e stars were i en and m d abo my script fr ard D ken to Jeremy er sitting on Oce own ideas ough. eyfuss in the lot uhine, I security I ream I an Dreyfu on my wal vs in fit kid. On 3,000. R gh, on my sever fall wh ith the peop e 1 filming seve e they 5 miles he director du g a b where they v ewhe o ng encl s nd to me t bring d somewhere t it t t was i e Cr ." I am the et, and they showe pulled er bi fearle d him on the sho h the ontin rdinated t back to the set late an ted to ming, "Congratula tin and ready s a child, but thos other an the nd someti ed I sh urposeful e nonsens po e has bee itting Dre te chno or misogynis nest of N caus y a gate. how p een a whole new set of filmi hat build gular where ogical issues, nexpec ur big ye ke the e harder the o get to g d some as I had a a usiasm le v ermin d as I had a ederator an deter d n t mb e harder s o answer ns we re d siasm as I had a w lt joy at the th ts were lit

" These letters are a reminder of what happens when you stay true to who you are and what you want, no matter how much life tries to rattle you or how impossible getting to that next level feels in the moment. "

-Lauren

Your Mindset Is Everything!

What I Learned About Luck From Surviving A Plane Crash

To people who need a little inspiration,

It was a cold day on January 15, 2009, the day I began to realize that I am one of the luckiest people on earth. My girlfriend dropped me off at Laguardia Airport for a flight I had booked in an emergency the day before. My grandfather was diagnosed with cancer for the fifth time. I was flying through Charlotte, North Carolina to Myrtle Beach, South Carolina, to help my grandmother take him to some doctor appointments.

I boarded the plane, and we took off, just like any flight. Approximately two minutes into the air, there was an explosion. It was scary. We lost power. I looked outside the left side of the plane, and the engine was bursting into flames. Then we had a weightless moment. It felt like we were about to nosedive.

Next, the pilot started to turn the plane, which made me feel like he had control over it.

But then, he got on the loudspeaker and said, "Brace for impact."

When you hear that on a plane, it basically means you're about to die.

The flight attendants started to chant, "Brace! Brace! Keep your head down."

I could hear the fear in their voices.

The whole time I was glancing out of the window, watching New York City inch closer and closer to us. I was confused and scared, but something inside of me made me feel that I was going to be fine.

We hit the Hudson River hard, skipping like a rock on the water.

The lights turned off, and the pilot yelled, "Evacuate! Evacuate!"

Then, the smell of jet fuel punched me in the face. But I still made it to the front of the plane and slid down into a raft. I like to say I had a luxurious plane crash because I didn't even get wet.

Once I detached from the plane, I knew I was going to be OK. Sitting on the raft, looking around at this incredible scene was surreal.

I high-fived the guy next to me and said, "Dude, we just fucking survived a plane crash!"

I have been laughing and smiling ever since.

The crash is now famously known as the "Miracle on the Hudson." We landed in a body of water, and miraculously, no one died. All 155 people aboard the flight survived.

After that day, I began to truly understand age-old sayings like, "You never know what's going to happen tomorrow" and "Nothing is impossible."

See, I know whatever I go through in life, no matter how grave or scary the situation, I am going to be just fine. I no longer allow fear or adversity to hold me back, flying on more than 600 flights since landing on the Hudson River.

In my life, I can see the light at the end of the deepest and darkest tunnels. And the world has most certainly tested me.

Nine years after my plane crash, at 36 years old, I suddenly lost feeling in my face from my chin to my lips. My friend, Dr. Matthew Lorber, a psychiatrist, suggested I get some bloodwork. Shortly after, he called to tell me I had cancer. It took 10 days of testing to actually diagnose me with stage 4 Burkitt lymphoma, a lymphatic cancer that goes through the entire body. The doctor told me without treatment, I had two to seven days to live.

From the first moment I was diagnosed to when I went to Memorial Sloan Kettering for chemotherapy, I never stopped thinking positively or smiling.

I was given some of the most intense chemo. And while going through my treatments, I would tell the nurses how I am the luckiest person in the world.

They would say, "What do you mean? You're getting chemo right now."

I just knew that I was going to survive.

I knew beating cancer would be another experience I could use to inspire people.

Sure enough, I was right. I am now 15 months in remission. Getting sick taught me additional life lessons, as I have started living a healthier lifestyle, eating well, and exercising daily.

While many people would say I am unlucky for being in a plane crash and getting cancer, I consider myself extremely lucky, considering most people don't survive either.

And I am not the only one with luck.

You are lucky, too. You simply have to realize it. If you take the time every day to think about how lucky you are for the opportunities and people in your life, you will genuinely be happier.

Gratitude is key. Smile through the toughest moments, even when you're looking up at a very steep hill. There is always hope. Once you know that, see that, and feel that, you become capable of so much more in life.

So, when I tell you I am a lucky person, I want you to understand that luck is not about randomly avoiding bad situations but rather choosing to see endless possibilities in all circumstances.

Today is your lucky day! Go enjoy it!

Adir Freilich

To The Dreamers, Not Everyone Will See Your Vision

To the dreamers,

I am a comedian making a living uploading videos of funny sketches with me and a puppet.

When I look at it from the outside, sometimes I am like, "Hold up, this shit really worked?"

But the truth is I always believed. I just felt it. I woke up from a nap one day, and it was in my head, so I started writing everything down. Sometimes you just know that your dream is meant for you, even if going for it feels like you are jumping off a cliff.

My dream started before I could even recognize it. In middle school, I used to draw cartoon characters, and I would do these little newspaper sketches of my teachers or people in class. For a long time, I had no idea I would transform those skills into a career.

Instead, I went to college for engineering. My junior year, I dropped out for six months to try and figure out what I really wanted to do with my life. When I went back, I took a communications class and started editing videos. At first, I thought I wanted to be an editor. So I began practicing editing videos and figured I might as well try to be funny. It was just like the stuff I was doing in middle school but for adults. I posted one video onto the internet, and people liked it. So I posted another one, and from there, it started snowballing.

Soon after, somebody asked me to host a show, and I said, "No, I never hosted a show."

He said, "We will give you $300."

I was like, "Alright, cool."

Once I felt the stage for the first time, I told myself, "This is it. This is my future."

It was 2009.

I said to my roommate, "I am going to be a comedian."

He responded with a straight face, "But you are not funny like that."

My mom wanted me to sign up for the airforce.

When I told her I wanted to be a comedian, she said, "You gotta be logical about things. You can't make no money being a comedian."

My dad didn't say anything, but he didn't have to use words. You could see it on his face. His energy was very negative.

I pursued it anyway, and the doubters continued to appear.

I was in LA, and I was dating this girl who saw a puppet on my futon in the living room. She asked why I had a puppet.

So I explained, "Oh, I'm going to be in a relationship with the puppet. I am going to do this whole online skit."

She said, "That shit sounds wack."

She couldn't see it. If you are a dreamer, you gotta remember that not everybody's going to be able to see what you can see. You have to trust yourself before you trust anybody else.

The very first video I uploaded with a puppet got a million views. The second video I posted with the puppet got two million views.

So I bet my house on it, literally. I needed to go on tour, which meant I needed to pay for the venue, plane tickets, food, and every other expense since I had no experience.

I sold all my shit: my computer, camera, and whatever else I had that was valuable.

But there was a problem. I called around to comedy clubs to book myself. I told club owners that I had a strong social media following and that I could sell out. No one called me back. So I was like, fuck it.

I felt every single emotion possible. I did not have a safety net because I walked away from my other businesses to do comedy. Comedy was how I wanted to make money. It was moments like this where I felt crazy. I would look at social media and see all my friends buying houses and cars and getting engaged. Meanwhile, I am over here with no job, just trying to figure shit out.

Then one day, I was ordering food over the phone, and the guy called me "buddy" like I was a kid. Clearly, he thought I was young. So I realized that must be how I sound to club owners. And let's be honest, if I was a guy who could sell out clubs, would I really be calling myself?

The agents and managers I met with couldn't see my vision, so I made up this fake guy named Scott Rothenburg. I would call as Scott and use this fake Jewish agent voice. That's how I booked my shows.

When you have a dream, you got to figure shit out.

My dad always said to me, "There is more than one way home."

If one way isn't getting the job done, you have to find another way.

After I booked my first club, I released the tickets on Saturday, and I sold like three.

I said to myself, "Damn, maybe I was wrong."

I didn't know what I was going to do if I couldn't make my money back. I sold all my belongings, and I would have been completely broke.

Thankfully, I posted the tickets again on a Tuesday, and the first show sold out. Then, the second show sold out.

I had never headlined a tour before, so I took a featured act that had been on the road for years. He knew more of the game than me. Even though I was the leader in a sense because I headlined the tour, I still was able to pull back. Sometimes you've got to know to step back a little and play another position for the betterment of the team.

Ultimately, it all worked. We sold out the entire tour.

My proudest moment was when I realized I came up out of those rocky and uncertain moments and proved that my vision was right.

What I learned is going out on your own and pursuing your dream can be similar to being left on a deserted island. Your survival instincts kick in. Humans are built to survive. If you have never built a fire from scratch, but you're stuck on a deserted island, I bet you will figure it out because you know it's possible.

So my advice is to go to the deserted island, jump off the cliff and expect there to be moments where you feel like you are going to smash right into the ground. I promise if you trust and believe in yourself, you won't let yourself die. Instead, you will find ways to survive, and you will be one of the few in life who experience what it is like to fly.

So stop dreaming and go find your wings!

Trey Moe

How Hope Helped Me Survive 16 Years Of Wrongful Imprisonment

To those who are losing hope,

For my first 15 years in prison, I had hope. But then, like you, I almost lost it all. I remember sitting down in a room with a closed-circuit TV — a video with three people. It was kind of like being in a bad sci-fi movie because there was a lag between the audio and the video. The people on the screen asked me many questions, including questions about the programs I completed and the plans I mapped out for my future. All of my answers seemed to go over well except for one.

They asked me if I was maintaining my innocence.

I said, "Yes."

When I tried to elaborate, they didn't seem interested.

Three days later, I got an envelope in the mail. Inside was a message that noted I had excellent educational and disciplinary records. It even mentioned that I had some letters of support. Nonetheless, they wrote that I was found guilty of committing a brutal and senseless crime. To release me, they said, would somehow lessen the seriousness of it.

That was the day I got denied parole. That was the day I started to struggle with hope. It was another door to freedom slammed shut in my face, and I was running out of doors to knock.

I began openly asking a pen pal — a stranger, "Do you think I should just quit? Should I go ahead and kill myself?"

It felt like I was never getting out. And the truth of the matter was, I should have never been there in the first place.

I grew up in Peekskill, New York, a quiet, diverse middle-class suburb about 50 miles north of New York City. In school, I skipped first grade, so I was younger than the rest of my class. Starting in middle school, kids bullied me. I was an outcast, as I was not interested in drinking, parties, or chasing girls like some of my classmates. It got so bad, my grades suffered, and the school held me back.

My life took an ever darker turn during my sophomore year of high school. One of my classmates went to the park to take pictures of foliage for her photography class. Then, she went missing. Three days later, they found her body naked from the waist down.

Our quiet town became an atmosphere of fear, paranoia, and constant rumors. There were multiple town hall meetings held where they discussed safety tips and updates on the investigation. Parents were driving their kids straight to school, picking them up, and bringing them directly home.

Everyone wanted to find the killer, including me.

The police interviewed a lot of students from the high school. Some of those kids told the police they might want to speak to me because I didn't quite fit in with everyone else. Also, I was a sensitive child. Despite not knowing the victim well, I cried a lot after she died. Some people found my reaction suspicious. And without realizing it, I quickly became a suspect.

At the time, my dream was to become a police officer, and the police acted as though they needed my help to solve the crime.

They would say things like, "The kids won't talk freely around us, but they will around you. Let us know if you hear anything."

Then, one day they told me that they had some new information that came into the police file, and they wanted to share it with me. But first, I had to take and pass a polygraph.

So the next day, without telling my mother, I went to the police station rather than report to school. The police drove me 40 minutes away by car to the town of Brewster in Putnam County. I didn't have any way of leaving on my own. They never read me my rights, and I had no attorney or parent present. They put me in a small room and attached me to this polygraph machine. The officer who gave me the test was dressed as a civilian. He raised his voice at me. He invaded my personal space. He kept asking the same questions over and over again. As each hour passed, my fear increased.

He said to me, "What do you mean you didn't do it? You just told me through the test result that you did. We just want you to confirm it verbally."

That's when my 16-year-old self really felt terrified.

One of the cops who seemingly befriended me told me if I told them what they wanted to hear, I would not be arrested and would be able to go home. Being young, naive, frightened, and not thinking about the long-term consequences, I made up a story based on the information they gave me during the seven-hour interrogation.

I falsely confessed to rape and murder.

Then, I collapsed on the floor in a fetal position, crying uncontrollably. I was arrested and charged.

At the trial, I had a public defender who rarely met with me and didn't allow me to testify. Although the DNA found in the victim's body didn't match mine, I was convicted based solely on my confession.

When they read the guilty verdict, I was 17 years old and completely stunned. I thought that only guilty people were convicted. Tried as an adult, I was sentenced to 15 years to life and sent to a maximum-security prison.

Prison was hell, especially as a convicted sex offender. Even so, for many years, I was able to hold on to hope.

For the first 11 years, I focused on my appeals. I always thought I only had a year or two more in prison. I kept telling myself I only had to make it to the next appeal, where I would for sure regain my freedom because, after all, I was innocent.

However, I lost seven appeals. After your appeals are over, the only way back in a courtroom is if you can find some new evidence. So, I started writing letters, trying to find somebody who would help me pro bono. Those letters got me through the next four years. But when nothing panned out, I started seeing the parole board as a way of regaining my freedom. That's why after they denied me, I nearly lost all hope. I nearly quit. I almost gave up because I couldn't see any other way to get out of prison.

But thankfully, I did find the strength to keep going. I did find a way to hold on to hope.

Sure enough, after I was denied parole, I received a response from a letter I had written the year prior. Ultimately, an investigator connected me to the Innocence Project. They took my case. A new district attorney allowed us to conduct further DNA testing and enter it in the New York State DNA databank of convicted felons. The DNA matched Steven Cunningham, a man already in prison for another murder he committed after I went to jail. When confronted with the DNA evidence, he confessed to the crime — he admitted to killing my classmate.

After 16 years in prison, I went back to court, and they dismissed all the charges against me. I was 32 years old.

When I was finally let out, all I could think to myself was, "Is this really happening? Has this day finally come?"

It felt surreal. But there were still many challenges ahead.

I felt like I was in a parallel world. The technology was different. The culture was different. Cities and neighborhoods looked different. Also, there was a stigma associated with being in prison. Even though I was wrongfully there, people were scared of me. Plus, since I went to prison so young, I never had a job. I never lived on my own, and I didn't have a Driver's License. Finding work became exceedingly difficult, and I nearly ended up homeless.

Ultimately, with the help of a dean at Mercy College, I finished my bachelor's degree. The school gave me a scholarship, allowed me to live on campus, and provided me a meal plan. After I graduated, I applied to law school, and I got rejected. So, Instead, I took out a loan and pursued a master's degree in criminal justice.

Then, I sued all the parties involved in my wrongful conviction, and I won. I won big. From two lawsuits (and a total of five defendants), I received about $24 million before lawyers' fees.

The money certainly was not worth all the time I lost, as I missed births, deaths, weddings, and rites of passage. I would have much rather had a normal life. But I decided when I left prison, I would not live my life bitter. I want to enjoy my life as much as I can. So, I channel my anger and hurt into advocacy.

With some of the money that I won in the lawsuits, I created the Jeffrey Deskovic Foundation. We free wrongfully convicted people and pursue policy changes to prevent more wrongful convictions. So far, we've helped bring home 11 people who were wrongfully convicted.

I am also an advisory board member for a bigger coalition called It Can Happen To You. We have passed five laws with the coalition. However, a few years ago, I became unsatisfied with sitting in the front row of the courtroom. I wanted to sit at the table, represent clients, and make some of the arguments. Again, I decided to apply to law school.

While I scored poorly on the LSATS, I got an interview at Pace University and knocked it out of the park. Six years after I started my foundation, I went to law school. In 2019, I graduated and passed the bar on the first try. Now, I work 50–60 hours per week as a lawyer and advocate, and I'm able to do so pro bono, thanks to my settlements.

I found my purpose in the world, which has provided me with some acceptance and inner peace. Helping others facing similar circumstances that I once did has allowed me to heal. It's given my journey meaning, as I am making a difference in the world.

But I would have never gotten here if I had let go of hope.

When you have a lofty goal in life, you need a realistic plan. But you also need to be flexible with that plan. Remember that the goal is the goal. The plan is not the goal. Also, you must work hard. And when you think you can't go any further like I did when I was denied parole, you have to tell yourself that the key moment could be right around the corner. If you quit, if you stop now, you will never know what's on the other side.

Hope is what will keep you going. Hope is what will stop you from harming yourself. Hope is what will fuel you to fight.

Hope is the reason I am here.

So, even if you can't see where your breakthrough is coming from, take it from me; it doesn't mean it's not there.

There is always hope.

Keep believing, stay strong, and when you make it through, don't forget to use your hope to help someone else.

Jeffrey Deskovic

How My Journey Can Teach You How To Unlock Your Dreams

To young people,

In 1995, when my daughter was born, I gave up football. I quit the sport I loved while playing at the level I dreamed about as a young boy in Franklin, Louisiana.

At nine years old, my dad and I were watching the Cowboys vs. Steelers play.

I told him, "One day, you are going to watch me play on TV. You are not going to believe it's your son because I am going to play so well."

From that day forward, I tried to be the best at every sport I played. I tried to seek the best coaching. I ran around with older kids, who taught me discipline. And I pursued life focused on my future success.

However, along my journey, I faced plenty of challenges that could have gotten in my way.

When I was in second grade, they desegregated schools. I transferred to W.P. Foster Elementary School, where I attended school with white kids. We couldn't use the same bathrooms. Rarely did we play together during recess.

One day in high school, I was walking home with three or four of my friends, who were Black kids. Two guys pulled up behind us in a pickup truck with shotguns. They were yelling explicit language, N-bombs here and N-bombs there, along with a whole bunch of put-downs.

We were pissed off. The next day at school, my friends decided to take it out on other kids, stealing their lunch money, beating them up, and smashing their eyeglasses.

Finally, I told my friends to cut it out. I explained that their behavior only created a deeper problem and a deeper hatred. We would only end up disliking the white kids more, and the white kids would end up disliking us more.

I tried to be a leader and encouraged everyone to respect each other. Regardless of what anyone decided, I knew I was going to do what was right.

I knew if I wanted to be great in life, ignorance would get me nowhere. Violence would be my worst enemy. So, I found ways to adapt to various cultures, people, and religions. With that philosophy in mind, I chose to go to Louisiana State, where I received a scholarship to play football, as opposed to an HBC school.

In college, there were plenty of distractions. To make it to the next level, I had to make good decisions. One bad decision could derail my whole future, which happened to my roommate. He missed curfew because he chose to stay outside and argue with his girlfriend instead of coming back to the dorm and dealing with the problem the next day. He got kicked off the team and never reached his goals in football.

However, I chose to follow the rules. During my four-year career at LSU, I had 180 tackles and five sacks. In my senior year, I was named the team's Defensive Most Valuable Player.

In 1983, just like I imagined when I was a young boy, I made it to the NFL. The New York Giants drafted me in the second round with the 37th overall pick. Getting drafted was crazy. It changed my whole life. I bought my parents a house and a car and gave them a nice fat check. Everything a kid could do for his parents, I tried to do.

However, even once I got to the NFL, I had to be focused and know my worth. In 1990, I held out of training camp and almost all of the preseason. Even though I was one of the best players in the league at my position, the Giants didn't want to pay me. I knew if I didn't get my money, I would never get it. And I knew the team needed me to win.

Sitting out was painful. I hated doing it. Ultimately, I got paid my money, but Bill Parcells had a vendetta against me. He wouldn't start me, which affected potentially record-setting stats. I was disappointed, but I remained ready by continuing to show up and put in the work. Finally, in week 13, after we lost our Monday night game against San Francisco, everyone realized they needed me. I got my job back, and we went on to win the Super Bowl, which was my second of two championships.

Today, I battle depression and memory loss, among other symptoms, because of chronic traumatic encephalopathy, also known as CTE, which is a result of the head injuries I endured playing football. However, I don't regret playing football, and I am proud of my accomplishments.

I am telling you all this because you are all pursuing your own goals. You weren't there for my football journey, but there is so much you can learn from it.

I want you to understand how you put your pants on every morning, in terms of your attitude, determines the outcome of your day, regardless of the challenges you face.

A lot of people told me I couldn't do shit, but I worked hard, and I shut a lot of them up.

Success starts with you. You can do no more than you believe you can. At nine years old, I believed I would become an NFL player, and that belief created opportunity and helped me navigate decisions and obstacles throughout my life.

Every success comes at a cost. CTE was the price I ended up having to pay.

Thinking back, I should have played a little longer instead of quitting. But when my daughter came into this world, I no longer wanted to be the best football player. I wanted to be the best father. And even today, my focus is no longer to live out the dreams I imagined as a child but rather to see all of you live out yours.

Your future is yours,
Leonard Marshall

How One Pitch Changed My Career And One Person Turned It Back Around

To those who doubt themselves,

I'm about 6'3", 6'4". When I was at the top of my game, I walked around the clubhouse like I was 6'6" or 6'7". But after one pitch rattled my confidence, I didn't walk as tall, and I certainly didn't walk as proud.

One decision. One pitch. One moment.

Before that pitch, I don't remember doubting myself.

I grew up in Holyoke, Massachusetts. My father brought me to my first practice when I was in second grade. The minute I stepped on a baseball field, I fell in love with the sport. At about nine or 10 years old, my parents got divorced. My father wasn't around a whole lot, and my mother was working, trying to support and raise my sister and me. Baseball became my escape. When I wasn't playing organized baseball with my team, I'd catch with my buddy across the street or play Wiffle ball or watch other teams and players.

By middle school, I knew I was the best player on my team. In my sophomore year of high school, I made varsity. Then, during my senior year, we were getting ready to play our rivals. They were the next town over. It rained on the morning of the game. So, I drove over there to see the condition of the field. I ran into a couple of scouts from the Boston Red Sox, who ended up talking to me.

I didn't know who they were at the time.

But they asked me my name, and when I told them, they said, "We're here to see you pitch today."

That's when I knew I would have a future in baseball.

Sure enough, later that year, in 1988, I was home alone, and the phone rang. It was an area scout for the Atlanta Braves.

He said, "Congratulations, we drafted you in the eighth round. We'll be in touch."

After I got off the phone, I sat in silence, with my mind going a million miles an hour.

I felt great!

Three years later, I got called up to the big leagues. At 21 years old, I was thrust into the middle of a pennant race, and it was everything I dreamed it would be.

My confidence was certainly on the rise.

That season, I was part of a combined no-hitter. Kent Mercker went the first six innings. I pitched the seventh and eighth, and Alejandro Peña pitched the ninth. It was the seventh combined no-hitter in MLB history.

We made it to the World Series, where we lost to the Minnesota Twins. But that year, the Braves didn't put me in too critical of a role in the postseason. I don't think they wanted the world to fall on my shoulders at such a young age.

I pitched well in 1993. In 1994 there was a shortened season because of the strike. So, I thought 1995 was going to be my breakout year. A rookie named Brad Clontz won the closer's role out of spring training. But in early June or late May, I became the closer. My confidence kept climbing throughout the season.

Ultimately, I found myself on the mound for Game 6 of the World Series. We were in Atlanta, up 1-0 over the Cleveland Indians with two outs in the top of the ninth. Bases were empty. Carlos Baerga was on the plate for the Indians. I tried to downplay the whole situation as I reminded myself that I still have to get an out. I tried to think of it as another regular-season game.

I threw a fastball. Baerga hit it to left-center field. When I saw the ball go up in the air and I knew my center fielder, Marquis Grissom, was going to catch it, my confidence reached its peak.

Being at the bottom of that big pile after everybody ran out to the field is an experience I'll never forget. I won a World Series. That's when I felt 6'7" or 6'8". That's when I felt tall and proud. Also, I became widely considered one of the best closers in baseball.

But one year later, my confidence took a complete 180.

We were back in the World Series but with a different outcome. This time we were facing the New York Yankees. It was Game 4, and we were at home with a 2-1 series lead. In the top of the eighth, we were up 6-3. I was on the mound, and Yankees catcher Jim Leyritz was at the plate. I was throwing him fastball after fastball, and he kept fouling back. I thought I needed to mix it up and throw something different. I still believe it was the right pitch. It was just a bad location. I left it up. I made a mistake, and he took complete advantage of it. He hit a three-run game-tying home run, and the Yankees went on to win the game and the World Series.

That home run was not only a turning point in the series but also in my career.

One decision. One pitch. One moment.

While I pitched the rest of the series, and I didn't give up any more runs, the worst thing that happened to me was the offseason. I would hear people talk about the pitch, and then I'd see TV stations play the highlights repeatedly.

When I returned for the next season, I started to think, "OK, here comes a reporter. He is going to ask me about last year's World Series," or "This fan is going to say something about last year's World Series."

No longer did my mind contain positive thoughts. Instead, the negative thoughts were compounding daily.

In '97, I lost my ability to throw strikes. I completely lost all feeling in my hand to throw a baseball. And that's not easy to do when you're in front of 30, 40, 60 thousand people.

I thought I could physically battle my way through it. So, I kept working, and I kept throwing. The Braves sent me down to the minors in '98 to relieve some pressure. It didn't help.

In '99, they wanted to send me down again, but I didn't want to do that. So, I forced their hand to either release me or trade me. They traded me to the Cincinnati Reds, which was a great change of scenery, but I still struggled.

Finally, my elbow blew out, and I needed Tommy John surgery, which was devastating at the time. However, without a doubt, the injury became a blessing in disguise. I couldn't pick up a baseball, which meant I had to beat this adversity mentally, not physically.

Throughout about 10 months of rehab, I convinced myself that the reason I couldn't throw strikes was that I had nerve or ligament damage in my elbow. That's why I could not feel a baseball.

I told myself, "OK, you had Tommy John surgery. They repaired the ligament. So now everything is going to be OK."

Deep in the back of my mind, I knew that wasn't the truth. But I had to think that way, so I could get out of my head and just play baseball.

I kept telling myself over and over, "Your elbow is going to be fixed. You are going to be good to go."

When I came back, I started slow — playing catch from maybe 15 or 20 feet apart. Then, as I regained my strength, I simultaneously rebuilt my confidence.

Most people thought my career in Major League Baseball was over. But at the end of 2000, the Cincinnati Reds called me back up to the big leagues. I don't even remember my first appearance when I returned, but once I got that call-up, I was like, "OK, I'm back."

I stopped doubting myself.

I knew they were not bringing me up to embarrass myself or the organization. Instead, I knew I earned the opportunity, which was one of the most significant accomplishments of my career.

That year, I pitched well against my former team, getting out Chipper Jones and Andruw Jones. There were still many people in Atlanta that supported me, so it was meaningful to me to play well in a place I still consider home.

In 2001, I agreed to be traded to the Yankees, which was a childhood dream. I didn't play a huge role on that team because they had a stacked bullpen. But I pitched OK, and it was a great experience.

After 1996, I could have thrown in the towel, but I am glad I did not quit. Instead, I gave it my maximum effort and proved that I could still pitch in the big leagues.

In the process, I learned how powerful our minds can be. So, if you doubt yourself or if your confidence has taken a hit in whatever it is that you do or that you are passionate about, remember what changed the direction of my career.

One decision. One pitch. One moment.

But also note, to change it back, I only needed one person. I needed just one person to believe I could do it.

And that person was me.

Give your best effort and believe in yourself.

You got this!

Mark Wohlers

Humble Beginnings

I Was A Homeless And Hungry Child Until These Miracles Came Into My Life

To those who are considering becoming a mentor,

I am so incredibly thankful for all the miracles that came into my life.

Without so many miracles, I would be dead right now. Maybe, if I were lucky, I would be in jail.

My mom is from Spain, and my dad is from Cuba, but I was born in Tampa, Florida. Early on, I lived with my mother. Even though we were poor, my mother was a rock-star parent. She worked hard as a nanny and housekeeper for a very wealthy family. All day, she washed their clothes, cleaned their house, and took care of their kids, only to come home and do it all over again for my brother and me. My mom signed us up for sports and never missed our games. Our Christmas tree was always drowning in gifts. Come hell or high water, if my brother or I needed something, she would find a way to get it done.

However, when I was 10 years old, the family my mother worked for moved, and everything changed. My mom lost her job and became an alcoholic. No one knew what was going on because my older brother ended up moving in with my grandparents. So, it was just my mother and me.

There would be times when my mom would go missing for a few days, leaving me without food. Sometimes, I would come home from school, and I would be locked out because she was passed out drunk. When she had seizures, I was the one to call 911.

One day my mother told me we were getting evicted. She said I should head over to my friend's house, stay there and wait for her to come back in a few days. When I went to my friend's house, his mother didn't know anything about watching me. So, I returned to our apartment, climbed up the gutter, hopped through the window, and stayed there. I figured my mom would be back soon.

Every day, I'd rush home from school, thinking, "This will be the day she comes back."

But she never came back.

For 10 years, I didn't have much of a relationship with my mother. She was sick, homeless, and repeatedly admitted to the hospital. Extremely thin and losing her hair, whenever I saw my mom, it was traumatizing, as she was so far gone from the Wonder Woman I knew as a young child.

With my mom mostly out of my life, at 11 years old, I was in survival mode. I started asking older dudes in the neighborhood to help me out and get me something to eat. First, they gave me a little money for some McDonald's.

Soon after, they said, "Look, man, I can't give you any more money, but you do what you can with this 'stuff.' Bring me back this much money, and the rest is yours."

That's how and why I got into illegal activity. I was just a hungry kid trying to survive.

Eventually, I couldn't stay in that apartment by myself, and I asked my friend Leonard if I could stay with him once in a while. Too embarrassed to tell him what was going on, I often slept in a dugout at a nearby baseball field on the days I wasn't with him.

My very first miracle came when Leonard's mom, Andrea Daley, realized I was homeless and made me stay with them permanently. She bought me clothes and took care of me. When I was sad or angry, she consoled me. All the kids in my neighborhood had a pass to a local water park, and she bought me one, so I wouldn't feel left out. I don't know how she did it, as she was a single mother herself, but she was like a mother to me. She made me feel safe and loved.

Despite Andrea's efforts, I still got in trouble. Trouble was all I knew.

In school, I got expelled from eighth grade because I frequently got into fights. Violent and regularly involved in criminal activity, at 12 years old, I assumed I'd ultimately end up in prison just like many other members of my family.

Then, more miracles came into my life.

All this time, my dad didn't know what was going on because my mother pushed him away. Only by luck, he found out. After two years of living with Andrea and Leonard, my father told me to come live with him.

Around the same time, I started high school, where I was looking forward to playing football. Football had been the only constant in my life — a safe space and a regular schedule. I loved it so much that I paid for my own $150 entry fee and pads through the years. In youth football, I didn't need good grades to play.

Through a nonprofit program called Play It Smart, our high school football program had an academic coach named Kent Wilson. During my freshman year, Coach Kent saw me screaming at a girl whose mother owed me money. Coach Kent pulled both of us aside and told the girl that if I didn't apologize to tell him. He then told me to see him in his office the next day.

That's when Coach Kent started to look into my background. In our meeting the next day, after we spoke about the argument with the girl, he wrote this number on a teal sticky note.

He said, "You see what this number is?"

I said, "Yeah, it's a 0.5."

He responded, "That's your GPA."

I was like, "OK, so?"

He explained, "You can't play football with this GPA."

Immediately, I started dry heaving. Football was all I had. So, from that day forward, I began to put in some effort. For the remainder of high school, I got straight A's.

Throughout the next four years, Coach Kent told me that I was smart and special, because school came so easy to me. He gave me confidence in the sense that if I had a problem, I knew I could go to him. It made me feel like neither my background nor my family history mattered. There was someone there that would help me with whatever I needed.

But as my life started to take a turn, my father went to prison for a year. My dad didn't want me to get a job, and he wanted me to stay out of trouble.

He used to say, "As long as you do well in school and you play a sport, you don't have to work. If you want to go on a date or want this or that, I got you."

My dad was doing what he did because his full-time job wasn't enough. He knew I needed a car and money to pay for college. So, he was getting involved with all this illegal activity to save my life.

When he went to jail, that was the moment I decided I wanted to be a lawyer. I knew so many people who got in trouble, and the world simply viewed them as criminals. In reality, they were really amazing people who made the wrong decisions for all the right reasons. Those are the types of people I wanted to help.

However, I still needed many more miracles to make it happen. Sure enough, another one soon came into my life.

While my dad was in prison, I was having trouble finding a stable place to live. Tracy Donovan, the mother of my friend Seth, told me to stay with her and her family. She was the first person to teach me about God, and she also helped me with life skills like finances and addressing an envelope properly.

While I was with Ms. Tracy and her family, I received a letter inviting me to attend the National Young Leaders Conference in Washington, D.C. I was the only one in my school invited, but I was about to throw the letter away because it was expensive. Ms. Tracy saw the envelope and asked me about the program. I told her what it was, but I said to forget it. She refused to let me lose this opportunity. Instead, she orchestrated a fundraiser through her church and took me shopping for suits.

Her determination to get me to Washington taught me not to make excuses in life. There is a way through every obstacle. She also taught me to believe in unconditional love and kindness. I never thought that people who didn't know me would give me money. When you grow up in such violence and turmoil, that is all you expect. My life was always every man for himself. When I received those donations, it helped me see the good in the world.

Plus, the conference was a surreal experience. I flew to Washington, D.C., saw snow for the first time, walked the halls of the Capitol, and sat on the floor of Congress. The trip broadened my horizons and made me realize the possibilities that existed outside of my neighborhood.

When I returned, I continued to get in less and less trouble. For a long time, I was so reckless with my life.

There were moments where I was like, "I am dying tonight."

I had bullets graze my t-shirts and guns pointed at my head.

As more and more people stepped up to help me, I moved further and further away from that life. Seeing how much people cared about me made me start to care more about myself.

In my senior year, I hit yet another roadblock. I got injured, and I didn't have a great season in football. As a result, I didn't receive a single offer for an athletic scholarship. Coach Kent set me up at a college recruiting fair. That's where I met the coaches at John Carroll University in Cleveland, Ohio. They told me I would get to play right away. While John Carroll didn't offer athletic scholarships, they were able to put together both an academic scholarship and a financial aid package so I could go to college almost for free, which was great. But once I got there, I realized there were still thousands of dollars of expenses: flying home, tuition increases, school supplies, and basic living necessities.

Thankfully, more miracles came my way.

When I went home for Thanksgiving during my freshman year, I told my Uncle Sebastien that I was thinking about transferring closer to home to a more competitive football program. My uncle didn't believe that was the reason, so he kept prying. Finally, I admitted that it was also too expensive.

Before I went back to school that weekend, he tracked me down at a Chili's restaurant in Tampa, where I was eating with another family. He asked me to come outside and wrote me a blank check. Then, he told me to fill in the balance on my tuition. Also, he said he would cover any tuition balances for the remainder of my four years.

I was completely blown away as he explained that he did not want me to quit because of money and said that he and my Aunt Carolynn believed that I was destined for great things.

When I went back to school, I worked even harder because I did not want to waste their money, and I did not want to let them down.

After four years of college, I went to law school. Now, I have my own practice where I do criminal defense and civil police brutality cases. I have defended kids in similar circumstances that I was once in and parents who committed crimes for the same reason my father once did.

At 33 years old, I am happy to be alive. Financially stable as a successful lawyer with a beautiful wife, I no longer am just surviving, but I can actually say that I am living.

Daily, monthly, quarterly, and yearly, so many stars had to align just for me to have a shot in life. I had and needed many more miracles than the ones I named in this letter. Each miracle showed me that the ultimate form of love is giving to others who have nothing to offer you in return. That's one of the reasons I try to help people every day. It's also why I am writing this letter to encourage you to do the same.

So, if you have the chance to offer guidance and support to a child, do it. Be consistent. It won't always be easy, but if you show someone you care about them, it will carry a lot of weight.

Every child deserves a chance in life. Every child deserves and needs miracles.

And for kids who come from neighborhoods or situations like mine, our miracles start with our mentors.

You, too, can help save a life.

Christopher Rivero

To Struggling Single Moms, This Is How I Found My Way

To struggling single mothers,

I used to have this recurring dream of a little girl sitting on the steps. I wondered why no one would rescue her.

I would pray, telling God, "She needs help. She needs someone to come get her."

While that dream returned for many years, in my waking life, I struggled. I quit school after ninth grade. At 16 years old, I had my first child. Crippled by anxiety and depression, I would look in the mirror and see a young woman who I thought was worthless. I wanted to end my life. I didn't want that person looking back at me to exist anymore. With no education, no money, no job, and parents who were drug addicts, I had no idea how I would take care of my baby.

Now, I have five amazing children. I found a way to provide for them, love them, and raise them to be successful, good people.

I promise you can do it, too, but I will admit — it's not easy.

Sometimes I wanted to give up, but then I thought, "What would happen to my children?"

I had to do everything by myself. To stay motivated, I would leave quotes in the bathroom. I saw them every morning, and they reminded me that I was not a failure.

For 20 years, I was on welfare, but at age 29, with five children, I wanted to plant the seed for a better life. That's when I pursued my GED. It took me seven times to get my GED. I was so determined because it was my opportunity to show my children that you can always change and improve your life.

Often I felt overwhelmed. Creating a schedule and becoming very disciplined helped me. Everyone went to bed and ate meals at certain times, which gave me designated times to just mellow out.

For five years, while my children grew up, I stopped dating. From sexual abuse to neglect, I needed time to heal from all the different situations from my childhood that still impacted me. I went to therapy and let go of all the anger I felt toward people who hurt me throughout my life. That doesn't mean I excuse what they did, but I released them so I could release myself, so I could move on and focus on my children and me.

I took advantage of programs that taught me lessons like budgeting, being on time, and patience. People think because we are moms, we already possess all these tools, but I wasn't equipped with all the knowledge needed to run a household. I realized it was OK if I asked for help or read books relevant to my children and me.

I truly fought to give my children everything I did not have as a child while also trying to believe that I was worthy of a good life. As I fought, I taught my children to do the same. I wouldn't let them quit any of their commitments. Quitting wasn't an option. They had to find ways to get past their obstacles.

They all had their moments where they wanted to give up on something, but a lot of people talk about my son Malik Hooker and his desire to quit football during his sophomore year of college.

Malik was a star athlete in high school, but when he went to Ohio State, where he received a football scholarship, he was fourth on the depth chart. He didn't know how to handle it. He often called me upset. I wanted to rescue my son, but I knew I would ruin the journey he was meant to travel.

So, I told him, "You can do this."

He would come home and say he didn't want to go back to school.

I would say to him, "You can't stay here."

There was a lot of crime and young people dying in our neighborhood. Nothing good would have come from him moving back home. He needed to stay.

Ultimately, he became a starter for the Buckeyes, a first-round draft pick in the NFL, and he now plays for the Indianapolis Colts. To see my son in a stadium with his name on the back of his jersey is incredible.

My children and I have broken a curse that lasted generations in my family. All five of my children went to college, and I, too, am returning to school to get my degree. We are no longer eating tuna casserole just so we can get by for two days. My granddaughter is five years old, and unlike my mother, me, and my children, she will never live in the projects.

I am so proud of my entire family.

I wouldn't say we made it, but as a family, we are making it. We have all come so far, especially me. For the first time in my life, I am working in a position that I love. I'm a Personal Care Assistant, helping kids with learning disabilities and behavioral problems.

As single moms, we can be so hard on ourselves, but I want to tell you if you need a break, take it. If you need help, ask for it. If there are resources available to you, take advantage of them. If people are telling you that you can't make it, please know that you can. Don't give up on your children, and don't give up on yourself.

Today, I'm proud of the woman that I see looking back at me in the mirror. That's what I want for you. I have learned to be self-confident and an advocate for myself and my children. While I still remember dreaming of that little girl waiting on the steps for someone to rescue her, I now realize that she was waiting for me.

With strength and motherly love,
Angela Dennis

If You Listen To This Advice, You Won't Spend Two Decades In Prison

Dear Face (my 16-year-old self),

You're 16 years old, and you want the world to know you aren't afraid of anything. But that's not true. There is one person who scares you, and I am writing to tell you that your fear is ruining your life.

It is the day after Christmas in 1996. You have not been going to school, and you just recently started robbing people, selling drugs, and smoking weed. Face is who you are right now, but Face is not the person you should be.

Face is your street name — a friend gave you the name because people always say you have a baby face. But with the name comes a different persona.

It all started when you were six. Your family went back to D.C. You moved into an apartment building that your grandparents owned, and you could hear gunshots down the block every night. It was like growing up in a war zone.

When you started school in D.C., the class bully hit and pushed you. Even though you were tiny for your age, you defended yourself like Dad trained you to do, and you whooped him. The bully became your best friend, and together you both bullied other kids.

At a young age, you knew you were the smartest kid in the class because you always knew all the answers and raised your hand first. You took your PSAT at 11 and scored very high.

You also knew you had a talent for the arts. At the last minute, the school needed someone to recite a poem called "The Creation." You told the guidance counselor you could do it. You only had a day to memorize it. So, you studied all night. After the performance, many people in the crowd cried, and your guidance counselor grabbed you.

Through tears, she said, "Oh, my God! You are so smart, but you're just going to waste your life with your attitude. "

She wasn't far off.

When you were 11, your dad left. He moved to Las Vegas, leaving you feeling empty and hurt. Around that time, you started to also feel a lot of peer pressure. You wanted to fit in with other kids. So you began to cause trouble — acting like a class clown.

In school, you started to dumb yourself down. You got kicked out of the gifted and talented classes and sent to lowest-level classes where kids couldn't even spell their names.

In the streets, a kid told you to jump someone for nothing.

He told you, "If you don't, you won't be with us."

You chased a guy down the street and beat him up for no reason.

Unfortunately, you don't know how to stand up for values or morals because you don't want to be alone and become a target in your community. Your environment is influencing so many of your decisions. A friend of yours teased you about the condition of your sneakers. That was another catalyst that led to this street lifestyle you are living now.

You feel a sense of empowerment — because you think making your own money, by whatever means, allows you to make your own rules.

However, being Face, living this thug life will lead you to today, December 26, 1996, a day that will change lives forever. You are about to lose money shooting dice. One of the guys will suggest robbing those men selling drugs in what you consider your territory. He will give you a gun. You will go to their apartment, pull out the gun and order the men to give you cash. They will throw the money on the floor. When you bend down to get it, one of the men will grab the gun, which will go off but hit no one. You will fight these men and get out of there safely with the gun but without any cash. When you tell your friends what happened, one of them will go back to the apartment and fatally shoot a 51-year-old man.

Weeks later, you will get arrested. You will laugh when they tell you you are there for murder because you know you didn't kill anyone. However, that's not exactly how the law works.

Prosecutors will allege you went back to the apartment where the killing occurred.[1] Even though you will tell them that you didn't go back, you will be charged and convicted of felony murder because anyone involved in

---

[1] Ryals, Mitch. "How to End a Sentence." Washington Post, 10 Oct. 2019. https://washingtoncitypaper.com/article/178137/how-to-end-a-sentence/

a felony crime that results in death can be charged with murder — even if you're not the one to pull the trigger.

The following year, at 17 years old — still looking like a child at 5'1" and 100 pounds — you will be sentenced to 40 years to life. But you won't be shaken by the reality of your situation. This is normal to you. In your neighborhood, young men either get killed or charged as an adult for a violent crime. It is a future you expected. You will simply follow suit.

The first two years in prison, you will still be Face, a thug, letting people know that nobody is going to prey on you or your property.

However, when you get to prison, a woman who works there will ask you if you can read. She will bring you books. And you will consume one after another. By 18, you start to notice that all those people you were trying to impress in the community have forgotten about you. The people that genuinely love you, like your mom, don't care if you are a gangster or thug or what type of sneakers you own. They genuinely just love you.

Once you realize this, you will have a dark moment. You will smoke some weed in prison. You will sob in your cell as you finally recognize and accept that your whole life has fallen apart.

But then you will make a promise to yourself. Every day you will say one prayer, read at least one verse, do one push-up, and work towards your legal case and GED.

That night in the winter of 1999, you will decide to stop being Face and start being Halim. You will decide to be better — you will decide to just be you. Halim is the name you were given at birth. You never liked it because the name made you stand out from everyone else. But Halim is not a thug. He is not a murderer. He is a smart, poetic, artistic, nerdy guy who loves books.

You will stop smoking weed and gambling. You will pray, and you will read scriptures. You'll learn about Confucianism and Taoism, and you'll start to learn about all these various ways to heal yourself spiritually. Once people realize you are intelligent, they will respect you. They will ask you to write poems for their girlfriends and explain what their lawyers are trying to tell them about their cases.

In prison, you will write 11 books. You will write letters to kings, prime ministers, deans, and professors.

These relationships will help you stumble across research that provides evidence that a juvenile's prefrontal cortex is not fully developed, which makes them more impulsive, more susceptible to peer pressure, and less able to make thoughtful decisions.[2]

Because of your progress in prison, you will become the poster boy for new legislation in D.C. for people who got life sentences for crimes committed under 18. The new law will say anyone who served 20 years for an offense committed under 18 will have the opportunity to go back to court and petition for resentencing and release. From prison, you will get to read your testimony on the matter to lawmakers. The law will be enacted in 2017, and two years later, after 22 years in prison, you will finally be released.

First, when you get out, you will hug your mother tightly. Then, you will ask your family for a computer so you can get to work. All those people you wrote to in prison will provide a network for you, and you will launch a public speaking business, sharing your truth with the world in a poetic way.

---

[2] Tsui, Anjali. "How to End a Sentence." PBS, 2 May 2017. https://www.pbs.org/wgbh/frontline/article/how-brain-science-is-changing-how-long-teens-spend-in-prison/

You will start taking pictures of articles from the Wall Street Journal and writing poetry and commentary on them. That will be your first piece of visual art. After speaking at an Apple store in San Francisco, a man will offer to buy 10 of your pieces at $2,000 apiece. Crazy right? He will turn out to be an owner of the Golden State Warriors, and he will take you to a game and introduce you to the other owners. He will continue to encourage, mentor, and text you daily.

You will share your interest in fashion with him, and he will help you launch a fashion brand. And then, when the pandemic hits, you will start to paint. People all over the world will buy your art, and prestigious galleries will sell your work. Your art will bring you around the globe, building relationships with people from all walks of life. You, a kid from Washington D.C., will be commissioned by a newspaper in the U.K. called the Evening Standard to create art for the late Queen for the Platinum Jubilee celebration. In your first three years out of prison, you will sell about $2 million worth of artwork.

You will do well in life, and you will even have a beautiful little girl. But I need you to listen to me. Don't take that gun. Don't go to that apartment. There is no reason for you to spend 22 years of your life in jail. Please, go to school. You can become an engineer or work in finance since you love math. Stop selling and abusing drugs. Stop the violence.

Don't wait until you're in prison to be a poet. Right now, be an artist. Let the world know that you are smart. If you can have the courage to explore your gifts instead of trying to be a "gangster," you will be able to fill the emptiness your father's absence left you with the love of all the new relationships your art can help you create. If you excel in school, it will keep you safe. Your intelligence can be your ticket out of the hood and your passport to see the world.

83

You came up in a mosque and the church, reading scriptures. Stay connected to your spirituality and honor your family values.

I promise, greatness is inside of you.

The world is so much bigger than the 61 square mile radius of violence and prison and despair that you know as Washington, D.C.

Right now, you think you're tough because you're not scared of drug dealers, police officers, or gang members — many who are much bigger than your diminutive child-like frame. But the reason you will suffer in life — the reason you are not happy — is because there is one person — one thing — that terrifies you right now. And that is your true self.

If you want to be brave, the most gangsterest thing you can do is Love who you are and all that you are and let the light follow.

Don't be Face. Be you!

I know you got a hard head, but I hope you listen.

With love,
The man you are and the man you should have always been — your 42-year-old self — Halim

To Young Immigrants, Here Is How I Am Reaching My Goals

To young immigrants,

I don't know who you are or where you are from, but I, too, know coming to this country is not easy.

My very first words in English were "A McChicken meal. Medium, large, or small?"

At the time, I worked as a cashier at a McDonald's in Miami, Florida. It was not what I wanted to do, but it was what I needed to do.

See, I lived in Venezuela until I was 14. Venezuela had been under an authoritarian regime for over two decades but later became a total anarchy — the government controls everything. A lot of people struggle economically. Going to school is a privilege there, not a right. You can't speak out against the government without the risk of getting killed or persecuted.

Because the law is so non-existent in my country, as a child, I became fascinated with it: Why is the law necessary? What is the rule of law? How do we apply that?

I knew at 10 years old I wanted to be a lawyer. I wanted to save people from unfairness. However, I also knew it wouldn't be easy to become a lawyer living in Venezuela.

When I was 14, my mother worked as a sales representative for a pharmaceutical company. They sold and distributed psychotropics and other medicines and miscellaneous wholesale products to different pharmacies, clinics, and hospitals throughout Venezuela. My mother was the lead representative for the northern area of Venezuela. At that time, the government wanted to take over the company. In February, July, September, and October of 2016, my mom was persecuted by a group of people known as the collectives, which are thieves that the corrupt, and repressive government in Venezuela pays to abuse, harass, kidnap, and even kill people that work for companies that protest against the government. Attempting to coerce her into providing information about her company, she experienced physical, mental, and phycological torture. After that horrific experience, she knew we needed to move to the United States as soon as possible.

We left the only home I ever knew, and we came to South Florida with only one $100 bill. At first, we stayed with my mother's friend for about five months. Then, unexpectedly my mother and I were homeless for the next year and a half. We stayed in eight places — friends and even strangers willing to give us a place to sleep for a month or so. One of the most challenging memories was getting groceries. We didn't have a car, so we'd have to walk miles and miles, which wasn't easy in the Miami heat — especially during the summertime.

My mom always told me education would be the escape from all of my struggles and obstacles. Also, I knew I needed an education if I wanted to become a lawyer. But that first semester of school was tough. Every day I would go home with a headache because I didn't know the language. During the first nine weeks, I almost failed three classes. But then, I started to write down what my teachers would say, and when I got home, I would use Google Translate. Also, I was working at McDonald's so my mother and I could afford a place to live, and working there helped me learn the language faster. After six months, I had a good handle on the language — so much so that McDonald's promoted me to a supervisor and crew trainer of the store. After a year, I was fluent in English, and thanks to my promotion at McDonald's, my mother and I eventually moved into a one-bedroom apartment of our own. Paying rent for the first time with my mom will always be my proudest accomplishment. It was a major step into the rest of our lives.

As we became more and more settled in the U.S., I continued to focus on becoming a lawyer. I had a goal and no plan B. I was determined. Every day, I showed up to school on time and stayed after class to ask my teachers questions about how to live a successful life in the United States. I even started a student organization to help raise money for school supplies for kids in Venezuela. Thanks to my hard work and help from my teachers and mentors, I graduated with a cum laude distinction. Florida International University (FIU) awarded me a full scholarship. My mother cried when we received the letter. People I didn't even know cried. While I didn't show as much emotion, I was excited, proud, and grateful for everyone who helped me along the way.

Now, in my junior year of college, I am getting closer and closer to my goal of becoming a lawyer. I am among 20 students around the world that were accepted into a pipeline program at Stanford Law called Stanford Law Scholars Institute. It is a new program catered to underrepresented communities. Also, I have already completed eight internships and three fellowships. Right now, I am in D.C. working for the Bipartisan Policy Center.

After law school, I want to focus on constitutional law and, one day, become the first Hispanic male Supreme Court Justice. I have so much work ahead of me, but I am focused and determined, just like I have always been.

For you, life may seem so hard and so overwhelming right now. Your goals might feel out of reach, as you might simply be more concerned with where you will sleep tonight than the career you wish to have in 20 years.

Even so, I want you to understand that the steps you take today, big or small, will help create opportunities beyond what you may currently be able to imagine. To get there, here are some tips that have helped me along the way.

For starters, breathe. Just breathe. There are so many emotions that you are currently feeling and will feel. I have been meditating twice a day for 10 years — when I wake up and when I go to sleep. It helps me control my emotions. You could also try hiking, exercising, or a hobby — something to let your mind relax a little.

Curiosity is essential. I was curious about becoming a lawyer, learning the language, and getting internships. Curiosity will lead to knowledge, and knowledge will lead to growth.

Understand that this isn't going to be an easy journey. So, don't be afraid to ask for help, especially if you start to feel desperate or like you don't know what to do next to move forward. People will give you the tools to help you pave your path.

Also, read, read, read, read, and read some more. Listen to a podcast or Audible book if you don't like to read. There is so much valuable information in books and podcasts that you can use to your advantage.

Lastly, don't be afraid to tell your story. Your story has power, and your delivery (of your story) is the most powerful tool you can ever have. It will connect you to other people, empower you to overcome upcoming obstacles, and inspire others.

A few years ago, I worked at McDonald's, only knowing a few English words. Many people would have never guessed I would be where I am today. And I'm not even close to done. I am still very much writing my story, as are you. But I want you to know — no matter what people say or how hard this moment in time feels — that America is a great place, and it's exceeded all of my expectations. And that is because no matter who you are or where you are from, in America, if you stay focused and remain true to yourself and your values, you can become whatever it is that you want to be.

Keep pushing!

Luis F. Moros

To The Executives Who Didn't See My Talent, This Is What Happened

To the executives who didn't see my talent,

Mama would always say, "You are never going to go up until you hit rock bottom because when you hit rock bottom, there is nowhere else to go but up."

Well, thanks partly to you, I hit rock bottom. But I didn't stay there.

My dream to be on the radio started when I was a kid growing up in Philadelphia, long before I met any of you. Like most parents, my mom wanted me to be a doctor or a lawyer, but I always loved music. I have always been a DJ at heart, so I was determined to make it.

In fact, I had no plan B because if I did, I wouldn't have worked as hard, knowing I had another option to fall back on. Instead, I just believed in myself, even though you all did not have any confidence in me.

When I graduated college, I was interning at a local radio station in Philadelphia while djing at clubs. I was making about $1200 to $1500 a week. And that was back in the late 90s. That's around when I started approaching you all for jobs. You all saw me only as a mixer. When I told you I wanted to be an on-air announcer, you basically laughed in my face. You thought I was a joke. You didn't see any potential in me at all.

I didn't let you all stop me. I took a leap of faith, packed up my car, and moved to Gainesville, Florida, without even knowing where I would stay. The boss at Magic 101.3 was willing to give me a shot, paying me $250 a week. However, it didn't last. I got fired in three months after regrettably saying something I shouldn't have on the air.

I was too embarrassed to go back home. Plus, I still believed in myself. I knew I could make it work. A Jacksonville station had an opening, so I went there to interview, but I didn't get the job. I crashed at my cousin's for a couple of days before his wife kicked me out. That's when my rock bottom period began.

Homeless and living out of my car, I got a gym membership just so I had a place to shower. First, I worked as a telemarketer, which was painful for me. Then, I started pushing around a cart and selling items. It was humiliating, but I needed to save up enough money to get an apartment. That job led me to work for a company where I sold products door-to-door. But after an incident where I got in a fight with a bus driver, I ended up moving to South Carolina, where my uncle lived. He owned a strip club, and I started djing there.

At this point, I was sitting there thinking, "Why does God hate me? Why is all of this happening?"

I know what you are thinking right now. You are thinking it was happening because you were all right about me. But you weren't.

A new radio station started in Columbia, South Carolina. I gave them a call, and the person who answered was best friends with the guy who gave me my first internship in Philly when I was 17. My old boss gave me a recommendation, and I was back on the air. Five months later, a station in Greensboro, North Carolina, offered me a job.

In North Carolina, a newspaper reporter asked me about my next goal in radio, and I said nights in Miami. I had no clue how I was going to get to Miami, but I knew that's where I wanted to be. Three weeks later, a former co-worker from the Gainesville station, the one where I got fired, hit me up about an opening at 99 Jamz in Miami, so I sent in my tape. Coincidentally, her boss, the station's program director, was driving through North Carolina. He heard me on the air and called his boss and said I think we found our guy for our nighttime job. When he got back to Miami on Monday morning, my tape was already on his desk. Three weeks later, I was in Miami.

That's how I made it! You didn't think it would happen, but it did. My struggle was part of my success story. While I have had some bumps in the road since landing in Miami, I am still on the air, as I am currently with Hot 105 Afternoon Drive.

My wise mom also told me, "If you believe, you receive. If you doubt, you will be without."

In life, if you don't believe in yourself, you might as well forget about it.

I definitely didn't forget about my dream, and I know at least one of you won't ever forget me, either. See, you may have never hired me, but you have definitely heard me on the air. I am the guy on the competing station, kicking your ass.

Never bet against me. I never did.

The kid you turned down,
Alex Chisholm

Abandoned At Birth, This Is How I Have Been Able To Thrive In Life

To those who had a rocky start to life,

During my senior year of college, I decided to run for class president. I went to a meeting in a room full of people I had never met. On one side of the room were a bunch of frat guys and people in ROTC. On the other side, it was many girls who knew each other from their sorority. I was the only Black person in that room.

I thought to myself, "I'm not getting this. Everybody knows each other."

But I decided to go for it anyway. The other candidates promised to raise a specific amount of money for our senior class.

Not me.

I said, "My name is Angel Thomas. I've been running boards since I was 13 years old. I was on the youth and adult board of directors for a nonprofit organization where I also managed my own firm, Hip Hub (a local music and art distribution service). I've raised this much money over the past couple of years, but I'm not going to promise anything. I'm just going to get out there, and I'm going to do my best."

Doing my best has always been how I have lived. Because of that, I have come so far from where my life began.

See, I was born under horrible circumstances — pure darkness and evil.

For many years, I had no idea. My childhood was seemingly normal. Growing up, I had two loving parents. My dad was my best friend. He let me do whatever I wanted. My mother was a bit tough on me, but that's because she wanted the best for my life. Like many other young girls, I loved Barbie and Bratz dolls.

My cousin told me I was adopted at four years old, but I don't remember the conversation.

In the third grade, I told my mom, "Hey, my friend from school is adopted from Guatemala."

And she responded, "You know, you're adopted too."

I said, "Really?"

I was never treated any differently than my siblings, as I always felt very loved. However, sometime after that, I started to learn more about my past. In elementary school, I found a baby book of mine. That's where I discovered a newspaper article with the headline, "Deep December: What Child Stirs Under The Stars?"

The article said a newborn baby was found abandoned outside in an Anastasia blanket with an umbilical cord still attached on the coldest night of the year in November 1999. It said the baby suffered from severe infant hypothermia. I knew the article was talking about me, and from that moment on, I always thought that my biological mother just didn't want me.

But that's not what happened. It took me a little longer to find out the truth.

One night in middle school, I went to my mother's room. She was watching the news about some court case, and I felt her energy was off.

I said, "Hey, Mom! What's wrong? You alright?"

She responded, "Yeah, I'm OK. Just go to sleep. You have school tomorrow morning."

Knowing she was upset about something, I told her I loved her and went to bed.

I was in therapy at the time because I was bullied at school and suffered from self-harm. My dad lived in Durham, an hour from my mother and me in Greensboro, North Carolina. Unexpectedly, he showed up at one of my therapy appointments.

I thought to myself, "Oh my, my dad is here. What did I do?"

After my mom, dad, me, and my therapist sat down, my mother picked up her purse and took out a manilla folder.

She pulled out an article and pointed to the picture of the man in the story.

She said, "That's your biological father."

Then, she took out a picture — which wasn't a part of the article — and said, "That's your biological mother."

She told me to read the article. Hurt and shocked, I couldn't believe what I was reading. My biological father raped my mother, who gave birth to me when she was 13 years old. My father took me from my mother and abandoned me in an apartment complex because he didn't want people to know he was molesting my mother.

The son of the lady who found me said I was his angel. My mom kept the name because she said angels were watching over me that day. It was a miracle that I was OK.

But at that moment, I didn't feel like an angel. I felt so guilty. For all these years, I resented my biological mother for not wanting me. And that wasn't the case at all. Years after learning about how I came into this world, I met my biological mother — but it was tough. We didn't have a lot in common. Our life experiences were different.

As far as my biological father, I never met him. But one day, shortly after I learned my whole story, Child Protective Services left a note on our front door to call them. They wanted my DNA. We gave it to them, and I found out a few years later that my DNA put my biological father away for life in prison.

While I was already struggling to cope because of bullying, I simultaneously was trying to process the idea that I was the product of horrific violence. As a result, I started to act out. I talked back to my mom. I was angry. I was sad and frustrated. Luckily, no matter what happened, no matter what I did, my mother always loved me. She made me want to be a better version of myself.

Thanks to my mom, I became less of a dreamer and more of a doer. She encouraged me to get good grades and be a leader.

See, at first, I was one of those kids that sat at home, ate up all the food in the house, and didn't do anything.

When I was in sixth grade, my mom said, "Just get in the car."

I responded, "OK, Where are we going?"

She told me I was joining an organization called The Chosen 50, which aimed to develop young leaders in Greensboro, North Carolina, where we lived. I was a shy, reserved kid. I barely spoke.

In an interview, the organization asked me, "If you had to be one color, what would you be?"

They said I could only pick one, to which I responded, "Well, that doesn't make any sense. I'd be a rainbow because I'm not limiting myself."

They said that answer is why I got into the organization. After that, I started to build confidence, try new activities, meet new people, and make connections. I became a leader and mentor in my community, getting involved in many other organizations. In fact, in 2018, I was crowned Miss Teen Greensboro and was the first runner-up in Miss Teen North Carolina.

My mom also played a significant role in my academics. If I ever struggled with a class, she was at the school talking to the teacher and helping me work through any challenges. Also, my mom is the one who told me to become a pilot, suggesting I attend T. Wingate Andrews High School. Despite years of bullying in middle school, I made many friends in high school and began to plan my future. On my first day, I saw a poster advertising Embry-Riddle Aeronautical University. Right away, I knew that's where I wanted to go to school. Many people told me not to bother because it was so expensive and I would need to take out loans. But I knew if I did my best, I would find a way to do it. I'd be OK.

And sure enough, I was right, and ultimately, I attended Embry-Riddle Aeronautical University.

During the first few semesters of college, I struggled as I realized I didn't want to be a pilot. I switched my major to aeronautics with minors in business and safety. That's when I started to excel at school. By my senior year, I got my GPA up, and that's when I ran for class president and won!

Despite not knowing anyone else in that room, I won!

We raised about $10,000 in three months with only four fundraisers. Ultimately, I graduated from college. Now, I work for Amazon as a workplace health and safety specialist.

Long term, I would like to start either a business or a nonprofit that helps other people. I am proud to say I am doing very well in life.

While I don't know where you are in your journey right now or how you feel at this very moment, if you're someone who is hurting, I want you to know everything is going to be OK. Always stay true to yourself and stick to your path. Lean into the people that love you, support you, and want you to be happy and succeed. Don't worry about what anybody outside of your circle says or thinks. Your past is a part of you, but it's not something that defines you. It's another stepping stone that you have to walk over. But once you walk over, it's behind you.

At times, like me, you may need to sit with your emotions. Let yourself feel them.

But then, ask yourself, "What can I do to get to that next step? What can I do to feel better? And how can I positively deal with these emotions so that they don't keep resurfacing?"

One day, I had to sit down and have a talk with myself, addressing the darkness surrounding my early life.

I said to myself, "You had nothing to do with what happened. Yes. It was so bad. But out of that terrible thing that happened, a beautiful and strong person — an Angel — came to be."

I am not my biological father. On the day I had this conversation with myself, I decided I would always be the opposite of him by adding love to people's lives.

While I am only 22 years old, I have learned from my story that no matter how dark your past may be, if you do your best, you can always be the light that the world needs.

With love, hope, and happiness,
Angel Thomas, formerly known as Baby Doe

How I Made It With The Odds Heavily Stacked Against Me

To those with the odds stacked against them,

When I was in high school, I had a football teammate named Darren, whose father was the superintendent of schools in Paterson, New Jersey, where we lived. Darren came from a very stable family and lived on the "nice" side of town in a house with his parents and two siblings. We lived in the same city but were seemingly worlds apart. I was the youngest of six children. My father never lived with us and died when I was 12 years old. We didn't own a home or have a lot of money, but somehow my mother provided what I needed. We lived in subsidized housing or housing projects in communities plagued by low academic achievement, unemployment, drug abuse, and violence, among other things.

If you put my profile next to Darren's, nine people out of 10 would bet on Darren to beat the odds for Black men and for me to fall victim to them. But Darren, an All-State football player with a full-ride to an ACC school, developed a drug habit that resulted in a 10-year prison sentence for armed robbery. Since Darren and I graduated high school in 1986, I was blessed to play Division I college football and attend law school thereafter (I wasn't good enough for the NFL). I worked as a lawyer at big firms and as an in-house counsel for a large company. I served as a state and federal prosecutor and as Chief Operating Officer in the city where Darren and I grew up. Now, I am what I call a "lawyer-preneur," where I practice law and am involved in different charitable and business endeavors that provide me further opportunities for meaning.

I remember meeting Darren in prison — Darren was an inmate, and I visited him while a top prosecutor.

At the time I thought, "Why did Darren go to prison while I was able to pursue a career in law?"

I am still a work in progress, but, as I have heard some say, I managed to overachieve. And I still can't help but wonder, "Why me?"

Transitions, The Cycle Of Life

When I was a child, I initially wanted to be a firefighter, a police officer, or a construction worker because those were the people I saw making money in my community. We didn't have family or friends who were doctors, lawyers, accountants, or engineers. But in fourth grade, my mind shifted. I had a teacher named Wyzetta Jones. She knew how to motivate kids. We played different academic games, and I was extremely competitive and argumentative.

One day she said to me, "You would make a great lawyer."

And I asked, "Why did you say that, Ms. Jones?"

She said, "Because you talk too much."

The idea of becoming a lawyer stuck with me. Because Ms. Jones planted the seed, I began to have a dream, a vision.

My family moved five times by fifth grade — from one part of the city to another. Fortunately, I was a good athlete, playing football, basketball, and baseball, which gave me confidence and made it easier to connect with new people and make friends. I also played on city-wide teams, which helped me build a network around the city and beyond. Because I learned how to adapt to new environments at an early age, I became unafraid of change.

A Perfect Storm — Drugs, Disease, And Mandatory Minimums

During my teens, the crack cocaine epidemic spread through the "hood" like wildfire. I witnessed family, friends, and classmates, who were perfectly healthy and vibrant, become a shell of themselves almost overnight. One of my brothers died from a drug overdose, and another brother succumbed to HIV AIDS. I loved those guys, and they apparently looked out for me more than they did for themselves.

Also, the implementation of mandatory minimum sentences for drug and gun-related offenses disproportionately impacted Black and brown people. Once a person got into the criminal system, the cycle started and seemed inescapable. And I wasn't exempt. I've had a few close calls. One time, in particular, a local drug dealer accused me of holding his stash, so a police officer stopped me and reached for his gun. In another incident, the police raided my block the day after I left for Rutgers. One day earlier, I would have been arrested in that sweep just for being there.

With that said, I was not dealing drugs or using them, but I lived in the community with those who did. They were still my friends and neighbors. Thankfully, I knew I wanted more out of life than what I saw, and my mom, coaches, and teachers told me that more was possible if I applied myself.

Mentorship Has Its Privileges

Because I listened to the people who invested themselves in my success, I received several Division I scholarship offers for football. My oldest daughter was born at the beginning of my senior year of high school, which certainly impacted my life, but I was determined to be a good father and follow my dream from fourth grade. I decided to stay close to home and accepted a football scholarship to play at Rutgers University in New Brunswick, where I initially struggled academically before I began taking law classes. Rutgers is where I met the late Mr. G, a Rutgers alumnus and fitness buff who loved supporting and employing student-athletes. Mr. G was a lawyer by trade, but he parlayed his law degree into a remarkably successful business career. He introduced me to lawyers and judges and helped me get my first internship with the late Clive S. Cummis. He planted the seeds of entrepreneurship to leverage opportunities with Emil J. Solimine, a confidante and business partner of Mr. G.

At first, I didn't know if I could trust Mr. G. I was an insecure Black kid from the inner city and was mistakenly taught not to show weakness or trust anybody, let alone a man who didn't share my ethnicity and background. Mr. G was a Caucasian Jew. I wondered what motivated him to mentor me. Despite my doubts, I continued to invest in the relationship with Mr. G. I couldn't afford all my books and housing for law school, so he helped me. But even more memorable was this one phone call I made to him after my first year of law school. There was pressure in law school to perform at a high level. One day, I was down because I didn't feel like I scored high enough on a final exam. I called Mr. G to deliver the "bad news." His response caught me off guard.

He said, "Kid, I am proud of you."

That's when I knew he really cared about me. Our relationship evolved through the years from mentor-mentee to more like father-son. And to this day, even though he is no longer alive, his influence echoes throughout my life through his family, his long-time friend, my mentor, Emil, and others. Because I trusted the process and allowed myself to be vulnerable, I developed faith in God and His ability to use family, friends, and mentors to help others. By the grace of God, I survived and made it to adulthood.

Focus, Focus, Focus

If the odds are stacked against you, as they were for me, it is important that you find one thing or one person to help keep you focused because distractions are everywhere. You cannot get rid of some distractions, but you can learn to focus regardless of their presence. Sports kept me disciplined and focused, but for you, it may be science, technology, engineering, the arts, or math. I was motivated to stay in school and do well because I wanted to play on the team. My coaches would sit or suspend players who did not meet behavior or academic expectations. I was benched a few times and am thankful to them for doing so. I learned that there are consequences to action or inaction.

Get an education. Don't quit school because it will severely limit your options and opportunities if you do. Create a network for yourself that will help you grow and develop in your chosen field. "Play Up" by using your gifts, talents, skills, and abilities to leverage an opportunity or solve a problem. Growing up, I played on teams with older kids who were more skilled, but it taught me to constantly challenge myself to compete and get better at something every day. Seek guidance from people in your school, community, church, club, or other organizations who have what you want or have access to those who do. Join a team, organization, or club where you can grow in the community and be surrounded by supportive adults who will invest in your success and development.

A Promise Made And Kept

Darren's experience taught me this: There are no guarantees in life. In many instances, we are defined more by the choices we make than the choices our parents made. It is undeniable that parents can set children up for success, but the power of choice can destroy the best-laid plans. While in prison, Darren promised his parents he would complete his college studies. In May 2022, almost 36 years later, Darren graduated with honors from Lincoln University. His parents passed and were not there to physically witness his remarkable comeback, but I was there beaming with pride while wondering what Darren's life would have been like if he had made different choices. I shifted my thoughts and decided to stay in that moment because he can't go back. None of us can.

Giving Thanks With A Grateful Heart

Today, I am 53 years old and am gaining a deeper understanding of God's purpose for me in this life. Mentoring, coaching, and serving are all a part of my portfolio as a lawyer-prenuer

I have a grateful heart and often marvel at God's grace upon my life. I have a wonderful wife, three incredible children, and a lovely grandchild. When I think about "Why me?" I am not sure I have the right sociological answer, and I have learned to accept that. The important thing is that no matter where you come from or how many people count you out, success is closer than it may appear if you remain faithful to your vision, surround yourself with supportive people, and get after it.

You can do it!

Vaughn McKoy

P.S. For more information on Vaughn, please check out his book "Playing Up: One Man's Rise From Public Housing To Public Service Through Mentorship."

To Students At Ginn Academy, This Is Why It Is So Important That You Listen

To the students at Ginn Academy,

Several years ago, I looked up the percentage of foster kids who receive a bachelor's degree. It's less than two percent. And if you factor in me being an African-American male, it is even lower. Like many of you, I have had the odds stacked against me in life.

But I know now to beat those odds, all you have to do is listen.

You probably think I don't know about your problems or that I couldn't possibly understand your specific challenges. Maybe that's true. Maybe it's not. But, like you, I certainly didn't have it easy.

I don't remember much of my early childhood — only that there was a lot of moving around. My mother battled drug addiction, and I never met my biological father. He passed away when I was a baby. While I initially lived with my mom, I was taken away from her, and I started going into group homes and foster care.

Group homes felt somewhat institutionalized. We ate buffet style, with people putting food on our plates as we moved down the line. For clothes, they took us to a huge room where we picked out whatever we wanted to wear that day. I did not have clothes of my own.

On weekends, I would often go to different people's houses. I think they were inquiring about adopting my little brother and me, but at the time, I just thought we were going to my friends' houses for the weekend.

At first, I didn't feel any type of way about my situation. I thought bouncing around and living with different people was normal because that was all I knew.

Then, one Thanksgiving, when I was eight years old, my friend invited me to spend the holiday with his family. He had a mom, a dad, a brother, and a sister.

As I walked into their house, I remember thinking, "Dang, this is crazy!"

They had a big house and a bunch of game systems, and all the kids played sports. Both parents lived in the house and cooked a lot of food. Everybody was close-knit. It was a family environment, which was a really good feeling. That was when I realized something was missing from my life. And from that point on, more than anything, I wanted parents of my own.

Later that year, my social worker came to my school in Arizona and told me that my brother and I were going to Cleveland. I had never heard of Ohio, let alone Cleveland. An aunt we didn't know lived in Cleveland. The social worker told us we were only going for a few weeks, but we never went back to Arizona. And I never saw my mother again.

My aunt was older and single. She did not have children of her own, but she adopted a few of my cousins before taking in my brother and me. For the first time, we regularly had home-cooked meals and our own clothes. I wouldn't say it was necessarily a family vibe like I imagined, but I did feel like I found a home.

Once I moved in with my aunt in Cleveland, the struggle was different. I was already used to poverty, but now I was living in poverty. I could see it. I am sure you understand. Like me, you, too, probably have got friends who have been shot, killed, or gone to jail for life.

Where we are from, it's easy to go down a bad path, but I know now there is so much more out there for all of us if we just listen.

In middle school, I was always cracking jokes and playing around. During that time, I got adopted, and my auntie changed my name. Two of my cousins who lived with us had the same first name as me, Brandon. So, they made my middle name, Xavier, my new first name, and switched my last name. I wasn't happy about the name change, and I think acting out was my way of dealing with all my past and current struggles.

Football was my only real passion, and I was very good. Many of the Catholic schools recruited me, but my auntie didn't want to pay money, only for me to get kicked out. So, my principal suggested Ginn Academy — the same school you attend right now.

During my freshman year, a scout from the University of Southern California came to our school to see our players. I couldn't believe it. Then, our coach and the leader of our school, Ted Ginn Sr., invited some of his former players, such as Pierre Woods, Donte Whitner, and Ted Ginn Jr., to come back and share their stories with us. These players graduated from college. They played in the NFL, and they won championships and Super Bowls.

That's when I realized I, too, could have a future. And Coach Ginn wanted to help me get wherever I wanted to go.

The only thing I needed to do was listen.

He was constantly speaking about life and real-world situations. For example, I was very immature, and I liked to joke around a lot.

He always said to me, "The world is serious, but you're the only one playing."

Also, he knew my story.

He'd tell me, "The world is not going to care about your problems."

When Ginn would talk to us, there were times he had tears in his eyes, trying to make us understand.

Ginn, Ms. Parker, and so many other people at Ginn Academy believed in me, and they believe in you too. They believe we can do anything, and they want us to believe that as well.

But you've got to listen.

During my senior year of high school, Ginn sat us down after practice and told us he had cancer. I was hurt and scared. However, he was still focused on me, my classmates, and our future.

I, along with my teammates, all wanted to play Division I football. We worked hard. We pushed each other. We held each other accountable. But when my senior year came around, the Division I offers weren't exactly rolling in as I'd hoped. While many of my teammates got scholarships from big-time schools, I got more interest from smaller schools.

When smaller schools came to talk to me, I had a bad attitude. I didn't want to speak to them. Ginn wanted me to meet with them. He kept trying to explain to me that I had a great opportunity.

Unfortunately, I didn't listen.

I ended up committing to Lake Erie because they gave me a scholarship to play football. As a freshman, I started, but I wasn't going to class or taking school seriously. In my first semester, I had all C's and one D.

Ultimately, I got academically dismissed from school, lost my scholarship, and missed a year of football. I went to Tri-C, our local community college, with the intent of going back to Lake Erie without a scholarship. After Tri-C, I had to take two summer classes at Lake Erie and bring my GPA above a 2.0. This time, I put in the effort, but I got two B's, and it wasn't enough. I had a 1.9 GPA. I missed another year of football. Then, I failed a bio class, and that was it. The school dismissed me again.

I packed all my stuff up and didn't tell anyone I got kicked out. It was heartbreaking. I didn't know what I was going to do next.

This was the moment a lot of people probably would've quit. But instead, I started thinking about Ginn and all the lessons he shared with me. This was the moment I began to grow up, and I started to listen.

The very next day, I began applying to colleges.

Luckily, someone suggested I apply to Notre Dame College in Cleveland. I got in right away, but more bad news came when I found out that you have to sit out a year when you transfer academically ineligible. So, for the third straight year, I missed football. And if I wanted a shot at playing the following season, I damn near needed to get straight A's.

I knew it wasn't going to be easy, but I kept telling myself, "I've got to make this work."

In the fall of 2015, I met with my coaches every day after class and focused on my school work. I ended up getting all A's except for one C+. I did well enough to become eligible. Finally, I got over that hump.

That's when I started to believe that whatever life throws at me, I can handle it. It's also when I realized all Ginn was ever trying to tell us was that things will go wrong in life. But whatever adversity we face, we do have the courage and the strength to persevere.

I ended up playing well in football and got the opportunity to participate in an NFL Pro Day. In school, I had another setback, trying to get my credits from Lake Erie to transfer over, but ultimately we figured it out, and I graduated from college. I became one of the two percent of foster children who grew up and got a bachelor's degree. Ginn was there nearly every step of the way.

Ginn was there for my first spring game at Notre Dame and my senior game. He showed up when I gave a speech about my story. When I walked across the stage on graduation day, I looked out into the crowd, and there he was, pointing proudly at me. As much as Ginn has going on in his life, he showed up every time I asked him to be there for me.

I may not have had parents like I always wanted, but I did have Ginn. We all have Ginn. He cares about me just like he cares about you, and I am forever grateful.

Currently, I work in the finance department for Tesla. Next month, I will graduate from Grand Canyon University with my Master of Business Administration (MBA). My GPA is above a 3.0.

I tried looking up the odds of a foster kid getting a master's degree, but I couldn't find any stats — probably because there are so few of us.

The reason I am telling you all this is I want you all to know that if you listen to Ginn — if you really lean in and listen — what you will hear is him not only giving you the blueprint to beat the odds but also giving you the love, unconditional support, and self-confidence to set new standards.

Good luck!

Xavier Dowdell-Fullbright

Unseal Your Superpowers

LAUREN'S THOUGHTS

Pursue What You Want Like It's **Destined** To Be Yours

Since I could walk, I was an athlete, as I was faster, stronger, and more coordinated than most other kids, male or female. Plus, my dad and I bonded over sports. After sitting next to an ABC sports television executive at a New York Rangers playoff game when I was nine, I knew I wanted to be a sports reporter.

A few months after I met that ABC executive in 1995, I was in fifth grade and ready to start my career. It was early in the school year. The leaves had not yet begun to fall when my mother and I were driving from soccer practice in her minivan in a busy suburb about 35 miles northwest of New York City (Rockland County).

As I gazed out the window, we passed a building enclosed by a gate. The building had the letters "TKR" written on it. I asked my mom if she knew what was inside that building. She said it was a local TV cable station for Rockland County.

That next week, I pulled out our big yellow phonebook, placed it on our island in our very white kitchen, flipped through the pages to get to the T's, and found TKR Cable Company.

I thought to myself, "Yes! I got it!"

Filled with enthusiasm, I grabbed the phone on the wall next to our little kitchen TV and called the station When an operator answered the phone, I asked if they had any sports reporting opportunities for kids. The person who answered transferred me to a producer, who told me they had a kids' news show, but it didn't yet have a sports segment. She told me to have my mother call back the next day.

When my mother came home from work, I screamed, "Mom, I got a job!"

In the mid-'90s, I hosted the sports and fitness segment on "The Kid Report" for TKR Cable in Rockland County.

Once I got a taste of being on camera, I wanted a bigger bite. And despite being a normal kid who played sports and hung out at local malls with friends, I continued to hustle for opportunities.

When I was 13, I was vacationing in Miami Beach with my family, and I went for a walk on Ocean Drive. I knew they were filming a movie called "The Crew" about old retired mobsters. Big-time stars were in the film: Burt Reynolds, Richard Dreyfuss, Jennifer Tilly, and Jeremy Piven. We had spoken to Jeremy Piven in line for the bathroom at a restaurant called Grillfish, and we ran into Richard Dreyfuss in the lobby of our hotel, The

Loews. Through them, we heard about the movie. Sure enough, on my walk that day, I stumbled upon a small boutique hotel right on Ocean Drive where they were filming several scenes.

Barricades blocked off the entire set, but I told security I was staying at the hotel where they were shooting and didn't have my key because I was just a kid. Once I got on set, I found somewhere to sit that was out of the way. Then, I started chatting with the people who worked on the set, and they showed me who was directing the movie. I walked up to the director during a break, tapped him on the shoulder, and asked if I could be in the film. He said yes and told me to bring my parents back to the set later that night to discuss the details. If you ever watch "The Crew," I am the preteen screaming, "Congratulations" in the wedding scene at the end.

I love that confidence and fearlessness I had as a child, but those qualities were threatened later in life. As time moved on and I got older, it often felt, and sometimes still feels, like the universe was trying to break me down.

One of my English teachers implied I should major in math in college because I wasn't a good writer. A TV agent took a meeting with me only to sit on his high horse and tell me he didn't think I was pretty enough for a job in TV. A few co-workers were so competitive that they tried to sabotage me by pulling my script from the prompter or purposefully cutting me out of shows. There were even bosses who shut down ideas because of corporate nonsense or misogynistic beliefs.

As an entrepreneur, which is another dream I am now pursuing, there has been a whole new set of challenges. I started my company with only $3,000.

Regularly, there are technological issues, unexpected expenses, and not enough time in the day.

It seems like the higher the climb, the harder the hike. And I know I am not alone.

I know you had the same determination and enthusiasm as I had as a kid. I know that when you were little, you believed your dreams were possible and felt joy at the thought of them coming true. I know that when you were young, you didn't think anything could stop you from your happily ever after. Then, life happened. People questioned you. Resources were slim. And your own family or friends told you to "be realistic."

When you feel frustrated, broken, or like the path to success doesn't exist, I want you to remember these stories and their messages. These are stories of people who have faced extreme challenges: plane crashes, homelessness, foster care, abuse, and wrongful imprisonment. They didn't give up. They didn't stop dreaming. They kept going, and they found a way. And you can, too.

These letters are a reminder of what happens when you stay true to who you are and what you want, no matter how much life tries to rattle you or how impossible getting to that next level feels in the moment.

While you, your dreams, and your circumstances may change over time, I hope these letters ensure your fearless, hopeful, and determined mindset, the one you had as a child, always remains the same.

Lauren

- chapter 2

his book, and my life's work
started with a secret. Not a s
ne shared with me, but some
happened to me, something a
years ago. I was the last co in of
place in my town, and my
ess co n't, wou't, a
Maybe small sort me w
rassed. But mostly, wouldn
the rea of the boys
e. I su t had what
ened from others; it was som
ouldn cept within self
t too only lf my life to
hat secret into my superpow
n 20 wo d
a New York renl
Hudson River. As I opened
d looked at this incredible w

" I hope these letters allow you to give yourself grace in the grieving process as you realize that healing isn't a straight path. "

- Lauren

Loss Of A Parent

Dear Dear, It's Me

Dear Dad,

It has been almost exactly four years since you passed away, and there is not a day, not a second, that I don't miss you. More than anything, I just want to tell you that I love you. I vividly remember the day I lost you. Mom and I were holding your hands when you passed. I literally felt my heart drop. I felt numb, and I almost lost feeling in my legs. That was the worst feeling that could ever happen to anybody. It was really tough.

You told me weeks before you died that 2015 would be the hardest year of my life, and if I could get through this, I could get through anything, but I thought you were just talking about basketball. When you died, it felt like my life was over. I didn't care about much of anything except taking care of Mom and Nana. I lost the love for the game, a love that I had had since I was a baby.

Mom always said I was basically born in Madison Square Garden. When I used to hear your name in the stands, I would get excited. You and Mom introduced me to every other sport before basketball, but I always wanted to play ball. Whether it was AAU, Niagara, or Auburn, you were always watching, even if you weren't there. After you died, it felt weird to play ball and not have you there.

When we talked after games, you always went to the bad first. You told me what I needed to work on. Then you would go to cracking jokes and making stuff easy and funny again. There was never a dull moment with you! You were my best friend. I don't even have a favorite memory of you. All of them mean so much to me. But I do remember the first time I scored 30 points. It was against Iona, and we (Niagara) won in overtime. I was excited we won.

I figured you were going to be like, "Yeah! Congrats!"

But instead, you said, "Why the fuck did you shoot so many threes?"

I was like, "Dang! I just scored my career high!"

I think I am doing well, and you said, "You are just messing up your own percentage. If you are going to take threes, you got to take them at the right time."

Even when I was at Auburn, you still said I took too many threes. In my mind, the challenge was I had to make the threes. So, I had just played against Kentucky, and I think I hit five out of six, a very high shooting percentage from the three, and then my coach, Bruce Pearl, told me that I was leading the SEC in three-point percentage. Right after the game, I flew out to see you. At this point, you were in the hospital and had a tube in your throat, so you couldn't talk.

I told you, "For someone that you say can't shoot threes, I am leading the SEC in three-point shooting percentage."

You just looked at me and shrugged your shoulders like, "So what?" and we just started smiling.

It's just things like that, memories like that, that always make me miss you because it was just always fun.

When you died, I asked myself, "Do I really want to do this? Do I really want to play ball?"

I was home for a while, and I knew you wanted me to finish my season at Auburn, but I was taking my time sulking and everything.

Mom, who has really stepped up since you've been gone, finally said, "It's time for you to go back to Auburn."

She pushed me, but deep down, I knew all along I would play basketball again.

There have been some tough days, but any time I have a bad day, I just think about you, and you cheer me up. Any story about you makes me smile. It could be as simple as thinking about you coming into the house or me coming into the house and you just saying something outrageous and making me laugh. Basketball fans saw you as a tough, hard-nosed player, but off the court, you were one of the most heartwarming people you could ever meet. You were honest. You always wanted to make people laugh, and you never wanted to disappoint anyone.

There are times you come into my dreams, and you talk to me. I can hear your voice. Sometimes when I work out, I can see you talking to me just like how it was, like you are here. People probably think I have lost my mind, but we were that close, so you are going to appear in my life regardless of the separation.

Dad, in the last four years without you, I have definitely matured and grown up. As a man, I am making sure Mom is OK. Before Nana passed away, I took care of her, too, just like you would have wanted. In basketball,

I have become a better shooter (still shooting threes). I have learned the game more, studied it more, and I have focused on having a good pace. I have played in Cyprus, Canada, and China, and now I am about to head overseas again, but I haven't made a decision as to where yet.

In your process of making it to the NBA, you proved everybody wrong. You didn't take a direct route to the NBA. You played in the CBA and overseas as well. You were somebody that defeated a lot of odds, and I think in a weird way that is similar to the path that I am going through. I want to make it to the NBA. I want to carry on your name and still have it out there.

Although, to be honest, Dad, what makes me most proud to be your son is not even the fact that you played in the NBA. It is that I got to spend my whole life with you in the house, dropping knowledge to me as I grew up. The time you spent with me is what mattered most.

Because you ended up having so little time, just 48 years, I treat life differently now. I put more urgency in my life. I don't procrastinate. If it's time to do something, I just do it. Life is too short. If I believe I can do something, then I am just going all out.

And Dad, I believe I can achieve ALL my goals in basketball. I am never going to quit, and I am going to keep fighting until I can't fight anymore. Losing you has made me hungrier to achieve the dreams that we envisioned together, and when I do, I am going to smile because I know you'll be watching over me, saying, "We did it!" I know more than anything you are proud that I found the love for the game again, but the truth is I did so because where there is basketball, there is also you.

Love, your son,
Antoine Mason

This Is How I Rediscovered My Purpose After I Lost My Dad

To those struggling to cope with a loss,

Six years ago, I was on a serious downhill path. I never thought I would take my own life, but I did feel as though life was not worth living. All I wanted to do was sit and stare at an unpainted wall.

I was so lost.

On December 4, 2014, my father, who was 57 years old, died from a heart attack.

My dad was more than just a loving, involved, and protective father. He was my mentor. He had a big personality and a determined attitude.

Shortly after high school, my dad found a lug nut on the sidewalk on his way home from a catering job. He turned that lug nut into a ring. That's when he decided to apply to the Fashion Institute of Technology in New

York. After getting rejected, he showed up at the dean's office with the ring he created, insisting that the school give him a shot, which they did.

When my dad wanted something in life, he was relentless.

One time he read me a quote that said, "He didn't tell me how to live. He lived, and let me watch him do it."

It wasn't until I started to cope with grief that I realized the gift my father gave me was the example that he set for me.

My father was Scott Kay, a world-renowned jewelry designer.

My dad introduced me to jewelry when I was five years old. By age nine, he started taking me to the office. It was so exciting to me. We had a small workshop in the back. It was amazing to see somebody's hands create these designs. Then, I would look up on the wall and see pictures of jewelry that my dad had created. His work was in magazines. So, as a little girl, my dad seemed like a hero. And his company was magical to me.

I don't know if I ever really said, "This is what I want to do for the rest of my life." I just knew it was going to happen.

In college, I studied jewelry design at the Fashion Institute of Technology. At the age of 21, I started working for my dad's company. The second that I stepped foot into that building, my passion took over. I felt as though I had tripped into a world made for me. Everything was interesting to me. Every day, for nearly 10 years, I watched my dad work harder than I had ever seen anyone work before.

When my father died, it was completely unexpected.

My family and I were so lucky to have an incredible support system consisting of friends and family. But as life started to move forward and fewer people stopped by the house, the reality of my dad's death began to sink in, which was very hard.

Shortly after my father passed, a decision was made to sell the company, but I continued to serve as a vice president. It was a confusing time for me. I struggled to focus on projects that I had previously worked on with my dad. Depressed and not healthy, every day was a battle.

After a year, I was drinking a lot and showing up to work late. My life didn't seem important to me anymore. My mom and several close friends and family members convinced me to go away for 30 days to a treatment facility for depression. Reluctantly, I agreed to go. I went through grief therapy and developed tools to respond to challenging situations and emotions.

Meditation was a large part of my treatment, but with ADHD, it was hard to sit still and concentrate. A therapist recommended knitting to clear my head. I loved it. It allowed me to be calm and present. It centered me.

When I left treatment, I felt like a different person. I had new tools to tackle my life and my pain. Also, I decided not to return to my dad's old company. Instead, I decided to move on from the past and start over.

After a few months, I realized I didn't want to give up my passion for jewelry design. And at the time, knitting was such an important part of my life and my healing. So, I decided to marry the two.

Inspired by the textures and patterns in my knitting, five years ago, I started my company, Tiffany Kay Studio.[1] We have grown tremendously through the years, with more than 250 designs in our collection.

Starting my company enabled me to talk about my dad again. It brought me back to memories of him working in the art room.

---

1 https://www.qvc.com/content/insideq/tiffany-kay-jewelry.html

Losing someone you love is never easy. But I want you to know that it's OK if you're not healing or moving forward as fast as other people. There is nothing wrong with asking for help. I wish I had asked for help sooner. Also, don't sweep your feelings under the rug by drinking or doing other self-destructive behaviors. Express yourself and lean on the people that love you.

When I lost my dad, I also thought I had lost my future.

Thankfully, I had friends and family there for me, along with my dad's example, which showed me never to give up. For me, that meant getting the help I needed to heal.

Once I did, I not only rediscovered my purpose, but I also found a way to stay connected to my father.

I am happy to be home again. It can get better.

With love,
Tiffany Kay

How I Am No Longer Allowing What Hurt Me To Hold Me Back

To those who are experiencing a setback,

No matter how discouraged you feel right now, don't quit. At some point, all of us will have our minds go against us. But these last few months have taught me that there is always one person who can beat your inner demon.

See, when I was eight years old, I saw my brother playing basketball, and I decided to try it. My parents signed me up for a rec league.

Right away, everyone was like, "Oh, she's got some skills."

So, I started playing in a more competitive league, AAU. That's where I fell in love with basketball. I enjoyed the camaraderie and competitiveness, as well as being in the paint and wrestling girls for loose balls.

The game was fun, really fun, and by fifth grade, I knew one day I wanted to play professionally.

My dad became my 24/7 coach. If I wanted to shoot hoops or if I had a question about basketball, he was always available. He also was my biggest cheerleader. However, we had to develop our own system.

He was a big man with a loud booming voice. As a former bodybuilder and a member of the National Guard, many people were scared of him.

Early on, he would yell simple things from the stands, such as, "Go rebound!"

But it sounded so aggressive, I told him, "Dad, you need to calm down."

So, as I got older, he started giving me hand gestures.

He would do a cranking up motion if I needed to up my tempo or a relaxing motion if I needed to take a breather and chill. We had our own little language. It worked for us.

By eighth grade, I was already getting looks from colleges around the country. In high school, I wasn't happy when coaches could directly reach out to me. I was trying to watch Netflix on the couch, and the phone kept ringing off the hook. I don't even know how many offers I received, but it was a lot. Ultimately, I decided to go to the University of South Carolina.

While college was a bit of an adjustment, I came in with the mindset that I would need to earn my minutes and my spot. And I did just that. I was the SEC Freshman of the Year, and I went on to be a four-time All-SEC player and four-time All-American.

My dad missed my freshman year because he was deployed, but he was there for the other three years, and he loved coming to my games.

We played Mississippi State my senior year. They were the team that we needed to beat to get to the championship. The game was tight the whole time. Within the last couple of minutes of the last quarter, I had the ball at the top of the key, and no one was expecting me to drive to the basket. But I ripped the ball through, went to the basket, and scored the layup. They panned the camera to my dad. He was super excited, high-fiving everyone, including my pastor, who was also at that game.

I loved looking up and seeing him and my whole family cheering for me and going nuts when I did well. They motivated me to put on a show for them, and they always told me how proud they were of me.

Up until my senior year, my basketball career went very smoothly. Then, in February of 2017, we were playing Missouri, and my journey took a turn. I went up for a block, and I ended up stepping on my opponent's foot. I twisted my ankle inward and landed hard on my inner ankle. It was painful and swollen.

After I got it checked out, I was able to come back for senior night against Kentucky. I felt fine, and then I got hit by what I call the invisible sniper. Literally, I was running on the court, and I just fell over. I tried to play one more time, but I made a wrong move, and it felt like my tendons ripped apart inside of my ankle. So, that was it. It was every senior's worst nightmare.

I had surgery and began rehabilitation.

My team made it to the National Championship game. I was so happy they won, but I couldn't even attend the game because I had to keep my leg still.

It sucked. But thankfully, my basketball career was not over.

In April of 2017, my family came with me to New York City for the WNBA Draft. I knew I was going to get drafted, but I thought I would go number three overall to Dallas. Instead, I was shocked when Chicago chose me with the number two overall pick. I had so much raw emotion, and I am thankful my father was there for that moment because my dad never got to see me play again.

By the 2017 season, I was healthy enough to get on the court, but I wasn't yet in shape to go up and down the floor. So, I missed the season, and I signed with a team in Hungary to get some professional experience.

In Hungary, on the day of the last game of our series, I was at shootaround when the owner of the team approached me. He told me I needed to call my agent. Then, my agent told me to call my mom. So, I went into the owner's office and Facetimed my mom. I could see my family around her. They were all teary-eyed.

My mom said, "Daddy died."

That's how I found out my father had passed away. He went into cardiac arrest while driving his car.

The following day, I got on the first flight home. There was a lot of anger, confusion, and hurt.

When I finally played in the WNBA, it wasn't easy. Father's Day and my dad's birthday both fell within the season. I tried to play through all of my emotions and use basketball as a distraction. But it didn't work.

I wore my dad's number, and I wanted to do him some justice. Throughout my time in the WNBA, I played with four teams.

With each team, I constantly was thinking, "What should I do?"

"What spot am I in?"

"Who is open?"

"Should I pass?"

I wouldn't allow myself to just play like I had done my entire life.

That's why this summer, I am home instead of with a WNBA team. But don't worry, I will be back. See, after this past season overseas in Israel, I looked at my numbers and watched film. I knew I could be better. I knew something was holding me back.

My mother and I talked after the season, and she told me that I wasn't separating my emotions from my work. She told me that I wasn't having fun anymore.

She was right. My emotions have no business dictating what I do on the court,

So, I decided to reach out for help. I began talking to a therapist about my life and my grief.

Already, I feel so much better. I don't want to say I never thought that I would get to this space of understanding, but I certainly didn't expect to get here so soon. Now, I feel like I can get back to hooping without being in my head or nervous. I can just go out there and play the game that I love.

I am so proud to say that my strength is back, and so is my spirit. And I am confident it will translate on the court when I go to Turkey to play overseas.

So, if you're feeling down or you're not doing so well, take the time to figure out what's wrong. Is it mental? Is it physical? Figure it out and work on it.

What I have learned through my own journey is that the same person who created your inner demon is the one person who can beat it.

And that's you.

Your comeback awaits you, and so does mine!

Alaina Coates

Mom And Dad, Here Is What I Want You To Know About The Moment You Missed

Dear Mom and Dad,

In 2016, I had one of the greatest moments of my life. However, amid my joy, I felt sadness and disappointment because you weren't there to witness it.

Without you both, that moment wouldn't have happened for me.

Dad, as a kid, you used to make me go to work with you. I had to get my butt up at 4:00 in the morning during the summer and spend the whole day at your construction site. It was hard, and you never let me cut corners.

At home, Mom, you took care of our house and showed me how to be domesticated. I had chores that included vacuuming, taking out the garbage, and keeping my room clean. You made sure I didn't just get these chores done but that I did them right. When I swept the floor, I had to sweep underneath the cabinets and in the corners.

Both of you wanted me to understand hard work, laying a foundation for my future.

However, my dreams for the future were different than you envisioned. I fell in love with the game of basketball.

Dad, you said to me, "You will need to get you a real job, something that's going to allow you to make a living and do something with your life."

At first, you didn't want me to play. But Mom, you saw how committed I was to the game. For a long time, you let me play and didn't tell Dad.

As your son, I wanted support from both of you. I wanted your approval. I wanted you to be proud of me as a basketball player. And growing up, that's what drove me.

When I practiced, I never let my teammates outwork me. If we did sprints, I wanted to be the fastest. If we had a shooting contest, I wanted to win. Consistently, I was looking to gain an advantage, and even though I was a late bloomer, you saw it pay off on the court.

Dad, when you realized basketball could get me a free education, your feelings changed, and you became my biggest fan. You cheered me on in junior college. Both of you were thrilled when I received a scholarship to play at the University of Hawaii. When I ran out of the tunnel at the Oakland Coliseum wearing a Warriors jersey, you both witnessed it from the stands. You even got to see me start my business as a basketball trainer.

Thankfully, you saw a lot of my career. But you missed the best of it.

Mom, you passed away before I got hired as a coach in the NBA for the Lakers.

Dad, you were there, and even though you didn't like crowds, every time we played in Oakland, you got a ticket to the game.

You began to watch games at home, learn the players and even crack jokes, saying, "Hey man! How come Shaq can't shoot free throws?"

But Mom, Dad, my career didn't stop there. I earned the respect of the best players in the game, such as LeBron James, Kyrie Irving, and the late Kobe Bryant.

One time, when I was with the Lakers, we played in Charlotte. Kobe didn't have a great game. We had to fly to New York to play a back-to-back. I was asleep on the plane when one of the security guards tapped me on the shoulder.

He said, "Kobe wants to go to the gym."

At 2:30 in the morning, we got off the plane and went straight to the gym. We didn't leave until about 5:15 a.m. Our next game was later that day, but there were no questions asked on my behalf.

Dad, just like you taught me when you took me to work early in the morning as a young boy, my players know I am willing to work anytime and anywhere.

I am also very detail-oriented. A player could be handling the basketball, and their footwork might be wrong, or they might have the incorrect body position, I will point out the smallest details. Mom, similar to how you taught me to sweep the floor the right way, I always make sure my players do their workouts the way they're supposed to be done.

After I left the Lakers, I moved to Cleveland, and Dad, you had a stroke and passed away. Now, you were both gone. Shortly after, is when I had that moment that I so desperately wanted to share with you. That is when I won my first of two NBA championships. I won with the Cavs against the Warriors in Oakland, where you raised me.

All you ever wanted in life was for me to be able to provide for my family and be successful. And I so badly wanted to do that through basketball.

When I became a champion, I knew it was because of your love and your lessons. In that moment of glory, all I wanted to do was hug you both and say thank you.

I wanted to thank you not only for teaching me hard work but also for teaching me to be a compassionate, confident, humble, strong, and good person. The best way to show my gratitude would have been to show you that I achieved greatness.

So, as I celebrated with my team, I imagined you, Dad, standing proudly as you, Mom, smiled with excitement. And deep down, I held hope that somewhere you were watching because what hurts so much is that I know my success would have been your happiness.

Mom, Dad, because of both of you, I made it!

I love you and miss you.

Your son,
Phil Handy

Mom, I Know You Still Believe In Me

Dear Mom,

I know if you were here right now, you would pop me upside the head and say, "Boy, chin up, head up, and keep going."

But Mom, it hasn't been easy.

You are the one who taught me about wins and losses in life, especially early on. We lived in gang neighborhoods in Los Angeles: first, 52nd and Hoover, and then we moved to 5th Avenue and 60th Street. We lacked money. We were a lower-class family in a tough environment. I grew up seeing so many losses, including people getting shot, killed, beaten up, and drugged out. At 16, I watched my older brother go to prison. Two years later, my older sister's lungs collapsed, and she died.

You wanted better for me. That is why you put me in sports, which became my safe haven. Football was where I found my wins. I was a quarterback at Dorsey High School, and in 1982, my senior year, we won a city championship.

During high school, I watched you wake up at 4:30 a.m. You would take me to school, go to work as a school cook, pick me up, drop me off at football practice, cook dinner for our family, go to your second job, and then come home around 10:00 p.m.

You were trying to prevent the losses around me from influencing my path in life. It was your work ethic that laid the foundation not only for my city championship in high school but for my entire career.

You always told me I was going to be where I wanted to be. You would always say, "My baby is going to make it."

As you know, Mom, I wanted to be one of 32 NFL head coaches. In my career, I have gotten the opportunity to be an NFL head coach not once but twice. As a Black coach, getting those opportunities wasn't easy, but I found a way.

The first time around, I went 8-8 with the Oakland Raiders. Owner and general manager, Al Davis, believed in me, but he died during that season. The new regime wanted to go in a different direction the following year.

After I lost my first head coaching job, I had to start over. I went and coached on defense in Cincinnati as what was essentially a quality control coach and worked my way up to offensive coordinator. Mom, I tried to be the best I could be, like you taught me. Despite suffering a heart attack in 2014, I ended up being Pro Football Writers of America's 2015 NFL Co-Assistant Coach of the Year. At that point, my chance to be 1 of 32 resurfaced. The Cleveland Browns hired me as their head coach. This was my opportunity to show that the Raiders should have kept me.

By this time, in 2016, you suffered from dementia. You not only didn't know that I was the head coach of the Browns, but you no longer even recognized me. That was tough, but I was still trying to make you smile and prove you right.

The Browns were appealing because I already knew the division. At the time I accepted the job, they had a real nucleus of good players and just needed some tweaks. Plus, I thought I could build an unbelievable legacy there because the franchise had struggled for so long.

However, instead of winning, we lost a lot. In two-and-a-half seasons, we went 3-36-1. People are not built to lose. It leads to too many negative outcomes. Some athletes and coaches turn to alcohol, drugs, or other unhealthy habits because they just need that win for a moment. To be a good leader, I had to abstain from outlets that weren't productive.

To stand before a football team and keep them motivated to play, I had to stay motivated myself. Mom, people won't see it this way because I lost, but my time with the Browns was some of my best coaching. I took a group of men and kept them playing and competing at a high level. That takes a lot of skill and determination.

While there is a record that, for some, defines a lot of my wins and losses, my greatest loss during my time in Cleveland was you. You passed away during training camp in 2018, just two weeks after we lost your son and my older brother, John Jackson Jr. Even after you died, I could and can still hear some of the conversations we had when I was younger. Those conversations helped me endure the challenges I faced as a coach as well as the loss of my dream job, as I was fired during the 2018 season.

I realized that there is a human side to wins and losses. Whether it be the personal defeats or the ones on the football field, what is important is how you navigate coming out of all of them.

It's easy to become isolated, as people seem to have so easily forgotten all my hard work, progress, and accomplishments as an offensive coach.

You would be most proud to know that I haven't given up. My memory of you won't let me. If you were here, you would tell me tomorrow might bring another opportunity, and I need to be ready when it comes. You would tell me to stay focused on my goal, not to let people deter me, and not to worry about what people say. You taught me how to really believe in myself and to push forward toward whatever it is I want to accomplish.

All the losses didn't break me. Instead, I am making sure I don't let the past create my future. And that's because of you.

I know without question that you still believe I am going to be a successful NFL head coach.

I know you are in heaven saying, "My son is going to coach and win in the Super Bowl."

Mom, I don't know how my story will end, but I know it's not over yet. Many around me see my record and my personal tragedies as a lot of losing. However, you taught me that my will to continue to fight through all types of challenges and hardships means in life, I am winning.

I miss you, and I love you always,
Hue Jackson

How I Found The Courage To Keep My Crown And Pursue My Career

To those who have lost a parent,

My mom always used to tell me, "Get ready. God is about to bless you."

So, like many people, growing up, I never really thought about the negative in life.

Even early on in college, I thought to myself, "Nothing bad will happen to me."

Instead, I was ready for my blessings.

Now, after enduring the greatest challenge of my life, I not only realize bad things do happen, but I also learned that I have the ability to deal with them.

And I have Mom to thank for that.

When I was a little girl, I loved to write, and I was a chatterbox. So, in first grade, when my teacher asked me what

I wanted to be when I grew up, I told her I wanted to be a journalist. Luckily for me, my mother was an incredible writer. She worked as a journalist for the Indianapolis Star. Through the years, she would always scribble my reports with a red pen, helping me become a better writer.

When I was 11 years old, I didn't have a lot of confidence. My mom entered me into pageants.

At 19, I competed for Miss Indiana and won. Both my mother and I were so excited. But just two weeks after winning the crown, my whole life changed.

After seeing flashing lights in the corner of her eyes, my mom went to the Emergency Room, where she was diagnosed with Glioblastoma, a very aggressive form of brain cancer.

Immediately, I contemplated giving up my crown and passing on my title to the first runner-up. This way, I could stay home and care for my mom.

She told me, "Absolutely not."

My mother made me promise to stick with it and not miss a single appearance. She made no exceptions. A week after her diagnosis, she had brain surgery. On that day, I was scheduled to sing the National Anthem in front of 15,000 people.

She reminded me, "You won. You deserve this. And it's not going to do you any good sitting outside of an operating room."

My mother refused to let her cancer be the reason I didn't pursue my dream. Throughout my tenure as Miss Indiana, I became more confident in myself and more prepared for my career as a sports journalist. After my term ended, against the odds, my mom went into remission.

Everything appeared right on track heading into 2020. My mother was seemingly healthy, and I was getting ready to graduate. Unexpectedly, 2020 turned out to be an awful year — the worst of my life. First, in February, a friend of mine died by suicide. Then, the pandemic hit. In April, after three years in remission and many clear scans, my mom received the news that the cancer had returned. It was in one spot. They removed the tumor.

My mother healed wonderfully, and I thought we were in the clear. So, I went back to school for my last semester and interned at WISH-TV, a local station in Indianapolis. But then, in November, my mom went in for a routine checkup, and this time the MRI showed that the cancer was all over her brain.

When I took her to one of her appointments, she asked the doctor, "How much time do I have?"

He said, "Do you really want to know my guess?"

She said, "I really do."

He told her, "Three months."

When I first heard that prognosis, I thought, "Oh my gosh, my life is over. I'll never find joy again."

My mom had a different attitude. She was so strong. She wasn't scared of anything. She was not afraid of surgery, radiation, chemo, or even death.

As my mother fought for her life, she told me to keep doing what I loved. She told me never to settle.

I even asked her, "Do you think I'll be OK?"

She said, "Oh yeah. You are going to have the best career. You're good at what you do. You're going to keep climbing, climbing, and climbing."

On December 12, 2020, my mother passed away five days before I graduated from college.

After taking some time to grieve, I accepted a job in Rockford, Illinois as a sportscaster. To be honest, I wasn't excited about moving — not because of the job or the city. The problem was I did not want to leave my family, boyfriend, or friends. But at the same time, I knew my mom would want me to pursue my dream. I knew she'd want me to take the job.

Now that I am here and I am settled, I'm not only happy I accepted the position, but I feel my mother's presence all of the time. As I follow in her footsteps as a journalist, I believe I am continuing her legacy.

I am living my dream, and I want you to know you can still live yours too.

Take the time to heal. Focus on yourself first. Then, slowly but surely, introduce more tasks into your daily routine. Day by day, keep progressing.

When I realized I would lose my mom, I never thought I would be as mentally healthy as I am right now.

But before my mom died, I taped her telling me one more time, "Get ready. God is about to bless you."

And sure enough, she was right. God did bless me, just like God blessed you.

Even though we lost a parent, I realized we are still forever blessed with their strength and their love.

So, keep pushing!

Haley Jordan

How Two Strangers Helped Me Find My Purpose While I Was In Pain

To the two women I met on a plane in 2015,

We were only together for a few hours. I don't remember your names. I don't know where in the world you are today. And yet, I had one of the most important conversations of my life with you. It started with a simple question:

"How are you?"

Before I met you, I had plenty of meaningful conversations with strangers, but usually, it was other people telling me their stories — not the other way around.

My husband, Matty Mullins, and I got married at 18. A year later, while we both worked retail in our hometown of Spokane, Washington, Matty found out an up-and-coming band from Texas was hosting open auditions for a frontman. So, he flew to Dallas to audition. He was up against 180 other hopeful musicians.

From Texas, my husband called, saying, "I have bad news."

My heart sank.

I started to console him, but he interrupted me and said, "We have two weeks to move to Dallas because I am the new frontman for Memphis May Fire."

Within days, we left our hometown and moved to the Lone Star State.

I stood in the crowd at his first show a week later, glowing with pride. During the show, a young woman in her early twenties approached me. She was a fan and told me that Matty was a great new frontman for the band. Then, she went on to say that Memphis May Fire and other music like theirs saved her life. She opened up about coming from an abusive family, experiencing sexual abuse, and subsequently battling addiction and engaging in self-harm. Moved by her vulnerability and wanting to help, but unsure how, I listened and asked if I could pray for her.

Her story stayed with me over the years. As I traveled with my husband's band, I started hearing similar stories from more and more fans.

After a while, I said, "Ok, Lord, you're trying to tell me something, but I'm going to need you to give me direction."

I knew I wanted to help people like these fans, but I didn't exactly know how. I tried a lot of things. In 2008, I started a YouTube channel called "Ask Brittany Mullins," opening up about my relationship with Matty and what makes us successful. I noticed many people just wanted to be heard. So, I created an email address and told people they could write to me. I wasn't going to respond, but instead, create a safe place for them to get their feelings off their chests. However, I started getting thousands of emails a week. It became too much and too heavy for me.

In 2015, I was the manager of retail operations for Mac Cosmetics in Tennessee and Kentucky. While it was a great job, it didn't feel like the right fit for me. With no backup plan and a leap of faith, I quit my job. I was scared. For a long time, while Matty chased his dreams, I was the breadwinner in our family.

I thought, "What am I going to do now?"

I quit right before the Super Bowl, so I promised myself I'd have fun for the weekend and buckle down that Monday.

On Monday morning, I made coffee, sat down to figure out my life, and then my sister called.

When I answered, she said, "Dad is dead."

At 53 years old, my father died of a heart attack. I was devastated. My father was an alcoholic, and as a result, we didn't have the best relationship. I created boundaries with him for my well-being, but I had hoped for more redemption in our relationship before he passed away.

For the first time in my life, I felt like I touched clinical depression.

My mind raced with thoughts such as, "What is life? I just lost my father. There's no redemption. I don't have a job. What am I going to do?"

I felt hopeless.

After a sleepless night, I got on a plane to Spokane the following day. That's when I met both of you. I sat in the window seat, and you two sat next to me. One of you looked about 25 years older than me, and the other a little younger than me.

We were small talking, as strangers sitting on a plane together do, when one of you asked me, "How are you?"

Usually, when a stranger asks that question, most people say they're good or fine, even if it's not true. I know I've done that a million times before. But this time, for some reason, I responded truthfully.

"Not good," I said.

You both asked what happened, and I told you. It would've been so easy for you to give your condolences, then put your headphones on for the rest of the flight. However, that's not what either of you did. Instead, you told me you were sorry and asked if you could do anything.

When I told you there was nothing, one of you responded, "Well, the least we can do is make you smile."

We talked, but I don't remember what about. We played a game, but I don't remember what it was called. What I do remember is that we laughed. A lot.

During a quiet moment, I looked out the window.

I thought to myself, "If I hadn't talked to these women, I would have gone deeper and darker into my sadness. Instead, I opened my heart up. I was honest, and I received exactly what I needed."

Then it hit me. I realized people need people, and I figured out how I wanted to help others. On the flight to my father's funeral, I pieced together a vision for a nonprofit where peers could mentor each other through hard times. I didn't want traditional mentors giving advice but peer mentors who would be there for someone no matter what.

Shortly after landing, I called my husband and told him about my idea. He loved it. When I came home, I googled how to create a nonprofit.

Six months later, I started my nonprofit called Beneath the Skin. We provide peer-to-peer mentoring to young women who feel alone or isolated. Beneath the Skin is a place where women can build their confidence through genuine connection.

Since starting, we've had 400 matches and have changed the lives of both mentees and mentors. By simply showing up, a mentor showed her mentee how to find value, beauty, and confidence in herself. Another mentee spent years in toxic relationships. After meeting her mentor, she found a lifelong friend. Her mentor was even the Maid of Honor at her wedding. One mentee, who had suicidal thoughts, said the program saved her life by showing her that she does matter.

If I ran into both of you today, I probably would first bawl my eyes out. But more than that, I'm writing to you because I want to tell you both to keep being the type of people who are willing to put themselves in uncomfortable situations to help a stranger in need. You not only inspired me to be that kind of person, but you motivated me to encourage other people to be the same.

During a difficult time, you changed the trajectory of my life in such a beautiful way. You helped me find what I had been looking for for so long — a meaningful way to help people.

The odds of me finding either one of you again are pretty slim. Sometimes, I think about what would happen if God put you next to me on a flight again, like He did all those years ago.

I imagine you'd smile, maybe not remembering me, and ask, "How are you?"

This time, I'd smile back and say, "Blessed."

With love and gratitude,
Brittany Mullins

Loss Of A Child

To Children Battling Cancer, Your Smile Was My Son's Wish

To children battling cancer,

You may have never met my son Mikey, but he, too, knew how it felt to be stuck in the hospital for days on end. He knew how it felt to be pricked with needles and pumped with medicine while other kids are at baseball or soccer practice. Mikey knew what it was like to lose his hair and to experience side effects from treatments. Just like you, Mikey battled cancer. He was diagnosed one day after his 15th birthday.

I remember this moment while he was hooked up to a machine for his chemotherapy. At that point, he had relapsed, and his future was unclear. We were just living one day at a time. He told me he missed his friends. He told me cancer made him feel isolated from people.

Then, Make-A-Wish Foundation offered Mikey the chance to make a wish of his own. Mikey asked if he could start his own charity, providing electronics to kids like you, kids with cancer. The idea was to make sure you could remain connected to the world beyond your hospital bed. His aunt bought him electronics, which allowed him to see the benefits of these devices.

At the time, the Make-A-Wish Foundation told him starting his own charity wasn't an option. So instead, he cleverly asked for a shopping spree at Best Buy. However, the shopping spree wasn't to add to his collection of goods. He bought a bunch of electronics and went to the local hospital, where he gave them all away. That's how Mikey's Way, a nonprofit that travels the country providing brand new electronics to children with cancer, started.

With the help of the community, Mikey raised the first $250,000. He started Mikey's Way Days. That's where we go to hospitals to give you and your peers gifts. Mikey did 17 of those days, personally handing out electronics to children in hospitals around the country.

Mikey truly was an incredible person. Cancer never defined him, and he would tell you that it doesn't define you, either. He didn't let cancer stop him from becoming valedictorian of his graduating class, despite missing half of high school. Cancer didn't stop him from attending Harvard, where he was studying to be a scientist so he could cure cancer, so he could cure all of you. Despite only being able to go through one full year of college, his research and his writings were published in the Harvard Science Review as well as the Journal of Palliative and Supportive Care. As a child, you might not know what all of that is, but I assure you it means cancer didn't stop him from working hard to help you in every possible way that he could.

While Mikey was brilliant, I don't think his intelligence is the most remarkable aspect of his legacy. Mikey was the baby in our family, the youngest of three. He was treated as such and acted as such. But as he maintained his sense of humor, cancer transformed him into a wise old man. I think it's that wisdom that's left an indelible mark on you, the children that receive Mikey's Way gifts, and every person who knows his story.

Mikey truly embodied the words he spoke as he once said, "The best gift you can get is to give to another person."

That's why every time he gave a gift to a child like you, he felt the excitement of his Make-A-Wish coming true all over again.

Mikey wanted to instill hope. He wanted to encourage you to never give up, as he never did. Even though Mikey endured his own battle with cancer, he felt his journey wasn't and shouldn't be all about him, and he wanted to relay that message to others. Plus, Mikey didn't want to focus on his relapse. Instead, he wanted to devote his attention to positivity, which for him was providing kids like you electronics and seeing the smiles that followed.

Unfortunately, Mikey is no longer here to give you a laptop or an iPod Touch, but I am. Every single time I give a gift to one of you, I feel my son next to me. I love seeing your faces light up when you realize why I am there to see you. It probably brings me as much, if not more, joy to give you a computer or a tablet than it does for you to receive it.

Since Mikey's Way started in 2005, we have given away more than 7,000 gifts. Every one of the gifts we offer you is geared toward making sure you stay connected to people outside of the hospital. Each electronic has Skype or Facetime. We want to make sure you can get on Wi-Fi and download games and videos.

We have progressed quite a bit since Mikey personally gave out his last gift more than 10 years ago, but I am sure he'd say, "Dad, What took you so long? I could have figured out a way to get to 7,000 gifts way faster."

My son liked to tease me, but I know he would be very proud of how we've grown and how much we have given to all of you.

Mikey may have never gotten the chance to meet you, but he had you in his mind and his heart all along. He never wanted you to be bored or feel alone. And while he succeeded in finding a way to keep you all connected to the world, he also managed to keep all of us, especially me, connected to him.

If you don't have a new tablet to read this on, let me know.

Les aka Mikey's dad

Loss Of A Partner

How An F-Bomb Changed My Life

To those who read about my F-bomb,

My phone started ringing. Text messages from friends across the country began to pile in. Then, I saw for myself. My F-bomb became a national story. While you may have read in the paper or on the internet about my gaff on air, what reporters didn't write is that the F-bomb wasn't just a headline in the news; it was a breaking story in my life. Before and after the F-bomb feel like two very separate lives — not just a different chapter but a new book with a unique cover.

I would title the first novel "Thanks for the Journey."

When I said that inappropriate word across the airwaves, I was supposed to be giving the local weather forecast for NBC in New York. For 24 years, I was the local weatherman. But at that moment, I got lost in a conversation about my late wife, Nancy. I was talking about how when she died, a part of me had to go with her.

I told my co-worker, "It's a fucking weird thing."

That's the part you probably heard. That's what the media wrote about online and in the paper.

Nancy and I met back in first grade. The love bug hit me at our eighth-grade graduation celebration, where we started to dance and never stopped. We got married, had two kids, and lived an amazing life together.

My wife was a strong and liberated woman but still very rooted in family. While she gave up her career as a CPA to raise our children, which she thoroughly enjoyed, her brilliance was still quite apparent. I took three years of calculus in college, but I probably forgot all of it once I got a diploma in my hand. Not Nancy. When our son needed help in calculus, she remembered it all.

Her mission was always to guide our children to be their best in life. We had honest conversations at the dinner table because Nancy was a straight shooter. Your head would snap because she would be so blunt. While shocking to some, it kept the channels of communication open with our kids and with ourselves. Nancy was the center of our family.

In 2012, Nancy was diagnosed with myelofibrosis, a blood cancer. Cancer is very unforgiving. It was not only painful for me to watch the physical toll it took, but things like the loss of her hair seemed to rob her of her dignity as well. At work, I would do research, trying to find out if anywhere else in the world discovered an alternative method to treating her illness.

But I couldn't find a cure. I couldn't make her better.

On her last day in the hospital, I noticed her body movement was strange. Her eyes didn't move. She didn't blink. When I spoke to her, there was no indication that she could hear me. Then, just like in a Hollywood movie, I noticed the heart monitor. The beats were becoming more and more distant. She started turning blue. I laid down next to her and told her it was OK and that she should go in peace. I heard her last breath as I held her in my arms.

Nearly three years later, the F-bomb hit. Between Nancy's passing and the F-bomb, there were not only times of sadness but some real ugly depression. At first, I tried to be Dad and Mom for my children, but that wasn't possible. Also, there was a large sense of failure that I didn't fix her. I couldn't fix her.

I can remember finally starting to laugh, but even though I was physically laughing, I was still dead on the inside.

When the F-bomb hit, I was removing pictures from my work computer. They were from the last trip we had as a family, where Nancy was doing well. Three weeks after that curse word hit the air and then subsequently the entire internet, my bosses told me they weren't re-signing my contract after 24 years at NBC. My bosses were ending my employment but insisted their decision was unrelated to my slip-up. Nonetheless, the F-bomb impact was still there.

The F-bomb was the true start of the second book in my life. While it is still being written, I would title this story "The Sun Will Rise Again."

My wife will be with me forever. The time I spent with her and the love we shared is ingrained in me. It's a part of me. However, I continued to get out and socialize, which eventually led to me experiencing real joy again. I finally realized that I had to let go of the day-to-day emotional connection that I shared with Nancy. This is embarrassing to admit, but I never lived alone until my wife passed away, and I didn't know how to fill out a check until I was about 50 years old. I had to put on my big boy pants, which included paying bills and learning about our finances.

As I was forced to become more independent, I realized that, through the years, I may have lost a sense of self. My identity was tied to being a husband and a father, but when I step out of those roles, there is still me. There is this core of who I am that I had lost touch with through the years.

My approach to life right now is much less conservative than in years past. When I am confronted with a challenge or asked to try a new task, I dive right in as opposed to shying away.

I started to travel, which led me to a new lady in my life. We've been to Singapore and South Africa, trying different foods and meeting people from all over the world. Traveling has opened my eyes to humanity, helping me realize that all of us are a lot more similar than we think. People create differences by drawing lines, such as religion and race.

All my new experiences are not only enlightening me about the world, but they are helping me to learn more about who I am and what makes me happy.

Looking back, I wouldn't do anything differently in my life, whether it be my relationships or my career. On the surface, I have been through some terrible and hurtful periods recently, but on a deeper level, I am evolving, and I am growing.

These last few years taught me that if you love someone, don't bother complaining about little things.

I promise you, no one ever said to a person they loved on their deathbed, "Gee, I wish I yelled at you and busted your chops even more."

Also, I have come to understand that life is truly a gift, and I am going to enjoy it for as long as I have it. Right now, I consider myself in the bonus round. If it all ended tomorrow, I would have had an amazing life.

But to realize all of this — it took the F-bomb.

All of our experiences, good, bad, and devastating, make us who we are today. And while in the news, my F-bomb was the moment I said a foul word, in my life, my F-bomb was the point where I freed myself to move forward.

With clear skies and sunshine ahead,
Chris Cimino

CTE Took Your Mind, But I Still Have Your Heart

Zac –

You told me you'd never leave me. But you did. I know you were just looking for peace. Yet sometimes, I'm so sick with grief and sadness that I'm mad. I am mad that you're not here. I am mad that I'm alone. I am mad at every person, moment, and unknown that contributed to you developing that horrifying disease that ultimately took you from me and from the world.

The hardest part about losing you is trying to move forward in life peacefully and happily when I still feel so broken inside.

I loved you so much that it's impossible to describe. It was overwhelming. It started when we became really good friends in high school. I used to ditch fourth period just to go hang with you. It was my senior year after you graduated. That's when we became more than just friends. Even when we were miles apart, we spoke with such depth every night, and our connection grew with each passing word. Our relationship wasn't traditional, and at times, we kicked ourselves for it. But, as we always said, our story and our love were perfectly imperfect.

You were my safe space and my home. Affectionately, you called me by my middle name, Winslow. You believed in me so ferociously.

You once wrote to me, "Just know someday you will always have my vote for you to become president. Please go out and change the world. I love you more than words can explain."

That unwavering confidence in me scares me. What if I don't achieve all you believed I would? What if I do something disappointing? What if I can't carry on your legacy the way your legacy deserves to be carried?

You were my confidant, and to this day, you still hold secrets no one else knows. You made me feel strong and loved. I truly lost a part of myself when you left.

The night you died is still so fresh in mind. On December 19, 2015, I received a text from you at 12:24 a.m.

It read, "Thank you for everything. You have helped me through so much and never ever blame yourself for anything. I love you and will always be over your shoulder to look after you no matter what. Always keep having fun. Always remember me. Always keep striving for greatness, or should I say, first female president. Keep fighting for what you believe for. I love you, Winslow."

My heart dropped into my stomach. I knew what was about to happen, but I didn't want to believe it. Shortly after, you shot yourself in the heart, not only to end your own suffering but also to help prevent others from suffering, too. You were only 24 years old.

Some mornings I wake up, and it feels like it just happened; my gut wrenches all over again. The details are just so clear in my mind.

Almost everywhere I go and everything I do, there's a reminder of you. Of us. Discovering new music on Spotify, ridiculous dance moves at the bars, and watching a movie I've seen a hundred times all take me back to you and me.

I am angry at the disease in general. It began to develop likely long before I even met you. You started football in third grade. You loved football. You weren't as big as the others, but you were incredibly more powerful in your punch because you used your head. You weren't afraid to do that.

One story I remember is you had this drill at practice, and you went up against our very large friend, D. You definitely knocked him down, and he was twice your size. You were determined and unafraid to go head-to-head with anyone on the field.

But as much as you loved football, you also felt betrayed by it. Because the disease torturing you stemmed from all the concussions you accumulated playing throughout your childhood and through high school.

There were so many late nights where you kept trying to articulate your pain, and I kept trying to tell you to hold on. We used our connection and love for music to get you through the particularly rough nights.

You struggled to explain your disease. You had headaches and memory loss, among so many other symptoms.

I remember you told me, "I just don't feel right. I don't feel normal."

You didn't feel like you had control over your mind.

You went to different doctors, who gave you conflicting answers. One said it could be Bipolar Disorder. Another said you would end up homeless or in a mental institution. There were so many different answers but no answers at the same time. So, you did your own research and accurately self-diagnosed yourself with Chronic Traumatic Encephalopathy, also known as CTE, a disease that results in changes in the brain in response to repeated hits to the head. Once you realized you had CTE, you knew there was no cure and no way to even confirm your diagnosis until after you passed away. Nothing could be done, and you knew your symptoms were not going to improve.

Before you died, you wrote journals, documenting your disease. You also left behind a note, asking that your brain be donated to science to help researchers learn more about CTE. You did all this so you could lessen someone else's struggle. And by the way, the researchers who examined your brain did confirm you had CTE.

I know you wanted your family and me to also help spread your message. You wanted us to tell your story and to warn and help athletes. I am proud to share with you that we started a foundation in your honor. It's called CTE Hope. Our goals are to educate people about CTE and concussions, find ways to prevent CTE and create better return-to-play protocol.

Now I am sure you want an update on my life, too. It's been incredibly hard to navigate life without you. One minute I was embarking on a new chapter with you by my side, and the next, I had the wind permanently knocked out of me. I became a three-legged table, unable to keep steady. But I've had to learn. I've had to learn to be a three-legged table if for no other reason than that's what you wanted. I did it for me, but also for you because you couldn't for yourself.

Do you remember that you specifically told me I would make it through law school and I couldn't use you as an excuse not to graduate? Well, Zac, I not only graduated, but I also excelled in law school just as you expected. I won a national award, in part, because of the work you inspired. I interned for the U.S. Attorney's Office. I got hired by a great law firm. I moved to New York City, something we always planned to do together. I survived (and passed) the bar exam. I traveled the world. But as great as all those things have been nothing, I mean nothing, has been easy. I always feel a slight sting of sadness because you're not here to experience these moments with me.

You did tell me to move on and find someone great to spend my life with. Now, when I first read those words, I was annoyed and defiant — how could I ever find someone else? Well, a little more than two years after you passed, I did find someone. He is a great person who supports me and loves me and approaches my past and grief with such grace. I often wonder, did you send me this wonderful human? Do you approve? Do you even want me to ask that?

I still live in this constant state of guilt. I truly love my boyfriend. But I miss you every second of every day. How do I live with that? How do I reconcile these two extremely powerful emotions? It's tough to grapple with the hard fact that you had to die for me to find him.

Even though I am living my life as you advised and honoring your life as you requested, there are so many questions I still have unanswered. And some days, I'd rather crawl back in bed, shut my eyes, and remember what it was like to just lay on your chest and feel your steady breath under me. I'll forever have a piece missing, a piece only you hold. I'll never stop loving you, or missing you, or wishing you were here. But I have come to realize no matter how broken I feel or how much I miss you, I owe it to both of us to live my life for myself.

I have to show the same strength you did and live the life we both deserve. I have to accept this forever new normal and let myself be happy, let myself move forward, and free myself of the guilt. I have to be the best possible version of myself. Because by doing so, I honor you, I honor your legacy, and I honor the love we shared.

Zac, I would've done anything to heal you. Instead, I am now doing what I can to keep your memory alive while also trying to pursue my own joy in life. However, I still can't do that without you. I know you found your peace, but as I move forward in life, I keep you close because it is still you that helps me find mine.

I'll love you until the end.

Winslow (Alison Epperson)

Here Is Where I Found Hope When I Lost My Husband

To single parents who have lost their spouse,

Grief is a process, but I want you to know that you have all you need to get through it. When I lost my husband, Adam, it was a complete shock.

Our paths first crossed when I was 16. Adam was vacationing in the Catskills, close to where I lived. My father owned an ice cream parlor. One day, I served him a banana split sundae, and our paths crossed — just two strangers, no words. Twenty years later, my twin sister met his sister at a nail salon in New City, New York. She set us up on a blind date. He was the smartest and funniest man I had ever met, and we became more than just a couple. As Adam, a former Princeton football player, would say, we became a team.

Together, we faced some tough opponents. Our son, Jack, was born with a rare condition called familial

Dysautonomia. He can't control his autonomic system. That means his body can't regulate his breathing, heart rate, temperature, or the tear production of his eyes. He can't feel pain, and he can't swallow, requiring him to eat from a feeding tube. At birth, his life expectancy was five years old.

After Jack, we had twins Charlotte and Hunter, who were born 10 weeks early. With one baby weighing under two pounds and the other at three pounds, there wasn't a lot of hope. Doctors didn't know if they'd survive.

Each time we faced a challenge, Adam and I would grab ourselves by our shoestrings, hold hands and tell each other, "We are going to get through this."

And we did!

Jack is now 15, and our twins are 12. All three are thriving.

As a team, we jumped over what others might have seen as insurmountable obstacles. Our resilience together only made July 29, 2014, more shocking.

At 47, Adam died unexpectedly from a heart attack. He passed away in a split second.

I kept thinking to myself, "This can't be happening."

My oldest son, Cody, who is from a previous marriage, was 14. Jack was eight, and my twins were six.

The way I see it is I believe God came down and said, "I need to take someone from your family."

The obvious one to take is the one who's sick.

But I feel like my husband, as the captain of our team, stood up to God and said, "Take me and let him live."

Adam did not die in vain. He died so his son could live.

And that's precisely what he would want us all to do — he would want us all to live.

After Adam passed, I could still hear him say to me, "Don't you fall down. You're better than that. You are not going to cry in the corner and say, 'woe is me' and feel bad for yourself."

I didn't fold. My whole family went to grief counseling, and we started to move forward, but Adam remained with us.

Adam worked on Wall Street. He left early in the morning and came home late, which meant he didn't see the kids a lot during the week. However, on the weekends, he would watch and talk football with Jack, my son with special needs. He introduced Jack to fantasy football. My daughter remembers playing Tic Tac Toe with her father.

He told her, "You can tie in Tic Tac Toe, but you can never lose."

Regardless of their memories, I make sure they all know that their father believed in being a part of a team. And he was "all in" when it came to our team or, rather, our family. I taught my children that we need to keep our team strong by each doing our part.

My son Jack eats every three hours through a feeding tube. At 10 years old, my daughter, Charlotte, learned how to feed him and help him with his eyedrops. Jack's lungs and kidneys are compromised, and he has nerve damage in the back of his eyes. So, he can't walk very far and tires easily.

As a family, we bought Jack a golf cart, which he can drive independently. Jack takes his friends, nurses, and siblings on rides in our backyard, as it gives him a sense of normalcy.

My kids are all very mature and have stepped up to help their brother and assist me.

I recognize that now I am the leader of this team, and my kids are watching my example. Time management is essential. In addition to caring for my kids, I own a computer software training company. I do all my food shopping online and delegate to people, such as my twin sister and friends, that are willing to help. Also, whatever problem I am facing, I have learned not to get upset or angry. Instead, I always remain calm and remind myself that we can't go backward. We can only move forward.

It's been six years since Adam passed away, and I am so proud to say my children are doing well, discovering their interests, and excelling at them.

My daughter took the lesson that Adam taught her during Tic Tac Toe and interpreted it to mean that you don't have to be the best every time, but whatever you do, do it well. So, she danced and won many accolades and awards. My son Hunter is very smart and loves basketball. Jack still loves football, as it's a way to stay connected to his father. He created a Fantasy Football League called the Jack Attack Fantasy Football League. Also, he made a website called LTPF, which stands for Level the Playing Field. It aims to make people who are bullied or discriminated against because of a disability feel normal and welcomed. My son Cody has a firm grasp of many important life principles, including hard work and commitment.

What I want you to know, as another parent who lost their spouse, is that even though it feels like your significant other is gone, he/she does and will remain in your family's hearts.

My children don't feel sorry for themselves. Instead, they have found lessons in an incredibly difficult loss. They are all happy and loved, which makes me fulfilled.

You will have days that are long and that are hard. Grief takes time, and I am not sure if it ever fully ends. But in the most challenging moments, look at your children and know all you need to get through is the support of each other.

Even though Adam may no longer be playing this game of life with us, our strategy hasn't changed. We have continued to live our lives with strength and love, which is why our team is one that still wins.

If my family can do it, so can yours.

You are going to get through this.

Robin Fiddle Posnack

Other Losses

To All The People I Could Not Save

To all the people I could not save,

Eleven years into my career as a firefighter, I attended a wedding. Everything was fine at first. When the party got underway, they had a group playing drums, lots of strobe lights, regular lights, and lots of yelling and screaming.

Even though it was a celebration, to me, it resembled a call.

Suddenly, I got really tense, chewing my cheek, while I felt my feet and toes scrunching in my shoes. I started rubbing my thumb and getting jittery and anxious.

I'm sitting there thinking, "What the hell is going on?"

I went to my truck where I cried for a solid hour — the hardest I've ever cried in my life.

Simultaneously, I sprouted out phrases and words to my wife: "I should have done more. Why couldn't I have been better?"

I couldn't figure out what was going on.

When I decided to become a firefighter at 21 years old, I thought I would be a hero and save people like in the movies. Two of my uncles were firefighters along with my grandfather. It was in my blood. But I had no idea what was ahead. I had no idea how crossing paths with all of you would affect me.

Distinctly, I remember meeting one of you a year or two into my career. You went into cardiac arrest, and I tried to do CPR to save you, but I didn't save you. I couldn't save you. In the days and weeks after, I kept seeing your face over and over in my dreams and in my thoughts. I felt inadequate and helpless, as I wished I could have done more.

Throughout my career, I saved two people from cardiac arrest, and many of you are among the others that did not make it. I believe there are between 200 and 250 of you, people that I could not save. For most of you, I don't know your name, and I don't know your story. That's partly what makes it so hard. I can't remember the "good times" in your life because I don't know them. Instead, I am simply left with the memory of that final look on your face before you passed.

It all came to a head last October when I answered back-to-back calls. The first was a car crash involving a father and daughter, who I believe both survived. The second call involved an elderly man who, to spare you the graphic details, basically drowned in his blood.

On the first call, I remember holding the little girl. It was almost as if I was hugging her because she was so afraid. Truthfully, though, there was a part of me that was trying to comfort myself while holding her. On the second call, there was nothing we could do, but I also couldn't move.

I froze as I thought to myself, "I need to get out of here."

As soon as I could leave, I started crying uncontrollably.

I texted my wife and said, "I can't do this anymore. I want to go home. I can't do it."

After that shift, I never returned to work. First, I took a leave of absence for two months, but it wasn't enough. Ultimately, I parted ways with the fire department.

I realize now losing all of you led me to suffer from Post-Traumatic Stress Disorder, also known as PTSD. I went from a very social, friendly, and outgoing person to a guy who was deteriorating. I became very standoffish, irritable, and short-fused as I started to rely on alcohol to numb my emotions and help me sleep. After a while, I'd look in the mirror, and I could hardly recognize myself.

To this day, dreams and flashbacks with all of you are frequent and repetitive. It's like watching a movie on a five-minute loop.

Sometimes I wonder if the reason I keep seeing all of you is because there is so much I never got to say to any of you.

I want you all to know I did what I could to save you.

I want you all to know that even though I don't know your names or your stories, there isn't a day that goes by that I don't think of all of you and your families.

I want you to know that I may no longer be a firefighter, but I am still fighting in honor of all of you. Your loss of life is inspiring me to extend or improve the lives of others.

After I left the fire department, I got a job as a baseball coach at Buckeye Medina High School in Ohio. I grew up playing baseball. It's always been an outlet for me. All the lessons I learned as a firefighter I try to pass down to the kids. For example, when I entered a burning building, I needed to know the guy that I went in with was going to have my back as much as I had his back. When I coach, I try to convey the importance of creating a brotherhood and a family that's respectful, compassionate, and understanding of each other.

On an individual level, a lot of these kids feel alone. I was one of those people who felt alone. So, I want them to know that it's OK to not be OK and that everybody has their struggles.

It's the loss of your lives that is motivating me to find the strength to make a difference in the lives of people who are still here. That is why I am now in school, earning a degree in teaching.

As a firefighter, military personnel, police officer, or any other professional who protects people and communities, there is an expectation to be strong, brave, and invincible. If you show too much emotion, you can be ridiculed or crucified for it. It shouldn't be that way because that's what makes people ultimately become more symptomatic, more vulnerable, weaker, and more alone.

I am so lucky and thankful to my wife, Tara, who is a psychologist, for being by my side and helping me find my voice.

She taught me the importance of self-care and educated me about mental health. As a result, I am now on a path towards healing, helping others, and acknowledging the profound impact the loss of your lives has had on me.

I have learned the hard way that life will always throw you curveballs. How you take a pitch ultimately depends on if you get to first, second, third, or home.

While losing all of you felt like I was continuously striking out in life, now, through these kids, I feel like I am finally scoring runs for them, for me, and for you.

And while I so wish I could have been your hero, I have also learned that it is OK to be human.

While you are in my past, you inspire my future. I will never forget any of you.

Pat Michalik

To The Children Of My Fallen Classmates

To the children of my fallen classmates,

Smile. I know you lost a parent, but I want you to smile. Every day you can continue the mission your parents set out to achieve.

See, at 17 or 18 years old, your mom or dad decided to serve our country because they believed in being a part of something greater than themselves. First, they, along with me, and the rest of our 2003 class, had to get through four years at West Point. We quickly learned the only way we could do that was together.

West Point purposefully overloaded us in our academics to teach us how to deal with stress and sift through what's extraneous work.

Every Saturday, we had room inspections. They would come in with a white glove and rub every horizontal surface, from inside your CD drive to the lock that pops out of your door. And God help you if you were a freshman and they found dust.

To graduate, we had to complete a challenging obstacle course in a certain amount of time. It was a lot of upper body mixed with endurance. In the indoor portion, after climbing the rope, we had to run around the track with a 10-pound medicine ball.

West Point challenged all of us mentally, physically and emotionally.

One classmate told me years later that during basic training freshman year, she was struggling, and I told her, "Come on, you can do this. Just relax and breathe."

We all suffered together and supported each other. The bond we created was unlike anything else. So, when any single one of us got hurt, we all hurt. There was and is love and loyalty between every member of our graduating class. Unfortunately, we are no longer whole. We lost eight of our classmates in combat and two from the effects of PTSD. Among those we lost, of course, were your parents.

Our class motto is Protectors of the Free, and with the help of our class president, we started The Protectors of the Free Foundation. Together, we raise money to make sure you, the children of our fallen classmates, have money to go to college.

However, more than the money to go to college, I want to share with you why, when you smile, you continue a mission that led to the loss of your parents' lives.

At West Point, our leaders constantly told us to choose the harder right over the easier wrong. As a member of our 2003 class, your parents committed to making choices in life based on what was right and not what was easy.

Also, West Point taught us never to get overwhelmed. Whether battling an enemy or facing a math test, life is going to throw you a lot of challenges and sometimes all at once. But as long as your parents were alive, they always kept going and kept pushing. We all knew and learned that as long as you keep fighting, you will always have a chance to accomplish whatever you want in life.

While your parents' lives ended short, their mission and the mentality they possessed in the process can continue every day with you and with us all. Regardless of the conflicts in our lives or the tasks that we need to complete, we must always smile.

The greatness in our country lies in our everyday citizens. When we smile, we offer kindness, which brings the best out of people. And when your parents chose to go to West Point and later on, on the day they lost their lives, they weren't fighting for themselves. Your parents fought to better us all. When you smile, you can do the same.

We are all proud of you.

The class of 2003 is here for you if you need anything.

Boyd Melson
MAJ, FA
Public Affairs Officer
361st Theater Support

Unseal Your Superpowers

LAUREN'S THOUGHTS

You Can **Find Joy** In Life After A Painful Loss

I was sitting in the front seat of my father's black sedan, just a few miles from the house where I grew up when I opened Facebook to read a message my ex-boyfriend's friend wrote to me. The friend and I hadn't spoken in years, so I didn't have a clue what he wanted, but I certainly wasn't expecting the news he delivered.

My jaw dropped, and I must have looked like I saw a ghost when I read the message because my father immediately asked me what happened. My ex's friend wrote that he didn't know how to tell me what he was about to say, but he thought it was important I knew. In the next sentence, he told me that my ex died the night before. I was 30 at the time, and my ex was only 29 years old. I was with him three weeks prior, laughing and reminiscing while I was on vacation in Los Angeles. To say I was in complete shock is an understatement.

His funeral wasn't for another week or so, so I had to fly back to Ohio, work for a few days, and then fly home again for his funeral. I was a sportscaster for ABC in Cleveland at the time, and I must have looked like a zombie on air all week. I was just trying to put one foot in front of the other. I couldn't focus, at all. At moments, I felt like I could barely breathe.

His funeral service was in a big church and it was packed. His family and friends told funny and endearing stories about him, as I cried uncontrollably while squeezing both my mother's hands.

My grief was so intense that the week after his funeral, I lost the ability to turn my neck. And all of a sudden, without an incident, an old back injury flared up and impacted my ability to walk, run, or play any kind of sport. Doctors wanted to test me for an autoimmune disease, but I, along with my parents, knew I was suffering from a broken heart. And I had no idea when or how it would get better.

My ex loved me.

He wanted the best for me, even if it meant me being with someone else.

The last time I saw him, he told me he treated me how I was meant to be treated and loved me how I was meant to be loved. He made me promise that I would hold the standard he set and never accept anything less for the rest of my life.

When you lose someone you love, the pain is overwhelming. I was sad for all the life that he won't get to live: marriage, children, career goals, and so much more. But selfishly, I was also upset about the hole that he left in my life, a friend that loved me, cared for me unconditionally, and I could always count on for anything.

My neck returned to normal in about a month, and my back took about a year, but my heart — I am not sure if that will ever fully heal. Grief is so overwhelming, and it never completely goes away. But my parents, and even his parents, told me I had to keep going. They wanted me to fall in love again, be happy, and not let his death consume my life.

I hope these letters help you realize that everything you feel after a loss is normal, and valid.

I hope these letters allow you to give yourself grace in the grieving process as you realize that healing isn't a straight path.

I hope these letters help you wake up and get out of bed in the morning.

I hope these letters let you know that you can and will be OK.

In all of these stories you just read, people shared how they suffered tremendous losses but have courageously moved forward in their lives in a way that honors the person/people they lost but does not hold them back from a healthy and happy future.

I am confident that you can do the same.

Lauren

- chapter 3

"You can't effectively battle an enemy unless you understand how, who, and where it attacks. And the best way to understand a problem is to learn from the people affected by it."

-Lauren

Gender

I Don't Wear Glass Slippers. I Shatter Them.

To the old standard of beauty,

You told young girls like me to make sure we wear make-up, do our hair, and wear the perfect dress while we wait for a guy to change our whole story. The women you told us about include Cinderella and Snow White. No offense to Snow White, but she just laid there until some guy kissed her and woke her up.

You projected this idea that we had to be thin and polished to be beautiful. By your standards, pretty was defined by not only what you looked like but also what you did. Pretty girls weren't on the math team. Pretty girls did not play aggressive sports. Pretty was more than a look. It was an entire image. These strict rules for beauty made me question my reflection. While I thought I could be cute, I would have never called myself beautiful.

I have always loved sports. At first, I played tennis because I saw women playing on TV. As I grew older, I started engaging in team sports: softball and soccer. But it was at 22 years old when I signed up for football that I found the magic that ended your spell.

When I started playing football, I thought that meant I needed to be big, wear black, and look tough. At 5'2", that wasn't an easy mold to fit. One time I was on my way to a game with my coach.

Some guy goes to him, "How did you get so lucky to ride to the game with a cheerleader?"

He responded, "That's my linebacker, and she will kick your ass."

I realized it made opponents mad that I was small and feminine. So, instead of trying to create this football persona, I decided to be an extreme version of myself. I threw out my black undershirt. I stopped trying to look tough. On the field, I'd sport makeup, pigtails, and a pink undershirt. I couldn't get in someone's face at 5'2", but I could blow kisses to them on the sideline while telling them that I would be all over them the next play. While teammates thought I was hilarious, I threw off my opponents, giving myself a competitive edge.

Suddenly, I owned who I was — a woman who loved and played football. It worked for me and allowed me to embrace being a girl who didn't fit the mold. I felt comfortable in my skin, as I didn't have to choose between this unrealistic standard for women that you created and my passion for athletics. I could get my hands dirty but still get my nails polished. This revelation not only made me a more confident person but also a better football player.

I embraced being small and used my ability to get low and be quick to my advantage. Ultimately, I mastered the game, and I became the first female coach in the NFL. Now, I travel the country teaching other young women the sport while instilling in them the idea that their biceps can be bigger than their boobs and they can still be beautiful.

I am personally making sure our world gets further and further away from you. But I am not alone. Companies are featuring more models with different shapes and sizes. Young girls are playing sports at record numbers. Women are embracing their unique body types.

We are no longer defining beauty by our image but rather setting standards with our attitude.

As a football player and most certainly as a coach, I am honored that I shattered the glass sideline, but I am even more proud that I am a part of a generation that is shattering the glass slipper.

Living happily ever after,
Coach Jen Welter

Here Is Why You Need To Stop Being Nice And Start Being Loud.

To ambitious young women,

My life has worked in mysterious ways. It's zigzagged all over the place. I was supposed to be a violinist and then I wasn't. I was supposed to go to law school, and I didn't. Then, to my own shock, I became Miss America, which led me to television. But for goodness sake, there was nowhere in my mind that I ever thought that I would jump off of a cliff and become one of the poster women for sexual harassment in the workplace.

Through all the twists and turns, the one constant in my life has been that fire in my belly. You know what I am talking about — that feeling deep down, that drives you to do the right thing, compete and make the most of your life.

As early as five years old, I had to advocate for myself. When I started kindergarten, the teacher divided the children up into two groups: kids who could read and kids who could not read. My teacher wrongly placed me in the group with kids who couldn't read. I can still feel myself running home from school, slamming the back door and screaming for my mom.

"Mom! They say I don't know how to read and I do," I cried.

She called the school and the next day, I was in the right group.

If I hadn't spoken up, it could have changed my entire educational trajectory, my self-confidence, my self-worth and my ability to stand up for right versus wrong.

Little did I know that there would be much tougher battles ahead. Luckily, along my journey, different lessons and experiences prepared me for my career.

When I was six years old, I started playing the violin. It automatically clicked and became my life. I dedicated most of my childhood to practicing four to five hours a day, learning immense discipline. Seeing myself grow and get better allowed me to build my self-esteem from the inside out. Also, developing and owning a talent was something no one could take away from me.

Through the violin, I learned how to value myself for who I was, not what I looked like.

In tenth grade, I auditioned for the school play, Oklahoma, as well as for this singing and dancing group called The Whirlwinds. Also, I ran for class president. In one day, I lost all of them. I remember going to my grandfather, completely upset.

He said, "Do you know how many elections Abraham Lincoln lost before he became president?"

I said, "No."

He responded, "A lot."

He said, "Do you know how many times it took Thomas Edison to invent the light bulb?"

And I said, "No."

He said, "More than 2,000 tries."

I realized that most people who find success in their lives have done so because they failed.

I know now when and if I fail, I might have to take two steps backward to get back into the game, but eventually, I'm going to move one step forward.

Ultimately, my ambition led me to Stanford and Oxford before becoming Miss America.

When I started my career, I began to realize how many women enter the working world with fire in their bellies but leave burned by their bosses. During my reign as Miss America, I met with television executives, trying to get a leg up in the business. Before my year was over, two executives sexually assaulted me.

My first TV job was in Richmond, Virginia.

Ironically, one of the first stories I covered was the Anita Hill hearings about harassment and Justice Clarence Thomas.

I remember watching and thinking, "I don't know why these men don't believe her."

Right after I covered the story, I was promptly sexually harassed on the job. If that wasn't enough, I was earning $18,000 and soon realized the male reporters were making more than me.

Much of my young age of 22 to 23 was filled with coming to realize that there was massive gender discrimination and abuse toward women. But as women, we're taught to put our nose to the grindstone, work harder, don't tell anyone and stuff the hurt somewhere deep in your soul.

At the time, I focused on becoming the best reporter at the shop and ascending through the television ranks. Years later, I was offered the opportunity to be a host of a morning show at Fox, and I jumped at it. A national morning show gave me the opportunity to showcase my smarts, my journalistic credentials and my personality.

When I realized after a decade at Fox, it was all coming to an end, and it wasn't my choice, I was devastated. I had killed myself for 25 years in a career.

That's when I used my confidence, my ability to bounce back from failure and my work ethic to take a leap of faith and speak up for myself and everyone else. If I didn't do it, who would? That's when I sued Roger Ailes, who at the time was the CEO and chairman of Fox News and one of the most powerful men in television.

Now, I am advocating for my kids and all of you, so you can work in safe and fair environments.

The two major ways sexual harassment has thrived in the workplace is through forced arbitration clauses in employment contracts, which means you can't go to open court, allowing companies to cover up their dirty laundry and secondly, through nondisclosure agreements. For the last three years, I have been walking the halls of Congress trying to pass legislation to eradicate forced arbitration clauses in contracts with regard to gender discrimination and sexual harassment.

Also, I recently started a nonprofit called Lift Our Voices. We are galvanizing an army of women and men across the world, trying to get rid of nondisclosure agreements for sexual harassment and gender discrimination.

But while I fight for you, I need you to make sure whatever path your life follows, straight or zigzagged, your fire not only continues to burn but turns into a collective blaze.

Whether you are five and in kindergarten or you are 40 and on television, use your voice. Women are socialized to be quiet and nice. Stop being so nice.

Men have no problem asking for a raise when they only deserve it 10 percent of the time. Women don't ask for a raise or a promotion until they're 90 percent sure that they're ready for it. I want you to go for it.

Stand up and say, "I'm worth it and I'm going to ask for what I want."

Take risks. I'm not saying to be irresponsible, I'm saying to go outside of your boundaries and color outside the lines every once in a while because it's going to help you gain more self-confidence.

Lastly, and most importantly, band together. Include young boys and men in this effort to fix problems for women in the workplace. Men are still running 95 percent of Fortune 500 companies and in charge of most of the hiring and pay equity or lack thereof. We need them to help us.

My hope is that the fire that still burns in my belly will burn down the old ways in the workforce, so that the fires in your bellies, whatever it is you decide to do, can be the flames that light up the world with your brilliance.

We got this.

Gretchen Carlson

Update: Lift Our Voices led the way to two of the most significant labor law changes in the last 100 years. President Biden signed the Ending Forced Arbitration of Sexual Assault and Sexual Harassment Act on March 3, 2022, and the bipartisan Speak Out Act, eradicating pre-dispute NDAs for sexual misconduct, on December 7, 2022.

This Is What Happens When You Pitch Like A Girl

To the parents who thought girls shouldn't play baseball,

"Don't get beat by a girl."

That was the mentality you passed down to your sons simply by the way you treated me. You were the parents of players on the opposing teams. I heard the comments you made and the gossip that went around every time I stepped on the mound.

You wanted me to hear you when you said I didn't belong. At first, it was not easy when you would shout that I was about to get crushed. You tried to rattle me, but instead, I learned to tune you out because I sure wasn't going to give up.

I fell in love with the sport of baseball when I was five years old, thanks to my dad, who introduced me to the game. By elementary school, I knew the sport would always be a part of my life. As a pitcher, I love taking control and having the command of the game.

Throughout Little League, I got a lot of attention. I made the all-star team each year. Camera crews showed up at games to film me, but at times you refused to let your sons be on TV. It was not because you didn't want them to have the spotlight, but rather because you feared that I would dim their shine. You didn't want your sons to be embarrassed when I struck them out.

While my teammates and their parents supported me, many people through the years tried to convince me to play softball. But why should I switch sports? That's like asking a tennis player to become a ping-pong player. Yes, they have a similar idea, but they are not the same game.

I always remained determined to play baseball regardless of the many hurdles in my way.

I wanted to attend a private school in Southern California, but the coaches wouldn't even let me try out. So, I had to search for a high school that would be open-minded enough to give a girl a chance to play, which I eventually found. While my teammates had my back, there were still times I naturally felt left out. Sometimes, I sat on the bench by myself, and that was hard.

Inside jokes didn't always include me. If I had one bad outing, it was the end of the world for my coaches. I wouldn't get playing time for weeks. No other player would get benched that long for a subpar performance. But I fought through it.

At 15 years old, I finally got a chance to play baseball with women. I became the youngest player on the U.S. Women's National Team, and I won an international award for best pitcher. That was the first time I really felt included and truly a part of a team.

My teammates encountered people just like you. There was and is an unspoken connection between all of us.

We all know what it is like to fight for a spot we deserve and to feel like an outcast. The Women's National Team is truly a collective group trying to succeed as one.

After high school, I received a scholarship to pitch in college at Montreat College in North Carolina while still playing with the U.S. National Team. In 2015, the U.S. women won gold at the Pan American Games, and I led us to the championship game.

Throughout my entire life, you've snickered, and you've doubted me. But instead of holding me back, I have learned not to let your words, or anyone else's, negativity impact me. With your help, I have grown into a strong and independent-minded woman.

I am 26 years old, and I still play baseball.

I continue to play with the National Team. I run clinics at a facility, and I work part-time at Fenway Park for the Boston Red Sox. Baseball isn't just part of my life; it's a part of me.

When I see young girls, who love the sport as much as I do, I warn them about people like you. I tell them not to listen. I tell them to never give up and to stay true to themselves and their passion.

Because the truth of the matter is that no one, not even you, is truly mad that girls are playing baseball. What bothers you is that we are good.

So instead of teaching your sons to fear getting beat by a girl, teach them to respect a good athlete. Because despite your efforts, our population is only getting bigger, and our talent is getting even better.

Who is up next?

Why It's Important For Women To Ask For Free Pizza

To the owner of my local pizza shop,

You probably don't know my name, and I am sure you have thousands of customers. Even so, I think you might remember me. I am the woman in her mid-20s who, from time to time, visits your pizza shop on Second Avenue in Manhattan. When I come by, I order several pizza slices, and I always ask for an extra free slice. You are good-natured and usually laugh.

But for me, asking for a free pizza is far more important than you might think. I don't ask because I am out of cash. I don't ask because I'm extra hungry, and I don't ask because I am greedy. Usually, I give away any extra pizza to someone on the street.

See, I look very young for my age, and I am a petite woman. Looking young sounds enviable, but when you're a professional, it's not, trust me. It makes it hard to get people to take you seriously. When I was in college, large companies sent their first and second-year employees to recruit on campus. During networking events, students would circle these young employees, who often overlooked me, literally.

People rarely made eye contact with me. The men talked the most, and when women did engage in the conversation, it was usually the taller women that got the most attention. I felt so unimportant.

Despite graduating from an Ivy League school where I was a leader in my sorority and in my dance group, when I entered the business world, I faced similar challenges. During meetings with other companies, if a man or a taller woman from my company stood next to me, questions would usually be directed to them and not me.

These scenarios played out for years and took a toll on my confidence. I had to remind myself that I am smart, and I had to find a way to speak up even when people made it uncomfortable for me.

That's when I started asking you for free pizza.

Sometimes you tell me no. When you do, it is a reminder that when I speak up, even if you reject me, I am no worse off. I still leave with the slices I bought.

Other times, you say yes, which teaches me that sometimes to get what you want, all it takes is some guts.

Asking for free pizza in a pizza shop is a low-stakes scenario. It provides me with a perfect place to practice asking bold questions, so I can be fearless when the stakes are higher. I named this practice tool The Pizza Principle.

And it's worked.

Linda Babcock, a professor at Carnegie Mellon University, says by not negotiating, an average woman leaves $1 million on the table throughout her career, but that's not going to be me.[1] Already, on several occasions, I have successfully negotiated a higher salary.

Even the way I respond to day-to-day interactions has changed. Recently, I was at a conference for work, standing at my company's booth next to a tall male colleague (and friend), Will. A man walked up to our booth and asked a question. I had more knowledge about the topic than Will did, so I answered it. He then turned to Will and asked a more specific question. I answered it again. This cycle repeated for four more questions. When the man walked away, I wasn't discouraged like I might have been a few years ago. Instead, Will and I laughed, as I knew the way that man treated me was his shortcoming, not mine.

The Pizza Principle has given me the confidence to stand up straight, look someone in the eye, ask for what I want and speak when I have something to say.

Today, it is probably easy to remember me because I am likely the only young woman to ask you for free pizza. But it may not be that way for long. Now, by writing a book and starting a blog, I am trying to teach as many women as possible The Pizza Principle. This way, more women will not only get an extra slice at your shop but also get a fair share in life.

Thank you — not just for giving me pizza but for helping me find my courage.

Mikael Austin

P.S. Your pizza is incredible.

---

[1] Babcock, Linda , and Sara Laschever. Women Don't Ask: The High Cost of Avoiding Negotiation--and Positive Strategies for Change. Bantam, 2007.

To WNBA Players, I Not Only Know Your Name, I See Your Fight

To the players of the WNBA,

I understand when you take the court, you aren't just competing with each other. You are competing against the outside world. That world consists of people who say you are not as good as NBA players or people who know you can play the game but don't bother even to learn your names.

I want you to know that I know not only your names but also how you play and why you fight.

At age five, I began playing basketball, but it wasn't until middle school that I started to get serious about the sport. Around that time, my dad started taking me to watch the Dream play, the WNBA team near my home.

There was one game against the Dallas Wings where we had pretty good seats, but we got upgraded to the floor. Being so close — just feet away from you — I felt adrenaline and excitement. Not to mention T-Pain and a few other famous people were sitting near us, so I felt like a celebrity.

At that game, I got to see Skylar Diggins-Smith, who played for Dallas. She's a burst of energy on the court, and she never gives up. She hustles throughout the whole game. Even if she's not making her shots, she'll do something to make up for it, and then her shots will fall.

She wears number four, and because of her, so do I. Early on, she showed me the type of player I wanted to become.

After middle school, I began to dedicate myself more and more to basketball. From practice to one-on-one with trainers, I am trying to grow and improve every day. There are moments I try to picture myself on the court, doing what you do. I try and put the idea in my head that I can play at your level.

Before Sabrina Ionescu rolled her ankle, I saw a play on Instagram where she went from being on offense to running down and getting the steal, which led to another possession for her team. Throughout entire games, she makes plays similar to that one. Her consistency and her hustle remind me that even when I am tired, I still need to push myself to make those plays.

Also, I have watched how players like Angel McCoughtry lead. She is always composed while also cheering on her teammates. Her demeanor and attitude are qualities I have tried to emulate in my young career.

I just graduated from high school, where I experienced some incredible moments. In my sophomore year, I played in the state championship at Georgia Tech, the arena where the Dream play. Our championship game was in front of a large crowd filled with scouts and fans. While we didn't win, being there as a sophomore was memorable. In my junior year, we made it to the regionals. As a team, we prepared similarly to how you, as professionals, prepare. We watched film and created offensive and defensive plays to defeat our opponent and shut down their best players. Our plan worked, and we played so well together, which is why that game is my favorite of all the games I played in high school.

While I am not on your level yet, I have received a ton of accolades, including First-Team All-Region and Second-Team All-State. This year, I will begin my freshman year at the University of West Florida, where I received a scholarship to play ball.

Before heading to school, I have been watching you all battle each other on the floor while also using your voices to bring attention to social justice. With the #sayhername movement, you are honoring Breonna Taylor and raising awareness for Black female victims of police violence. Seeing you all advocate for what is right made it clear to me that in your careers, you aren't just fighting for respect for women's professional basketball. You are and always have been fighting for respect for us all.

Truly, I want to thank you.

Through the years, you have not only shown me your basketball skills, but you have shown me courage and character.

While I have always known your names, it's because you have allowed me to see what's possible, that one day you might know mine too.

Amara Newsom

This Is What I Hope You Learn From A Female Football Coach

To my players on the Oberlin football team,

I am probably your first female football coach. The idea of a woman running drills is new for a lot of people — not just you.

Recently, Coach Ryan Swingle, our running backs coach, and I went to a recruiting camp in Michigan. When we walked in, Coach Swingle started getting funny looks because he was with me. One coach came up to him, shook his hand, and introduced himself. I was standing right there, but he didn't look in my direction. It was like I didn't exist.

So, I interjected and said, "Hey! I am Coach Hanna. It's nice to meet you. What's your name again?"

He reached out his hand and looked back over to Coach Swingle as he said, "So what is she, your assistant or something?"

My hand tightened up around his knuckles as Coach Swingle looked him in the eye and firmly said, "No, not at all."

I knew I had Coach Swingle's support, as I said, "I'm the director of football operations as well as the corners coach."

When he realized I was serious, the coach chuckled, rolled his eyes, and walked away.

I share this story with you because if I can get you to understand the significance of this moment, I know I can help you grow as football players and people.

Growing up, my dad was a Browns fan, and neither my younger sister nor my older sister seemed interested in watching games with him. So, I threw on an orange and brown shirt and sat beside him. Right away, I wanted to have a deeper understanding of the game.

My dad didn't know the sport's intricacies, so I started asking questions to my friends who played football. I was drawn by the idea that a detail as small as a needle can control an entire game's outcome — just the position of an elbow can translate into huge plays.

First, I went to Florida Atlantic University, where I got involved with the equipment room and worked with a position before transferring to the University of Delaware. That's where I decided I wanted to be a coach. Taking notice of my interest, the defensive line coach at Delaware, Levern Belin, sat in a classroom with me and some of his players to go over film. He never shied away from teaching me as much as I wanted to learn. Safeties coach, Tommy McEntire, brought me into his group as more than just an equipment manager. Also, he talked me through the path of a coaching career. It was at Delaware that I realized that there are people out there who will not only help me but also give me a chance.

However, the realization that being a woman in football wasn't going to be easy came in waves. In the beginning, I was told that a good spot for me would be in a dress, helping out with recruiting, as opposed to being on the sideline calling plays.

The next wave came with being assigned to assistant work, all the stuff they didn't want to do but thought they could easily teach someone who never played.

Once I got the chance to be out on the field, I battled how I looked and how I was perceived. Players commented on my appearance.

They said, "Did you dress up nicely for me?" Or, "Why are you wearing makeup?"

A player on an opposing team once said to me, "Hey, girl! Turn back around here so I can smack that."

When I told people I was a football coach, many thought I was a trainer.

Others would encourage me to pursue journalism, telling me, "You've got a great face and personality for TV."

I even received comments like, "You're going to find yourself a great husband."

My first boyfriend heard that players were talking about me in the locker room. He told me I had to choose: him or football. I couldn't believe people wanted me to give up my passion simply because other people couldn't respect or visualize a woman in a male-dominated sport.

Quitting wasn't an option for me. There is no other job I could ever do with this much passion. Whether I'm pulling an all-nighter or working 20-hour days for two weeks straight, I love every single second that I am coaching football.

I coached at the high school level and with the Cleveland Browns youth programs before Coach Steve Opgenorth saw my love for the sport and hired me here at Oberlin. He believes in me. Coach James Mayden, our safeties coach, has helped me learn and develop an understanding of the secondaries.

If self-doubt creeps in before I go into a meeting, he'll tell me, "You got this."

And the second we get out, he will say, "You killed it."

While my fellow coaches' support may seem minor, I learned at that recruiting camp with Coach Swingle that, like football, the smallest detail can have a massive impact.

See, after Coach Swingle let that other coach know I was certainly not his assistant, we started to intermingle with recruits. Coach Swingle and I had a line of student-athletes waiting to talk to us.

One of the coaches from the same team as the coach who dismissed me walked by and said, "Wow, you sure know a lot of people out here."

I turned around, looked him in the eye, and said, "It's super easy for my recruits to identify the female with the long hair as opposed to trying to figure out which one of you white dudes is tweeting at him on Twitter."

This man started cracking up and said, "You are dead right about that."

I knew I earned people's respect.

At the end of the camp, the initial coach who shook my hand told me, "You did a great job out here, and I can't wait to see you next year."

When Coach Swingle initially made it clear that he had my back, it gave me even more confidence to hold my ground.

You may not be used to a woman on the sidelines, but I will not change who I am or tone down my femininity because I am working in a sport known for "masculinity."

Some days, I am going to come to practice in makeup. On other days, I'll be without it. I may wear leggings to a meeting or shorts to training camp. For some games, I might polish my nails or have my hair done. At an event, I might dress to the nines in heels and a skirt. I don't like tan lines. So, I wear a bikini when I go to the beach with my family.

How I dress doesn't change why I am here, what I have to offer you, or how I expect you to treat me.

There should be no whispers in the locker room, no chuckles on the sideline, and certainly no derogatory comments anywhere. And if you hear someone else disrespect me, I expect you to correct them.

It may only take a sentence, a few words, or even just a look to make a difference. But by always standing up for not only me but also for each other, we will empower ourselves to play and perform with confidence. And even more importantly, by fighting for what is right, we will teach ourselves to live with courage.

That's how we not only make ourselves a great football team, but it's how we become people who will help create a better world.

I can't wait to get out there.

Coach Alex Hanna

Race

To the Black And White Youth Of America, Let's Get Real About Race

To the Black and white youth of America,

On my first day of kindergarten, we stood in a circle and said the Pledge of Allegiance. The teacher asked everyone to hold hands. When I reached out to my classmates, no one would touch me. No one would hold my hand. At five years old, I looked around the classroom, and I immediately knew the reason.

I was Black, and everyone else was white.

My high school experience was unique because I was a star athlete. While my classmates respected me, some of my opponents from other schools still held my race against me. In football, players from other teams would sometimes call me a N***** after they tackled me, and in basketball, some fans from other schools would taunt me with racial slurs while I warmed up for a game. I was offended, but it never caught me off guard. This was and still is customary for a Black kid and man in America.

Now, you may look at me and see a successful Black man: a graduate from a top university, a first-round NFL draft pick, a 12-year NFL All-Pro, a Hollywood actor, and a CEO of a tech startup.

You may say racism didn't impact me on my journey. But that is far from the truth. I just so happened to have athletic skills that allowed some to push racism to the side because I benefited their team, city, or bank account.

Even with my status, when I am pulled over by the police, it's not just an annoyance like it is for someone who is white. For me, it could be a life-or-death experience, just like it was for Philando Castile. He was shot and killed in front of his girlfriend and her child during a traffic stop while his girlfriend says he was just reaching for his license.[1]

The police officer that killed him did not even go to prison. He was acquitted and paid nearly $50,000 as part of a separation agreement to end his employment.[2]

Black people are even hurt or killed by the police in their homes. Recently, a 28-year-old woman, Atatiana Jefferson, was shot through her bedroom window by a police officer.[3] Before the shooting, her family says she was playing video games with her eight-year-old nephew. As we await more answers, the police officer who

---

[1] Lopez, German. "Philando Castile Minnesota Police Shooting: Officer Cleared of Manslaughter Charge." Vox, 16 Jun. 2017, www.vox.com/2016/7/7/12116288/minnesota-police-shooting-philando-castile-falcon-heights-video. Accessed 22 Aug. 2023.

[2] Forliti, Amy. "Cop Who Killed Philando Castile to Be Paid $48,500 in Buyout." The Associated Press, 11 Jul. 2017. https://www.usatoday.com/story/news/nation/2017/07/11/cop-who-killed-philando-castile-paid-48-500-buyout/466918001/

[3] Melhado, William. "Former Fort Worth Police Officer Found Guilty of Manslaughter of Atatiana Jefferson." Texas Tribune, 15 Dec. 2022. https://www.texastribune.org/2022/12/15/fort-worth-police-officer-atatiana-jefferson/

killed her was arrested for murder but released hours later on $200,000 bond.[4]

Her story comes on the heels of the trial for Botham Jean. Jean was shot by an off-duty police officer while eating ice cream in his apartment.

The police officer who killed him received a 10-year sentence with eligibility for parole in just five years.[5]

Instinctively, I have extreme anxiety about the police, as the aforementioned stories are just a couple of examples that show me that the justice system was not set up to protect Black people. It was not set up to protect me.

Black people in America statistically don't receive the same treatment or opportunity as white people.[6] That does not mean that if you are a white child, you have to grow up feeling sorry for Black kids, and if you are a Black kid, you don't have to feel like, woe is me. But this is the society you inherited.

Whether you are a white kid or a Black kid, racism is not your fault. It started long before you or I got here. However, it is up to you to make sure it's not here long after we are gone. All of you can help dissolve racism.

Here is how:

First, we need to start over. To do so, we need to look back at our history. You have to know where you have been to know where you are going. Slavery is at the root of racism in America. If you study the atmosphere in

---

[4] "The Latest: $200,000 Bond Set for Ex-cop Charged with Murder." Associated Press, 15 Oct. 2019. https://apnews.com/article/shootings-us-news-atatiana-jefferson-police-tx-state-wire-2dc677322c7f4d1fb7 d1b94f119e1806

[5] Ortiz, Erik, and Alex Johnson. "Amber Guyger Sentenced to 10 Years for Murdering Neighbor Botham Jean." NBC News, 2 Oct. 2019, www.nbcnews.com/news/crime-courts/amber-guyger-sentencing-resumes-after-murder-conviction-death-botham-jean-n1061146. Accessed 22 Aug. 2023.

[6] Toppo, Greg. "Black Students Nearly 4x As Likely to Be Suspended." USA Today, 7 Jun. 2016. https://amp.usatoday.com/amp/85526458

which slavery was cultivated, it will give you a greater perspective on the racial dynamic between Black and white people in this country.

A part of the problem is the current curriculum in most schools doesn't efficiently address Black history. It gives us a couple of cool Black people that were assets to white culture and then focuses on men like Thomas Jefferson. Schools teach us that Jefferson is one of America's founding fathers. He even founded the University of Virginia, where I received a great education. What schools failed to teach me as a kid was that he was a slave owner, housing my ancestors on the same grounds where I ultimately attended classes and starred on the field. Therefore, he is no founding father or hero to me.[7]

I didn't learn much about African-American or African history until I searched for it either in college or in the last 15 years through resources online. I realized that Black history didn't start with slavery. Black people have a global history of greatness that started long before coming to America. Brilliant inventors and royalty are just a part of Black people's lineage. Africa is the richest continent in natural resources.[8] From its food to its music, African culture has a worldwide influence.

Even though you are just kids, you need to venture outside of your classrooms and your schools to learn African history as well as real American history. Go to the library, go to YouTube, or listen to podcasts. Expose yourself to the accomplishments of Black people while also acknowledging the ugliness of our country's past.

---

7 Whitford, Emma . "Reconciling the Two Jeffersons." Inside Higher Ed, 7 Aug. 2018, www.insidehighered.com/news/2018/08/08/new-uva-report-brings-thomas-jeffersons-racist-past-light. Accessed 22 Aug. 2023.

8 Sawe , Benjamin E. "Which Continent Is The Richest In Natural Resources?" WorldAtlas, 20 Aug. 2018, www.worldatlas.com/articles/which-continent-is-the-richest-in-natural-resources.html.

It is important that all of you, Black or white, understand that there is so much more to Black history than what you've probably been taught in school or you have seen on TV.

Secondly, be unafraid to talk about race.

Sometimes white people ask me, "Why does everything have to be about race?"

What they don't realize is that America was built on race and racism. It has been intertwined in nearly every aspect of our society since slavery.

Some white people will say, "Well, slavery is long gone. Let's forget it and move on."

The problem is that the damage has led to deeply-rooted systemic and psychological effects that are still very much alive and prevalent today.

So while some white people are tired of talking about race and racism, trust me, Black people are even more tired of talking about race and enduring racism.

But an open dialogue is necessary for change.

The other day one of my white producer friends said, "It's hard being a white man in America right now."

I initially looked at him like he was crazy, but then I decided to take it as an opportunity to have a meaningful and educational conversation about race.

If you are white, you might be uncomfortable asking questions about race. It's OK if you don't know about a Black person's experience, but to solve the problem, we all have to talk about it. We have to be open to listening and trying to understand each other's circumstances so we can be more aware and compassionate.

Regularly, I post on social media about Black love and Black excellence. Some people have called me racist because of it. That's not the case. In reality, I am trying to encourage and empower Black people to love and value ourselves and to realize we are not inferior like we've been told and treated throughout American history.

I want you all to understand that honesty is not racism. It's OK to speak the truth, and it's also OK to ask about the truth. The acknowledgment of race doesn't perpetuate our problems. Dismissing or ignoring that there are problems is how racism thrives.

I also hope you speak up, not only for yourselves but for each other. Even as kids, whatever your race may be, you can take a stand. If you see someone using racial slurs or mistreating someone because of their race, help them. Live your life with dignity and courage by not only supporting what is right for you but rather advocating for what is right overall.

A lot of successful people with large platforms won't talk about race because they are afraid of the backlash. They are afraid it will hurt their careers or their businesses. I always say integrity over income. You get a dollar; you spend a dollar. Your integrity is here forever.

That's the way I live my life. That's the way my parents raised me. And that is why I am writing to you right now.

Lastly, don't think because you have friends of a different race, you are not capable of being racist.

As a former star athlete, there are a lot of white people who call me their friend. They treat me with respect and acceptance. However, I will go out with a friend who is Black but did not play football, and right in front of my face, those same people will talk to him differently. They will judge him differently.

That is racism. Those people, in all likelihood, like me for my status. What if I never played football? I might be treated just like my friend. The way I see it is, disrespecting my friend is disrespecting me.

Never approach someone with preconceived notions of their character, their ability, or their background. Be kind and respectful to everyone.

Understand all white people are not racist, and not all Black people are criminals. When you meet people, give them a chance and take the time to get to know them as individuals instead of buying into stereotypes.

To end racism, we have to treat everyone equally and fairly. While it is a simple concept, it's not easy to execute.

Racism today is a byproduct of years and years of inequality and mistreatment in this country. But I believe in you, and I believe progress can happen.

See, the day I first recognized racism in my kindergarten class when I was five years old was also the day I realized how we can all fix it — by reaching out our hands and doing it together.

We can be the difference,
Thomas Q. Jones

To White Mothers, This Is How You Can Help Keep My Sons Safe

To white mothers,

I am asking for your help.

As parents, we all share some similar worries about our children. We want them to stay healthy, make smart decisions and be kind people.

We want them to have the opportunity to live a good life.

Right now, my children are doing well. However, this week, after seeing a video of a young Black man, Ahmaud Arbery, shot and killed while jogging, I am once again reminded that as a mom to three Black men, I have added worries even though I have great kids.

When my boys play sports, they always look for their mom in the stands. If they aren't playing up to their potential, I will put my thumb up, which means to turn it up a notch. As they have progressed to larger stadiums and crowds, it's a little different, but even if they can't find me, they always know I am there.

The night my oldest son, Malik Hooker, got drafted into the NFL, he invited his father, who was absent for much of his life. Watching my boys run around to try and find their dad a shirt and some shoes infuriated me. My children pulled me aside and told me they not only paid attention to the role I played in their lives, but they also listened to the lessons I taught them. One of those lessons was about forgiveness. At that moment, I was so moved and so proud.

When I look at my boys, I see strong, gifted, loving, educated, and kind men.

The problem is when some people look at my sons, all they see is the color of their skin. Some people believe all Black men are dangerous and uneducated, which in their minds, justifies potentially hurting them without cause.

My sons are athletes and regularly jog outside. Ahmaud Arbery could have easily been one of my sons.

There is a tremendous amount of fear that simply because my children are Black, that one night they won't make it home.

Mom to mom, parent to parent, I am writing to you because you can be a part of making the world safer for my children and grandchildren.

Talk to your children about race. The younger you start these conversations, the better the world will be. Identify that we're not all the same. Our cultures and experiences may vary. But tell your kids that being different is OK. Every race is still made up of individuals. We all must teach our children to get to know people. Let's tell them not to make assumptions about people based on what they see on TV, hear from someone else, or read on social media. All Black people are not the same. All white people are not the same. There is good and bad in every race, which is why we all must look past someone's complexion.

Throughout history, there has not only been violence toward Black people, but there has also been complacency with awful behavior. I came across an article in the Washington Times from 1908. It was titled "Bait Alligators with Pickaninnies: Zoo Specimens Coaxed to Summer Quarters by Plump Africans."[1] A zookeeper sent two Black children into an enclosure with 25 alligators to lure the alligators from one location to another. Besides using children as bait, also terrifying was the fact that the reporter who wrote the story didn't criticize or condemn the zookeeper.[2]

Even though today, we may not see situations as severe as using Black children as bait, we still witness a lot of people who allow or encourage violence and racism. In Arbery's situation, his alleged killers, Gregory McMichael and Travis McMichael, were not charged until a video of the murder was released publicly, and the Georgia Bureau of Investigation took over the case.[3] The charges came more than two months after the February 23rd killing.

Let's teach our children not only to do right but to stand up against wrong. Whether it's mean words or violent acts, we all must hold each other accountable.

---

1 "Bait Alligators With Pickaninnies." Library Of Congress, 13 Jun. 1908, chroniclingamerica.loc.gov/lccn/sn84026749/1908-06-13/ed-1/seq-2/#-date1=1836&sort=relevance&rows =20&words=ALLIGATORS+BAITS&-search&sequence=0&index=16&state=&date2=1922&proxtext=Alligator+bait&y=0&x=0&dateFilter&page=4. Accessed 22 Aug. 2023.

2 Foxworth, Domonique. "The Gut-wrenching History of Black Babies and Alligators." The Undefeated, 22 Jun. 2016, theundefeated.com/features/the-gut-wrenching-history-of-black-babies-and-alligators/. Accessed 22 Aug. 2023.

3 Audrey, McNamara. "Probable Cause "Clear" in Ahmaud Arbery Case, Georgia Bureau of Investigation Says." CBS News, 8 May 2020, www.cbsnews.com/news/ahmaud-arbery-probable-cause-murder-case-georgia-bureau-investigations/. Accessed 22 Aug. 2023./

Black men are dying. They are getting killed — not because of what they've done or who they are as people. They are losing their lives because of the color of their skin.

I, a mother to three Black men, don't just worry about my sons getting the chance to live a good life. I worry about them getting the opportunity to live at all.

As moms, you and I may look different, but my love for my children is just the same as yours. And one day, with your help, I hope my worries can be too.

Angela Dennis

I Want You To Feel What The World May Not See

Daschel,

You are only five years old, but I keep having this recurring nightmare about your teenage years. In this nightmare, you are in New York City, where we live with a bunch of other kids your age. The cops are questioning your friends, but they skip you. You tell everyone you have to get home. So, you dip out and head back as if nothing happened.

Every time I have this dream, I wake up sweating intensely.

Before you were born, your dad was all prepared, reading and learning what it would be like for a white man to raise a brown child. But when you were born, you weren't brown. You weren't Black. Instead, you were born with pale skin and red hair.

Embarrassingly, as your mom, I felt a sense of relief.

THAT conversation — the one forewarning you about potential bullies and struggles because of the color of your skin — we don't need to have with you. We don't have to worry that if you wear a hoodie, someone will assume you are dangerous and harm you. You are less likely to be hurt by the police without cause. Instead, you will live a life with more privilege and opportunity than if your skin color matched mine, which is Black.

However, I want you to know what you look like doesn't change who you are or where you come from.

You have a lineage and a legacy of conscientious objectors, including my papa, Madison Shockley, who was the most important man in my life before you, your dad, or your Uncle Sage came along. Papa was ahead of his time. He stood up for social justice and fought hard for civil rights. From Tennessee to Los Angeles, he advocated for the desegregation of lunch counters. He took part in the March on Washington when Dr. Martin Luther King gave his historic "I Have a Dream" speech in an effort to end racism. Decades later, he attended the Million Man March, which aimed to unite African Americans as they combated inequality.

Part of the reason you look the way you do is not only because your dad is white but because my great great grandfather is also white. In 1897, your great great great grandfather, Isaac Jolly, married a Black woman, Minnie Minor. At the time, this was remarkable. Back then, you didn't see couples that looked like me and your dad. People married people of their own race. Your great great great grandfather was socially disowned by his family, as he openly walked the world married to a Black woman. Together, they had 12 children.

More than 100 years later, I am sure you have already noticed moments where people upset me — like at school when your classmates' parents thought I was your caregiver or in the streets when people assume I am your nanny. There is nothing wrong with being a nanny, but I am your mom, and I am proud to be your mom.

In your life, you might hear mean words about people who look like me, people who are Black or brown. People will talk differently in front of you than they would in front of me because they will think you are white.

You, in all likelihood, won't be targeted by biased teachers or administrators. You won't unjustly miss out on a promotion at work. You won't be impacted by stereotypes that lead people to assume Black people aren't as smart or as educated.

Right now, you don't have much of an understanding of race or racism. But as a child, you are already picking up on subtle cultural messages that say black is bad and white is good. Often the good guys are dressed in white, and the bad guys are in black. As you move through the world as a good-looking and seemingly-white person, I am afraid of how society will influence you.

I am worried that one day you will say, "I'm not claiming my heritage."

I am worried you will say, "I am not Black."

I want you to know that you ARE Black. Even though you won't experience much racism and people probably won't even inquire about your background, as they do to me, it doesn't mean you are better than anyone else. You just have a plethora of genes that happen to sort themselves out in this way.

I still want you to identify with my family and be proud of the people who came before you, the stance they took, and the progress they made.

When you meet people, I hope you take more than half a second to draw a conclusion. Our faces are very similar, but when people assume I am your nanny, it is because they don't look past our complexion. When you had two Black girls in your class, who were both new and around the same height, you assumed they were twins, but they looked nothing alike. I want you to always pay attention to details.

You need to ask people questions about their cultures, look at how people interact with each other and listen to people when they tell you who they are and where they are from. It will show others that you respect them, and you will hopefully get that respect in return.

When you witness racism, you will have a choice in how to react. I don't want you to align yourselves to the point where you get locked up or hurt. However, I hope you call someone's parents or stay with your friends or even, if it's appropriate, place your body in the middle of a situation in order to de-escalate a potential problem.

My biggest fear is that you will walk through life with blind entitlement, unaware of the privileges you possess.

I want you to know that it's not appropriate to watch people being treated poorly or judged unfairly based on the fact that it doesn't happen to you.

My nightmare is not that you one day will abandon your friends but that you will not feel connected to the struggle of most Black people. My fear is that you won't fight against racism. And if that happens, you won't only be rejecting your heritage, but you will also be rejecting me.

We will figure this out together.

I love you.

Mama (Kanyessa McMahon)

LGBTQ+

What It Is Like To Be A Trans Woman Of Color In America

To whoever is willing to read this,

The other day someone asked me how I celebrate July 4th.

I said, "I don't celebrate Independence Day. I don't think there's anything to celebrate until we are all free."

I am a 30-year-old Black trans woman. Black and trans people in this country do not receive the same rights and opportunities as others.

According to a study in the Americas, trans women of color have a life expectancy of 30–35 years old.[1]

Sometimes I wonder, "Will I make it? Will I make it to 35?"

There is so much violence against Black trans women. In 2019 alone, at least 27 transgender or gender non-con-

---

[1] "An Overview of Violence Against LGBTI Persons." Inter-American Commission on Human Rights, 17 Dec. 2014, www.oas.org/en/iachr/lgtbi/docs/Annex-Registry-Violence-LGBTI.pdf. Accessed 22 Aug. 2023.

forming people were fatally shot or killed in the U.S., and the majority of them were Black.[2]

Since I was a child, I knew that life would be hard for me. I came from a very Catholic-oriented family that went to church every Sunday. When I came out as gay at a young age, maybe 30 percent of my family was OK with it, but the rest did not approve. As a teenager, I started presenting myself as gender fluid, buying women's jeans, tops, and shoes. Family members threw away or even burned my clothes.

At 17 years old, I left home.

I didn't start fully transitioning until about 10 years later. Since I was a child, I knew I was a woman, but I was nervous about presenting myself as one. I felt pressure from society, my family, and my job to live and be someone that I was not. And then, of course, I knew the statistics in terms of violence against trans women.

I couldn't help but think, "If I go ahead with this journey, that could be me. Someone could murder me."

However, pre-transition life felt like being a caterpillar who wanted to be a butterfly. I was stuck in a cocoon. Feeling trapped mentally and physically took a toll on me. It was as though I was walking around not only lying to others about who I was but, most importantly, lying to myself.

Transitioning lifted a huge burden, but life was not any easier. I pumped myself with hormones and medications that changed my physical appearance and also impacted me mentally and emotionally. That led me to bouts of depression and anxiety and made me very self-conscious.

---

[2] "An Overview of Violence Against LGBTI Persons." Human Rights Campaign, www.hrc.org/resources/violence-against-the-transgender-community-in-2019. Accessed 22 Aug. 2023.

Assimilating to society as a woman was complicated. Before I changed my name, I would get carded at a bar and receive strange looks from the bouncer. If someone called to collect a bill, they would be confused when my masculine name didn't match my feminine voice. When I went to apply for jobs, they would tell me they were no longer hiring even though they were still advertising a given position. Regularly, I had to explain myself to other people and advocate for opportunities.

I have since legally changed my name and gender markers, which was an expensive process. While I think I am very passable as a woman, now I always worry about people finding out that I am a trans woman.

Thoughts run through my head:

"How will I be treated?"

"Will I still be able to go to this bar?"

"Will I still be able to keep such and such job?"

There is also the never-ending worry about my safety. I'm not sure if I go on a date with a man that I meet on a dating app that I will make it home alive.

One time I went to a movie with a guy. After the movie, he refused to take me home, locked me in his car, and assaulted me.

It's hard to find love, as many people treat trans women more like an experience than a person. When in relationships, transgender people face violence at much higher rates than the general population (30% to 50% compared to 28% to 33% in the general population), which contributes to the high rate of fatalities.[3]

---

[3] Brown, Taylor N., and Jody L. Herman. "Intimate Partner Violence and Sexual Abuse Among LGBT People - A Review of Existing Research." Williams Institute, Nov. 2015, williamsinstitute.law.ucla.edu/publications/ipv-sex-abuse-lgbt-people/. Accessed 22 Aug. 2023.

This journey is not an easy one. There was a time after transitioning that I lost my drive and my sense of purpose. Thankfully, when I started to use my voice and speak on behalf of Black trans women, I began to feel empowered.

That is, in part, why I am so grateful that you are taking the time to read this letter, which is more than many people are willing to do. Hopefully, through my story, you find a sense of compassion, understanding, and empathy for what I, along with many other Black trans women, endure in our daily lives. My wish is that you will see that we deserve love, compassion, understanding, and empathy, not just as Black trans women but as human beings.

Hopefully, you will join our fight. Then, maybe one day, I will be able to join you in celebrating the land of the free instead of living in a world that I fear.

You can help make a difference. Thanks for your time.

Loud, proud, and beautiful,
Gabrielle Inès

Here Is Why My Journey To Living Life As An Openly Gay Woman Hasn't Been Easy

To those afraid to live their life authentically,

It's not always easy to live your life as your true self, and for a long time, I lived a lie and felt the same way you may now — frightened to live your truth.

My story begins in a nondescript town in Northeast Ohio. Rural and conservative, it's a small town on a big map. I grew up there on a large farm, and my entire childhood, I thought about leaving. A life of anonymity in a big city was much more appealing to me.

I didn't fit in. I knew I was different. I knew who I truly was wouldn't be accepted there. I've known since I was about five years old that I liked girls. My first crush was on a character named Joey on a show called "The Courtship of Eddie's Father."

I remember thinking, "She's a sassy tomboy, like me. I want to kiss her."

In school, I developed crushes on my teachers, and there was one teacher that I really liked. I used to bring her flowers, apples, and other little gifts. One day, she told me she appreciated the presents, but I needed to stop. I got the feeling that what I had done was wrong. I was just a silly grade school kid trying to figure things out. I was heartbroken and ashamed. The incident confirmed the need to keep quiet and hide my real feelings.

Years later, in junior high school, I hit the game-winning shot in basketball. Everyone was so excited, and I was feeling confident, connected, and emotional. Later, overcome by a sense of belonging, I felt the need to share.

Surrounded by my close friends and teammates, I said, "I love you guys. You are my best friends, and I want to tell you something."

I had their undivided attention and told them, "I am gay."

They all froze and stared at me. You could feel the air literally being sucked out of the atmosphere. I thought they were going to throw me into traffic.

So, I immediately reacted and said, "Oh my Gosh, I'm just kidding. I am not gay."

The look of relief on their faces confirmed the need to, again, keep quiet and hide my real feelings.

After I tried to come out to my friends, and it didn't work out, I did what was expected. I dated a guy who had a crush on me, but it just never felt right.

After high school graduation, I finally got the chance to leave Ohio. I attended college in Georgia and lived in Atlanta. In a big city, I could experience gay and lesbian bars, and it was all that I had imagined. I met a woman, moved in with her, and we were incredibly happy. But it was short-lived.

In the '90s, there was a lot of hate toward the LBGTQ-plus community. My favorite lesbian bar was bombed, and several women had to go to the hospital. Media outlets mentioned them by name. They were outed, and some were fired from their jobs simply for being gay. It was a terrible time, and I was terrified to the point of no longer wanting to frequent the gay gathering spots I once loved and felt safe in. The violence and shame deterred me from living an authentic life.

Things fell apart. I met a man and ended up marrying him. Years passed, and eventually, we had a baby girl. Being a mom is the best job ever, but it didn't take away from the feeling of being unsettled. I knew deep inside; I was living a lie. I wasn't being fair to my family, myself, or my queer community. My struggle took root in my body and began to show up physically. I gained weight and wasn't healthy. It got to a point where I didn't want to go anywhere or do anything. Eventually, I shut down completely. There was a lot of resentment and toxicity, and my marriage turned ugly. One day, I decided enough was enough, and I finally found the courage to get a divorce.

The healing process took time. Eventually, I felt strong enough to live my truth and began dating women again. I became more open about who I am and stopped denying I am queer.

In a few weeks, I'll return to the small Ohio town I grew up in, and there may be looks and whispers. But honestly, it no longer matters.

The fear of living my authentic life put me on a different path, and sometimes I wonder, "What if?" It's those moments that led to me writing "The Pink Divide," a work of fiction loosely based on my life and experiences as a queer woman. It's my hope that the book and story give you the confidence and courage to be free and love freely. While the story may not be unique, I believe it's the sad commonality of the tale that binds many of us late-to-the-party queers.

I want you to know it's ok to take baby steps, align with allies and seek safe spaces. It was tough for me to fully live my truth, and I am sure you will have your own challenges.

Just know that even though it may be hard, living and loving authentically will always be worth it.

Good Luck! I support you.

Robee

LAUREN'S THOUGHTS

An **Open Heart** Is The Healer Of Humanity

When I was a teenager I had a math teacher who taught honors pre-calc. He had a thick accent, was very quirky, and a bit disorganized. One day in class, he posted a problem on the board that was supposedly difficult and wanted to see if any of us could solve it. Sure enough, I raised my hand. When he called on me, I told him the answer and how I got to it.

Instead of simply praising me for solving the problem, he said, "Wow, you are a lot smarter than you look."

The whole class was surprised by the comment, and everyone just stared at me to see how I would respond, but I didn't say a word.

I was caught off guard and I had no idea what he meant.

Did I look like I wasn't smart? Is it even possible to look unintelligent?

At that moment, I felt embarrassed and a little upset, but I wasn't exactly sure why. So when I went home that day, I told my mother, and she was furious — next level mad. Just by my mother's horrified reaction, I realized the comment was sexist and wrong, and that's why it evoked a negative feeling within me.

The next day, my mom called the school and complained, and he apologized. But that was the first of many instances where I felt someone else's misogyny take a swing at my confidence.

Working in sports, at times, was like jumping in a pool of rats who try to nibble at your self-worth and sense of empowerment. I often felt like I was hired to look cute, and at times, my intelligence and hustle were more of a liability than an asset. Some people didn't like that I had a voice. Don't get me wrong. I met many amazing people and mentors who are still great friends. But plenty of people tried to silence my voice and control my every move.

Then, there was the harassment.

There was a sports executive who told me, "You give me a little love, and I'll give you a little information."

And an assistant coach who told me if I performed a specific sexual act, he would tell me who was starting.

But honestly, I could handle a few perverts. Sadly, I have dealt with those types my whole life. The worst was being put in a box by some people (not all) in the business, who, when deciding on postions focused more on looks and gender than ability and work ethic. There were people who I felt stereotyped me and limited me to roles that they believed suited my appearance and gender.

As I started to vent to friends and peers, it seemed as though my friends who were Black understood my frustration the most, and they opened my eyes even more to the challenges they faced. While I knew racism existed, I didn't truly understand how it impacted so many different aspects of life, including work, until I was trying to unravel the discrimination I suffered.

I remember talking to a friend, who I knew dealt with racism growing up in an all-white town in the midwest, and asking, "How are you not mad?"

She said, "Lauren, if I got mad every time someone mistreated me because of my race, I would spend my whole life miserable. And I don't want that for myself."

My experiences made me more compassionate and thoughtful about other people's circumstances. And while I don't believe racism, homophobia, or misogyny are the same, I do think they are all cousins, and their last name is inequality.

I assembled this collection of letters for all marginalized citizens. If you have ever been discriminated against, or if anyone has ever tried to lower the volume on your voice, these letters you just read are examples of people who have not let small-minded, hateful, or ignorant humans shrink their power or undermine their dreams. They are people who fought back and won in ways bigger and better than anyone ever anticipated. But that's not all.

Listening to other people's stories and circumstances has made me realize how unaware most of us are of other people's hardships. And that's not blaming anyone. Every person experiences the world so differently, and often we don't count or recognize problems we don't have unless it impacts someone very close to us.

These letters aim to help you understand how hate and discrimination operate, infiltrate our society, and hurt (sometimes even kill) kind and innocent people just like you. You can't effectively battle an enemy unless you understand how, who, and where it attacks. And the best way to understand a problem is to learn from the people affected by it.

Hopefully, you read these letters with an open heart and mind, and it motivates you to fight hard for yourself and also for someone else.

Lauren

- chapter 4

COPING WITH

HEALTH CHALLENGES, ADDICTION, TRAUMA, OR MENTAL ILLNESS

" I want these letters to remind you that no matter how grave a situation appears, you must acknowledge your pain while keeping hope in your heart. "

-Lauren

Disabilities

How The Loss Of My Dream Led To The Best Gifts Of My Life

To those of you losing hope,

In my worst moments, I would ask myself, "Why me? Why did this happen to me?"

I was trying to be a good person. My faith was strong, and I felt like I was on top of the world in every aspect. Why did my whole world just come crashing down?

I was a professional motocross rider living my dream of racing bikes. Life seemed perfect, and I thought I was invincible.

I vividly remember practicing for the upcoming 2015 Supercross season. I was doing a jump, and while airborne, my bike malfunctioned and turned off. It flipped, and I fell, landing face-first on the ground.

I don't remember anyone telling me I was paralyzed, but as soon as I gained consciousness, I already knew. So, when I awoke, my attitude was, "What do I have to do to beat this?"

I was certain I would find a way to get back to my old self.

My first low point came about a month after my accident. That's when it really hit me that I would never ride my bike again. Motocross was my passion since age five, and I struggled to come to terms with the fact that my life as a motocross rider was over.

At that moment, I thought, "What am I supposed to do with myself?"

My second low point happened about 10 months after my accident when I realized I wasn't getting better. I wasn't gaining the movement back that I hoped I would. Instead, I needed to relearn how to live and do basic life activities: cook, make my bed and shower. There was an overwhelming feeling of defeat. I had thoughts of suicide, thinking I would rather die than live my life in a wheelchair. This just wasn't the life or future I envisioned.

Shortly after my second low point, I went out to California to one of the biggest spinal cord paralysis recovery centers in the world, called Project Walk. That's where I met a therapist named Amanda. I thought she was gorgeous, but I assumed I had no chance. Before meeting her, I tried talking to a few women, but no one was really interested. I assumed it was because I was a burden. Ultimately, I just thought no one would ever want to be with me.

However, Amanda and I ended up meeting up at a Halloween party. I got some liquid courage and told her I thought she was beautiful and I liked her. She tried giving me her phone number, but I was too intoxicated to take it.

She reached out to me the next day on Facebook and said, "Hey, last night we talked a lot, and I wanted to give you my number, but I couldn't. So here it is."

We have been together ever since.

Amanda didn't see the activities I couldn't do. She thought of all the things I could do. She saw me for me and didn't see the limitations or the boundaries that I put on myself. She took my fear of trying new things away and showed me that I could do much more than I anticipated. Amanda brought out the best in me.

Then, one day, right before Christmas, we were at a friend's house, and the topic of pregnancy came up. While doctors told us it was unlikely I could have children naturally, we decided to get a pregnancy test. Sure enough, we were expecting. At first, we were scared and shocked, and then we realized this was a miracle.

We decided to get married, and we are now living in Ohio with our two-year-old son Rhett. If I had never gotten hurt, I would have never met Amanda, and we wouldn't have our son. Seeing him grow and accomplish new tasks with my best friend by my side is an incredible experience.

I still think about walking all the time, and I remain hopeful that one day that can happen. But my journey has taught me that the life you plan for yourself and the plan the big guy upstairs has for you are not the same.

So, if you are going through a low point or a tough time in your life, my advice is to just keep going, just keep moving forward.

After the accident, I thought there was no way I would ever be as happy as I had been as a motocross rider. While I have never again gotten that feeling that I got from dirt backs, through the love of my family, I have gotten so much more.

So, when I think back to the question I asked myself, "Why did this happen to me?"— all I have to do is look at my son and my wife, my life's greatest blessings, and I can see the answer.

Just keep pushing,
Todd Krieg

To My Body

To my body,

I remember the last thing I felt from you. It was your heels hitting the ground, and then you went completely numb. I remember laying there with the trainers asking me if it was my head or neck and if I could feel this or that.

I remember my coach looking down on me, saying, "E! You have to pray."

You couldn't move. You couldn't breathe. Honestly, I thought you were giving up on me and our life was about to be over. But it wasn't.

In just 29 years, you and I have been through quite the journey. But as our relationship has evolved and changed, my true purpose has been revealed.

As a kid, our existence together was simple. It was great! You made me the biggest, strongest and fastest kid around. Because of you, I hung out and played sports with a lot of older kids. Playing with older kids made me confident and popular. Plus, it made me an even better athlete.

As a freshman in high school, I got an offer from Rutgers. So I knew early on you were going to play Division I football. While later on, you also got offers to Notre Dame, Virginia, Maryland, Florida, Florida State, and Miami, you decided to stick with Rutgers.

My freshman year wasn't easy for us. You changed positions on the field several times. Plus, my girlfriend and I had broken up in the middle of October, so I was dealing with that, too.

Sophomore year was totally different. It was a blast. We found our home at the nose guard position and started to get really good.

I never really thought about you and all your talent. When someone is young, they don't think about their abilities until something terrible happens. Unfortunately, during my junior year of college, something terrible did happen to you.

It was October 16, 2010. We had the game tied up, 17-17, against Army with about five minutes left in the fourth quarter. We were running down the field, and I thought we were about to make a big play for the team. We were facing a double team that game, which meant two guys were coming at us at once. One tried to block us. He missed, and you were able to get right through him, giving you about a 30-yard head start on this guy.

We were about to make the tackle, and I said to myself, "Do I want to use my head, or do I want to use my shoulders?"

And I said, "This might be a huge collision. I am going to use my shoulders."

As we went to make the tackle, one of our teammates got there before we did. I put your head down, thinking we're going to use your shoulders to make the play. The guy's body twirled in the air, and the crown of your head went right into the back of his shoulder blade, and that is what caused the accident.

We got carted off the field, and I wanted to give the crowd a thumbs-up, but you just wouldn't let me. It felt like a thousand pounds of cinder blocks were weighing on my hand. I saw my mom and my sister in the endzone. My mom was hysterically crying. I tried to tell her everything is going to be OK. They put us in the back of the ambulance, and they put an oxygen mask on you. Then we tried to take deep breaths, but you couldn't make that happen. It scared me. From there, I blacked out and didn't gain consciousness until four days later.

I woke up to a room filled with posters, cards, and jerseys. A whole bunch of my friends and family came to see me. It was all positive energy.

I couldn't feel anything from you at all except your neck, which was a little sore from surgery. Because of you, my life turned upside down. At first, I questioned my love and my commitment to the game, but then it quickly turned to thoughts about trying to get us back on that football field. As we were lying there, unable to move, I was praying. I was believing. I had faith in God. But according to doctors, it wasn't looking so good.

I didn't find out until a few weeks later, but they told my mom that you had fractured your C3 and C4 vertebrae. They told her you would be paralyzed from the neck down for the rest of our life. You would need to be on a ventilator, unable to breathe on your own for the remainder of our life. You would be on a feeding tube, unable to eat solid foods for the rest of our life. And that was if you even made it through surgery, as they were concerned you weren't strong enough to survive the operation.

But you sure showed them. When we went to rehab, you started to take a turn for the better, and you were able to come off the ventilator just five weeks later. You also returned to eating solid foods and enjoying a good meal.

It's been nine years since your injury. You can't walk yet, but I believe you will walk again.

I try to do whatever you allow me to in therapy. While you have made progress, you have also hit plateaus over the years. But we work hard to keep your muscles strong, so when that cure does come, you will be ready for it.

The most important lesson I have learned is patience. As you know, I still don't have much of it, but I am learning everything isn't instant gratification. I try to fall in love with the process.

In the meantime, I sometimes get frustrated with you.

The hardest part is not being able to do what I want to do when I want to do it. Like, what if I want to take a pretty girl out on a date?

I have to be confident enough to say, "Hey, can you come to pick me up and bring me?"

I have laid in bed and just cried to myself, thinking, "If things were just easier."

I don't stay in those moments too long, though.

I get to have five minutes of pity towards you, and then it's like, "Alright, this ain't doing nothing for me."

I know you aren't fighting against me. Plus, I do realize how fortunate I am to not only be alive but to set an example for others facing challenges in life.

I remember back around 2011 or 2012 when a blind kid came up to us.

He said, "I may not be able to see the world, but after hearing you speak, I see that I can do whatever I want."

His words made me realize that while you were good at football, my true purpose in life is to influence people, motivate them, and show them through hard work and determination that anything is possible. I want people to look at me as a hero. I want people to see that I believe in my dreams and I am doing whatever I can in my power to make them happen.

When that cure comes, together, we are going to go back to MetLife Stadium where you were injured, and we are going to lay back on that 25-yard line, hop up off the ground, and hopefully, you can run off that field. If you can't run, you are going to walk. If you can't walk, you are going to limp like an OG pimp. Whatever you can do, we are going to get off that field, and we are going to finish that last play.

So if you take anything from this letter, know it's coming. Keep riding. We will get back to being Big Sexy again.

Please, just don't give up on me.

With great hope,
The mind of Eric LeGrand

How Hustle And Heart Helped Me Win Some Prestigious Hardware

To those facing an unexpected challenge,

To put my childhood in a nutshell, every weekend, I would go to church with my family and wear a dress. Underneath my dress, I'd wear a tank top and basketball shorts. The second church was over, I'd run to the gym, strip off my dress and start playing football with the boys. At any moment, I was ready to play sports.

As far as participating in competitive leagues, I would have done so in every sport in the world, but my mom told me to choose one sport because she didn't want to be driving all the time. I picked basketball.

In 2012, at 13 years old, I went to my first basketball camp. It was three hours away from home. By day three of non-stop basketball, I was very sore. The coach suggested yoga.

I was doing the move, downward dog, and my back really started to hurt. Immediately, I lost my appetite. During the next 12 hours, I noticed I couldn't use my hamstrings anymore. While warming up for a game and trying to kick my butt, I physically could not move my right leg. The next day, in a three-point shooting contest, I lost my balance. And then the following day, I woke up to some nasty hip nerve pain. When I tried to stand up, my legs didn't move.

That's when my life took a turn that I never saw coming.

I was paralyzed.

After months of being misdiagnosed, doctors told me I had a traction injury due to a tight tethered cord — a condition I unknowingly had since birth.

The magnitude of the situation didn't hit me right away. Doctors weren't sure whether or not my condition was permanent. So, in the beginning, I thought I might get better, and life would return to normal. But after a year or two, I began to accept that I would spend the rest of my life in a wheelchair. The most challenging part for me was coming to terms with the idea that I would never be able to play sports with my friends again.

Thankfully, a nurse introduced me to wheelchair basketball. At first, I didn't want to go. I didn't know much about it, and I didn't see the point. My mom pushed me to give it a try, and I am glad she did. A basketball wheelchair is very sensitive compared to an everyday wheelchair. It will turn on a dime and has a big metal bar in the front to protect your toes and essentially ram into people. I thought it was just the coolest thing to be able to go ram into people. Also, I could go super fast. I felt the breeze in my hair, just like I did when I could run.

I fell in love with the sport and the community and decided I wanted to be a Paralympian.

For five years, I shot 510 buckets three times a week. Also, I had three weightlifting sessions, three conditioning sessions, and dribbling drills. I spent about 25 hours a week training for basketball on top of my schoolwork.

It was all worth it, though. I received a coveted spot on the U.S. National Team's wheelchair basketball roster, winning a bronze medal in Tokyo. One of my favorite moments was listening to our national anthem as we lined up against the other team.

I felt this overwhelming sense of pride as I thought to myself, "I'm representing my country. I'm one of 12 that get to be here."

Also, I just won my first national championship with the University of Alabama, where I am pursuing a master's degree in nutrition. I hope to work as a dietician at Alabama.

I am very happy with my life. But I, of course, have my moments. There are what I call my paralysis days — days when my situation gets to me. I'll go to pick something up, and it falls on the ground, and then I go to pick that up, and something else falls. It gets frustrating not being able to do certain things as easily as I would like.

Then, there are also the times that people, unintentionally, are quite offensive. Some people speak very loudly to me, like I'm deaf. I'm not deaf. I hear just fine. When I am out with an able-bodied friend, some only address my able-bodied friend and not me, as if they are my caretaker. While it bothers me, there is too much negativity in the world for me to add to it. So, I ignore those people, and I move forward.

Instead, I focus on the aspects of my life that excite me and give me tremendous pride. I'm proud that I'm on the starting five for Team USA and that I received my college degree. I'm proud of the small things, like my tenacity, ability to accomplish my goals, and work ethic.

When people ask me if I hope to walk again one day, I tell them I hope I don't walk again. That's how much I love playing wheelchair basketball and being a part of the wheelchair basketball community.

See, just like mine, I know your life took a very unexpected turn. It may seem horrific and really suck right now. But what I have learned from my life so far is that if you keep pushing, this new path you are on just might be the start of a journey that is more magical than you can imagine.

Keep your head up. Embrace being different. And go after what you want.

You got this!

Lindsey Zurbrugg #24

This Is How My Team Lifted Me When I Lost My Leg

To the Sacred Heart girls basketball team,

Last week we took team pictures. These pictures were unlike any pictures I have ever taken. For me, they didn't just represent our season, but instead, they also captured our spirit.

Our team mantra this year has been, "And still I rise."

While it's a lesson I wanted to teach you, it's also one that each of you has watched me live.

On November 8, 2020, at about 3:00 p.m, I went to the mall on my motorcycle. It was a beautiful day. I remember I was about a mile from my house on my way home when traffic was coming toward me. Then, all of a sudden, I felt excruciating pain in my left leg. When I arrived at the hospital, they did an emergency blood transfusion to stabilize me before they amputated my left leg.

That day, I blacked out after a truck hit me. I am lucky even to be alive, but losing my leg has been devastating.

My whole life, people have known me as an athlete. I was a three-sport athlete in high school and college. Even as an adult, I dabbled in some semi-pro full-tackle football and have coached softball and basketball.

For the longest time, I couldn't even look at my amputated leg. I asked people to cover it with blankets because I didn't want to come to terms with it being gone. To this day, it is still difficult when I walk past a full-length mirror and see what other people see when they look at me.

But I want you to know how much all of you have helped me throughout these last few months.

During my first week home from the hospital, I had laid down in a dark room and was not in a good place. During that time, our captains came to my house with balloons and brought me a giant card signed by all of you. Constantly, I heard from all of you wishing me well and telling me how hard you were working.

During my low moments, I thought about how I tell you girls to get one percent better every day and push through adversity. As I watched you put in the work and develop your skills from afar, I didn't want to be a hypocrite. Each of you helped me realize that instead of feeling sorry for myself, I had to fight hard to return to our team. That is why I promised whether I could walk or not, I would be back.

Thanks to Covid, the start of our season kept getting delayed. But shortly after we found out that the season would definitely start February 1, doctors told me they couldn't clear me to be on the court. My wounds were still healing. I went into creative panic mode. Our assistant coaches, who have been amazing, suggested I coach virtually. As a team, we all made it work.

However, after coaching eight games via technology, on February 26, I finally returned to the court. My first game was at the same gym against the same opponent as the last game I coached before my injury. Rolling up to the game in a wheelchair was emotional. I had my moment when I approached the building. I had my moment wheeling into the locker room. I had my moment when I went out on the court. But when the game started, I switched right into coaching mode. It was pure joy. Mentally, it was like my accident never happened. I was back in my element again — back to my happy place with all of you.

Our team reignited that passion within me and got my brain working again — not to mention we won.

As the season has gone on, there certainly are some days that are harder than others. One day, I had a prosthetic appointment right before practice. It was a difficult appointment, and I started to cry because I was frustrated and in pain. I didn't want to show up at practice upset. So, I acknowledged my emotions and then focused on motivating and preparing our team for our next game.

Throughout the last four months, I have had to dig really deep. As a result, I have become more comfortable looking at and taking care of my amputated leg. I have tried downhill skiing while starting to immerse myself in the adaptive sports community. I still yell and scream from the sidelines, just like I did in previous seasons. Through losing my leg, I learned that I have more strength than I ever knew existed.

This week, I am starting physical therapy to learn to walk with a prosthetic. I am so motivated because I want to be a living and breathing reminder for all of you that you can be strong in your toughest moments. When you get knocked down, you can get back up again. While you can't always choose your circumstances, you can decide your attitude. It's up to you how you react to adversity.

So with that said, last week, when we took a team picture, I decided to surprise you. The photographer moved you to a spot so you couldn't see me get out of my car. Without anyone noticing, I put on my new prosthetic leg. Then, with a cane in hand, I walked for the first time outside of a doctor's office. When I started walking towards all of you, you all had shocked looks on your faces. Once it registered what was going on, you started clapping and cheering for me. Walking outside for the first time in a prosthetic was painful. I didn't even know I could walk as far as I did, but I was determined to try for all of you.

See, this is still very much the beginning of my journey without my left leg, but it is also just the start of the rest of your lives.

When you look back on these pictures, I want you to remember that in life, you may be alone when the world knocks you down, or in my case, when a truck crashes into you, but the reason we can always still rise is because we do it with and for each other.

Thank you for inspiring me.

Go Sharks!

Coach Carrie Owens

I Have Autism — Your Doubt Was My Motivation

To the people who thought autism meant I couldn't succeed,

Before high school, my parents sat me down in the living room and told me I had autism. I didn't even know what autism was at the time. But that's when I learned about some of you, my earliest doubters.

Back in 1993, my parents noticed that the stimulation from sporting events at arenas overwhelmed me. From the noise of the crowds to the buzz of the scoreboard, it was too much for me.

You diagnosed me with Pervasive Developmental Disorder, which is on the autism spectrum. I was only five years old, and you, a group of doctors, told my parents I wouldn't be much in life. You told my family I would barely graduate high school and I would never go to college. I would never be an athlete and one day I'd end up in a group institution.

When my parents told me what you said, I just sat there in shock. Who would say this about a five-year-old kid? Instead of learning more about autism, I focused on proving you wrong.

My parents set high expectations and taught me to work hard despite challenges. They used basketball as a metaphor for life, explaining that in practice, I find ways to get through a two-mile run or make 10 shots in a row. In games, if I fall behind, I don't take my ball and head home. I keep competing. And so I applied that mentality to life and developed this determined never-quit attitude.

But you, the doctors, aren't the only ones I am addressing in this letter, as you weren't the only people who thought I couldn't succeed.

In high school, I walked the hallways and found more of you. You were kids at school who told me I couldn't play basketball. You said I was too slow and that I had no skills. At 6'6" in ninth grade, my height, coupled with my autism, made me an easy target for bullying. I often didn't understand your sarcasm. You would make a joke just to spark an emotional response from me.

Frustrated and upset, I got in the gym every single day and worked and worked and worked. When my AAU coach, Anthony Stuckey, saw the time I was putting in, he decided to help. He showed me different footwork and ways to improve my vertical jump.

Heading into my sophomore year, he told me, "Every day you wake up, you look in that mirror, and you just keep thinking to yourself, 'Go and take somebody's spot on varsity.'"

Before my sophomore season started, I was ranked the number one center in the entire state of Michigan. I not only earned your respect but also the respect of the whole community. During my high school career, I helped get my team to a state championship final. But I wasn't done there.

With the support of my parents and my teachers, I graduated high school and received a scholarship to play at Grand Valley State. After two years, I walked onto the basketball team at my dream school, Michigan State. When I got there, I met more of you, more of you doubters and haters.

My dad was the deputy athletic director at the school, so some of you said I didn't belong. You said I was only there because of my father. Incredibly proud to be a Spartan, I was determined to prove myself.

At first, I did not tell my team that I was on the autism spectrum. Many of my teammates were very sarcastic, including former Spartan Draymond Green. As I mentioned, I often don't understand sarcasm. One day Draymond made a joke and drove me to a point where I got very upset. I wanted to knock his head off, and I let him know.

He said, "If you can't take a joke, you shouldn't be on the team — just go home."

My strength and conditioning coach then told Draymond that I had autism.

The next day Draymond said, "First of all, kudos to you because look how far you've gotten despite autism. Second of all, shame on you for not telling me. All of this could have been avoided."

After that day, everything changed. If I didn't understand a joke, I could go to Draymond or any of my teammates and ask them to explain it to me. On that day, my teammates became more than players on the same roster as me, but also allies in my quest to prove you doubters wrong.

I didn't play a whole lot at Michigan State, but through my work ethic, I made the program better. So much so that my senior year, the school granted me a scholarship. And then, a few months later, I received my college degree.

Everything all of you thought I could not do, I did.

Now, I am a motivational speaker, and I have a wife and two young boys. Of all my accomplishments, my family is the one of which I am most proud. And you all will have helped me teach them important life lessons.

See, my mom once asked me if I forgive all of you — if I forgive the doctors that said I wouldn't be able to graduate school or the peers that bullied me, or the fans that didn't think I belonged on the court.

I told her I not only forgive you, but I want to tell you thank you.

Thank you to the haters, doubters, and non-believers.

Thank you for motivating me to stay focused. Thank you for teaching me that winning isn't always meeting a challenge. It's having the courage to face it. And mostly, thank you for giving me a journey that shows my children and others that the words from outsiders don't dictate your journey. I am proof that it's the heart and passion from within that will determine your life.

I am not even done yet.

Anthony Ianni

This Is How I Hope You Will Treat My Son As He Enters The Adult World

To the world that my son is about to enter,

As a parent, I am scared.

For the past 18 years, I've been in front of my son, blocking and clearing the way for him. But now he is beginning to step into the driver's seat, literally.

When my son first asked me to learn to drive, I was like, "Bro! I don't know."

My instinct was to protect my son, but he was persistent.

Luckily, I am a part of a Black fathers group on Facebook. There was a dad who posted a video of his 18-year-old son, who was on the autism spectrum, driving. This kid was rolling, and I think he was non-verbal. I hit the dad up. We spent an hour going back and forth on the techniques he used to teach his son to drive. The most impactful piece of advice he left me with was to trust my son because he will surprise me.

See, my son, Gabriel, is an amazing young man, but he is also different. At two or three years old, we started to notice some delays. He wasn't speaking, and he didn't know his name. By age five, he was officially diagnosed with autism. My first instinct as a parent was to ask, "How?" and "Why?" But then I moved on to "What do I need to do to help him grow and develop?"

As a child on the spectrum, he has faced many challenges. Gabriel didn't speak until age five.

I remember saying, "Lord, help him speak, and I'll never tell him to shut up."

These days, I wish I could renegotiate that deal because he is a chatterbox.

At first, learning to read was tough. Now, Gabriel reads very well, and we focus more on improving his comprehension.

Throughout his life, he struggled with anxiety. At one point, he developed a debilitating fear of chickens. He was constantly worried that the chickens were coming to get him. We found a perfect school for him, except for the fact that there were chickens on the campus. Fast forward to his senior year of high school, he is entirely comfortable with chickens and other animals. Also, he is thriving at that very school.

My son has amazed me so many times. He's very artistic and loves to draw. Gabriel has been putting puzzles together, multi-piece puzzles, since two or three years old. He takes one look at the box and then builds the puzzle out from the middle.

When he was in middle school, I never thought about him taking karate. I was focused more on fundamentals. But not only did he participate in karate, he also won a trophy.

I remember him holding that trophy proudly and yelling across the room, "Dad, I did it!"

Two summers ago, Gabriel worked at a company in Chicago called Bargain In A Box. They have a program where they employ young adults with special needs. I figured they would have him do inventory or something that wouldn't require him to interact with a whole lot of people.

Sure enough, Gabriel ended up greeting people at the front of the store and helping customers find products. As his father, I was so worried that his quirks might make some people uncomfortable and they wouldn't be nice to him. In the end, he did well, and he was fine.

The more my son tries new experiences, the more I realize how important it is to let my son learn to drive — to sit in the passenger's seat and let him navigate his way through the world.

On May 21, Gabriel will graduate from high school. He is entering a post-graduate program that combines school and life skills, including helping him find a job.

We talk a lot about what he wants for his future, and he constantly says he wants a job, a family, and his own house. He still has not decided what field he wants to pursue, but he loves animals and art.

As he enters this next phase of his journey, I understand I will be in the seat next to him. Instead of being in front of him paving the way, I will be beside him, with the hope of one day being behind him.

The hardest part as a parent is all the uncertainty that lies ahead. He is entering a world where a typical functioning 30-year-old Black man in his neighborhood, minding his business, can still get shot by police.

There are so many harsh realities that worry me. However, I hope we've done everything we could for the past 18 years to put our son in the best possible position to be ready for the world. While I would love to shield him from all the negativity he could potentially face, I understand if I don't let him drive, I won't ever give him the chance to find his way.

So, as my son enters the adult world, I want to give you a heads-up that your paths may cross. He might talk to you out of the blue about whether Elmer Fudd is a good guy or a villain because that's what enters his mind at that moment. Please understand that while he may be different and quirky, he's still a human with feelings.

If you are a potential employer, please know my son is super smart. He may require more patience, and he may need to be prompted to do certain tasks, but you can stretch him and push him. He responds well to challenges. It's part of his personality. So, let him tap into that.

For the woman he likes (probably the one with the long curly hair he's liked since he was a toddler), he is a kind person. Once he finds the right girl, he will have a healthy and loving relationship.

My son is so excited not only to learn to drive a car but also to figure out how to navigate his life. There is a whole world out there he can't wait to explore. While I am scared, I trust he knows where to go and will surprise us all with what he can do.

However, as a father who loves his son, I ask that you help make his ride a little smoother. It won't take much. If my son pulls up to wherever you are, please open your heart and welcome him.

It takes a village.

Many thanks,
Ahmad Islam

This Is Why My Stutter Won't Stop Me

To the people I will meet for the first time,

I am so proud of the woman I am becoming, but I still want you to know why words matter.

In elementary school, I knew I was different when I realized I was the only kid in the class getting pulled out for speech lessons. We played talking games. They were fun, so I didn't fully realize I was there for a disability.

But that all changed in fourth grade.

That's when I was talking to a few of my friends, and two boys kept saying, "There goes the robot again. There goes the robot again."

Every time I spoke, they'd repeat, "There goes the robot again."

Up until then, no one said anything, so I thought maybe no one noticed it. When I realized people did hear it, it made me upset and self-conscious.

I have a stutter, a speech-related disorder where you have a block in words or repeat syllables. Many people think if you stutter, you don't know what to say, or you are stupid. But that's not the case. While I know what I want to say, sometimes I have trouble saying it. It gets worse when I'm around new people or in stressful situations.

In middle school, I began to get very frustrated. About once a month, I would come home upset because someone said hurtful words related to my stutter. My dad, who also has a stutter, would give me advice, but I felt as though he couldn't relate to me. I didn't understand why I had to deal with this. I didn't think it was fair.

My twin sister has always helped me, ordering for me at restaurants or doing anything else I ask. I even have a friend that found out in sixth grade that a boy teased me. He not only said something to that boy, but he told him to apologize. A few days later, I found a card in my locker from the guy that made fun of me, saying sorry.

While my sister's and friend's support meant so much to me, still, every single time I spoke, I feared someone would make fun of me. When I started ninth grade, I was afraid if I stuttered in front of new people, they would think I was weird. I developed social anxiety. I thought the people I hung out with were only nice to me because of their friendship with my twin sister. There were so many times I was out with my friends, and I would pretend to be sick so that I could go home. I just felt so uncomfortable.

This past year, during my junior year of high school, I started to develop more confidence. I grew closer to kids at school and began to stutter more in front of them, only to realize, as my dad told me, that they did not care. They would wait for an hour if needed to hear what I have to say. And if someone does say something mean, they stand up for me.

I realized that my fear of being made fun of was far greater than the reality of the situation. While I still encounter people who upset me, I have learned that there are far more people who care about me — not my stutter. But I had to be brave enough to give people a chance to recognize that. As I became more comfortable around my peers, I also became more courageous.

I decided to run for class president. We taped our speeches, which were then shown during class. Sitting at a desk watching my speech with my classmates made me so self-conscious. I had to hear myself stutter, which is my least favorite thing in the world.

After we heard all the candidates speak, so many people came up to me that day, telling me they were so proud of me. They told me my video was so good, and they loved what I had to say. I won the election. I am the reigning class president.

None of you have met me yet. Maybe you will be my classmates in college or my co-workers at a job. You could even be someone that I meet through mutual friends.

Whoever you are and however we cross paths, please be understanding. If you hear me stutter, don't make faces. Treat me like a normal person.

Eventually, I want to work in special education so that I can make a difference in a child's life. I'm proud of the confidence that has grown throughout the years, but I still remember every instance where someone commented on my stutter.

So when you meet me or someone else like me, and you hear a stutter, even if you want to say something, just don't. While, thanks in part to my friends and family, I am becoming a woman who won't care, someone else might.

What you say can impact how someone feels. That's why your words matter, so please always be kind with them.

I can't wait to meet you!

Morgan Shagrin

To Parents With Special Needs Children, Here Is My Advice

Dear young families with special needs children — I want you to remember this,

I had a choice to test for certain conditions when I was pregnant with my daughter, Amy, but I turned them down. My reasoning was that the results wouldn't matter to me one way or the other. I, of course, would love my child regardless. So, on June 27, 1994, the day I first touched my beautiful daughter, was the same day I found out that my baby had Down syndrome. Because she was premature, I had to wait a week to actually hold her in my arms. That week was very difficult, as I just wanted to take my child home and keep her close to me.

According to the National Down Syndrome Society, Down syndrome occurs when an individual has a full or partial extra copy of chromosome 21. It affects a child's development and physical appearance.[1]

---

[1] "About Down Syndrome." National Down Syndrome Society, ndss.org/about. Accessed 22 Aug. 2023.

A nurse in the hospital gave me advice that I want to pass along to all you young parents trying to grasp the reality of your child's diagnosis.

The nurse told me, "Take it one day at a time."

To this day, her words echo in my head.

Medically, Amy has endured some serious challenges.

Amy was 2.5 pounds when she was born and eight weeks early. Thankfully she was still healthy even though she was underweight. As she got older, she wasn't performing some of the milestones as other kids. They had her tested and found that she had cerebral palsy on her right side. Then shortly after, two years or less, she was diagnosed with hypothyroidism, so she is on medication for the rest of her life. When she was four years old, she was diagnosed with leukemia and underwent two and a half years of treatment.

How did Amy handle all the adversity? Well, Amy doesn't even know she's been through anything adverse. She is the happiest person we know. But Amy's condition has definitely been a challenge for me, even when she is in good health.

When my nieces, nephews, or friends' children, who were the same age as Amy, would reach milestones, I would always compare Amy to them. Don't do that! I know it's tough to get over the fact that while your friends' children are crawling or talking, your child is not able to do the same. It took Amy three years to walk! Your child will meet all those milestones, but he or she will do it on their own schedule.

Remember, one day at a time.

Also, I don't care who you are; I know it is very hard to accept that your child isn't going to live the life that you think they should live. But you must accept it. There is nothing you can do about it. You can't change it. It is not going to go away.

Your child may be differently abled than Amy, but for her, I thought it would be best to give her the same opportunities as my other children.

Amy still wants to sing, dance, run, and swim. She just does it at her own pace.

In fact, in high school, the swim coach included Amy on the team. I was a little scared the first time they let her go in the deep end because I am afraid of water, but they had people all over to pull her out if needed. In the end, she became such a good swimmer that she no longer required one-on-one attention while she was in the pool. She also ran track, the 50-yard dash. And her coach made an adjustment to the hurdles for one year so she could race.

I want to tell you that everyone will be kind and compassionate. The truth is that some people are very welcoming and other people are not, but I don't care anymore, and you shouldn't either. Focus on doing what is best for your child.

Amy was in the chorus, and she played sports. She did all the activities she wanted, and I think the benefits were immeasurable. She has a lot more confidence, and like any child who participates in team sports, she is a better person for it. Her experiences enriched her life as well as the lives of her teammates and friends.

You might think as our children grow into adults, it gets easier. It doesn't. Understanding social cues is a problem. Trying to understand what's right to say, what's wrong to say, what's good, what's bad, who is good, who is bad, and why is a constant struggle. You can't get angry because they just don't understand. If you get angry, it is detrimental. Patience has to be number one in my book.

Like I said before: One day at a time.

Amy is 25 now. She is in a day program that volunteers daily in the community. She is also involved in theater, chorus, bowling, and several social groups, which she loves.

I want you to know that even though your child may have a disability, it doesn't mean he or she will not be happy. As long as a child is loved and cared for, how can they not be happy?

Amy is not grumpy. She is a joy to be around, and I love spending time with her. She always asks to do things that she likes. I would say she gets what she wants 95 percent of the time because she doesn't ask for anything extravagant.

My biggest fear now is not only her happiness but also her safety. That will probably never change for me or for you. That worry is just a part of our lives as parents, and I feel the same way about my two older children.

Through all the ups and downs and the challenges and surprises, most of all, I want you to know that the love you feel for your child, the love that is so strong and overwhelming that you can't put it into words, that is what makes being a parent so special. That is what family is all about. It's not when your child achieves. It is not what your child accomplishes or how they stack up against anyone else. It's about love. On the toughest days, the days that test your patience or make you cry, that is what you need to remind yourself. Because the love I felt for my child when I was pregnant and didn't know her condition is not only even more present each and every day but very much returned.

From one parent to another,
Kathy

To My Little Sister With Down Syndrome – This Is What You Taught Me

To my little sister Ariel,

I remember the day you were born like it was yesterday. Your dad, my stepdad, pulled me and our brother to the side and told us you and your twin sister finally arrived. He then told us that you, Ariel, had a condition called Down syndrome. I was seven at the time, so I questioned what Down syndrome actually meant. My stepdad told me you were different. He told me people might make fun of you or laugh at you. As your big brothers, he asked us to watch out for you and take care of you. I have tried to guide you as best I can, but as I look back, it's actually you who has shown me the way.

We grew up in South Phoenix, which is among the roughest areas in Phoenix. There was a lot of poverty. My friends were dying. I went to too many funerals in high school. I didn't want to go down the same path I saw so many others go. I wanted to be different, and because of you, I wasn't afraid to be different.

I remember sometimes we'd be walking, and people would look at you funny and walk to the other side of the street because they didn't know what was wrong with you. That really hurt me. But it didn't hurt you. You thought that something must be wrong with them. Never once did you think it was you. You were never uncomfortable in your own skin or afraid to be who you are.

With you as my example, I proudly paved my own path out of our impoverished neighborhood. I worked hard on the football field and in school. First, I went to a community college, and then I transferred to Missouri State. In my junior year at Missouri State, I ruptured my hip. It required major surgery. I had to learn how to walk again. Because of you, I saw it as a hurdle, not an impassable barrier.

See, I watched you struggle with your speech growing up. You would get frustrated when people did not understand you. You started working with a speech therapist. They kept coming to the house, and you kept working. And now you are able to express yourself, and people can understand you. It's you who taught me how to jump over hurdles as opposed to turning back around.

That's not all you taught me. I achieved my dream of playing professional football, competing in the Arena Football League. I even got tryouts in the CFL and NFL. When I finished playing, I decided to start a foundation to help kids in our neighborhood. It's appropriately named The Adam Dixon Perseverance Foundation. I want to help provide children with the resources to go to college. I want to support them and encourage them through their challenges. And I want to help them see the world the way you see the world.

You don't see people or life the way others do. You don't see Black. You don't see white. You don't see gay, and you don't see straight. You don't see poverty, and you don't see struggle. You find the best in people, and you find the best in life by always having a positive and happy attitude. You don't judge, and you don't care who someone is or where they come from. All you care about is the kindness in someone's character and the affection in someone's heart. You genuinely love everyone, and you have taught me to do the same.

My charity has given out nearly $10,000 in scholarship money to my old high school. We have a scholarship for individuals with Down syndrome. We are working on a group home. One child I mentored is in his second year of college now. His parents were deported, and he has no family in Arizona, but he is persevering. I'm proud to say he made the Dean's List at Arizona State, where he is pursuing a career in medicine. We are making a difference in people's lives, and it's because of you.

There is a reason God made you my little sister. You helped me to find my purpose. You have helped show me the type of man and the type of person I want to be. And while when you were born, I questioned what Down syndrome would mean for your life, I had no idea it meant you'd have all the answers for mine.

I love you so much.

Your big brother,
Adam

How I Learned To Love Myself While Living With Marfan Syndrome

To a young person with a disability,

When I was a child, I played soccer every season it was available to me. That was my thing. Constantly, I was invited to camps and showcases. One of my favorite memories was at this tournament where my team wasn't playing well. We were frustrated. Then, we played a game, and the ball landed right at my feet. I took a shot, and it went over the goalie's head and into the back of the net. My team was so excited. It changed the trajectory of the weekend.

I truly loved being an athlete and dreamed of playing on TV for the U.S. National Team.

But then, one day, suddenly, my dream was taken away from me. My parents took me out of soccer and started to steer me into other activities, like recreational gymnastics. At first, I didn't know why, but I was miserable.

After hearing my parents talk about it and seeing it mentioned in medical reports, one day when I was in seventh grade, I decided to research Marfan syndrome. I visited the cardiologist often throughout my childhood, but I never thought anything of it. I was always tall and skinny, with long arms and legs. My vision was always bad, and I had joint pain. As I read the description of Marfan syndrome, I realized that I wasn't supposed to be this way. I realized I had Marfan syndrome, a genetic condition that affects connective tissue.

That's when I thought, "What is this monster in my life?"

I felt like I was a broken human — almost as if I wasn't a whole person.

My parents took me out of soccer because I am at risk of an enlarged aorta and possibly getting an aneurysm. Elevating my heart rate, aka heavy exercise, increases my risk. Also, until surgery recently, I had an indented sternum, which sometimes made it difficult to breathe.

Life with Marfan syndrome has not been easy.

It wasn't just soccer that was impacted. I was in a marching band in middle school, and sometimes I would feel tremendous pain from standing so long. It was hard to communicate that I had a disability and needed to rest for a minute.

Our culture is obsessed with these stories of coming back from an injury or not letting a disability get in your way. I thought I needed to push through — to keep going — even though it wasn't good for me — even though it could kill me.

When I watched people engage in activities that I loved or stopped an activity because of my pain, I felt like a failure. I felt lost — like I didn't know who I was or what I offered the world. As a result, my self-esteem took a massive hit.

But now, at 24 years old, I am learning to love myself. I have been more honest with myself about my physical limitations and have learned to give myself grace by setting goals and standards that work for me. Therapy has been beneficial. It's been a way for me to get my thoughts out in front of me and make sense of them instead of letting negativity just circulate in my head. Also, getting feedback from another person who validates my feelings has helped me heal.

Now, I realize I have interests outside of activities that dangerously increase my heart rate. I enjoy yoga, pilates, and ballet. I have also come to love many non-physical activities, like knitting, crocheting, reading, and writing. While I may not be able to challenge and push myself physically, I can do so with activities that don't put my health at risk. For example, I can try a new technique with crochet or attempt a more complicated design.

It's not easy for me to set big goals or have these big dreams since the first big one I had came crashing down. But one step at a time, I am working on it.

I have let go of my dream to be an athlete. And in its place, I have started to let myself develop new goals — like one day starting a business knitting sweaters. As I allow myself to lean more and more into these new dreams, I am becoming more excited and confident.

If a disability has forced you to give up on something you love, I want you to know that no one is defined by one aspect of themselves. There is so much in the world to explore and pursue.

For a long time, I felt like a failure, but I am not a failure, and neither are you. We are on a unique path to finding our way to our purpose.

So please, focus on learning to love yourself — just as you are. You will realize that your disability doesn't make you broken. Instead, your resilience is part of what makes you beautiful.

With love and compassion,
Marisa Hart

Health

I Was Given Six Months To Live. This Is How My Miracle Revealed My Purpose

To those who have been told they have no chance,

My dad would always tell me, "You are here for a purpose."

For years, I didn't know my purpose. I thought it was just a miracle that I was here at all.

I grew up on the south side of Augusta, Georgia, right between the country and the city. A middle child of three boys, I was active in sports, playing in pop leagues and regularly attending church. My childhood was pretty normal. But when I was 11 years old, I developed what felt like a knot in my hand. At first, it didn't bother me. I could still catch a football and dribble a basketball. So, I didn't say anything to anyone. However, as time went on, it became very uncomfortable, to the point where I felt severe pain if anything even touched it. Finally, I told my dad, and he brought me to a doctor.

The doctor did a small biopsy, revealing I had a rare adolescent cancer called epithelioid sarcoma, a soft tissue cancer.

At first, I couldn't fully process the severity of the situation.

I thought to myself, "Not me. I am a kid. I am not supposed to die."

However, my dad was very much a stone-faced guy, and on that day, I saw him cry for the first time. He didn't want me to see it, but he was crying. It was raw emotion, and that's how I knew this must be serious.

I was very scared.

Blunt and cold, the doctor told me I had about six months to live. He strongly suggested I amputate my right hand. I asked him what chance I had to survive if I amputated my hand.

He responded, "You might have a few more months, but if you make it to 16, it will be a miracle."

The conversation was cut short, and he didn't share any other options with me.

I told my dad that I didn't want to amputate my hand if I had no chance of surviving cancer. I wanted to live the rest of my life as normally as possible, playing sports and having fun with my brothers. Thankfully, my dad listened to me, an 11-year-old kid. And instead of amputating my hand, doctors cut out, hollowed, and burned the tips of my fingers, severely diminishing my sense of touch. Even so, the cancer was in my lymph nodes, so the doctors didn't think I had a chance to survive.

But from day one, my parents told me, "You are going to beat this."

They refused to accept what the doctors told us. My dad took me to a bunch of different doctors. A doctor in

Florida put me on a strict diet, no meat or sugar — just lots of raw fruits, shakes, and supplements.

Battling cancer made me so sick my skin became discolored. There were days I struggled to walk and control my bladder. Also, I lost a lot of weight — 30 pounds off my somewhat chubby 5'4" frame. Constantly, I was weak and tired, unable to play sports and run around with my friends. I had to learn how to write with my left hand.

There were some very weak moments when I thought about giving up.

Every day, I felt drained. It was a chore to get out of bed. I hated my diet and all the pills. The shakes were absolutely disgusting. And I couldn't get a decent night's sleep because I was afraid to go to bed. I was afraid if I closed my eyes, they would never open back up.

None of my friends knew what was going on because I didn't want people to feel sorry for me. I didn't want to be treated differently.

People always asked me, "Why don't you eat meat? Why can't you come outside and play?"

Part of me wanted to say, "Screw it all. I am going to do what I want and eat what I want, and whatever happens, happens."

No matter what I did, the doctors weren't giving me much hope anyway. But then, I used to think about this bible verse I heard. To summarize, it said if you have faith the size of a mustard seed, you can move mountains.

So, I took a tiny mustard seed and taped it inside my wallet. Every time I opened my wallet, it reminded me that I could push through this if I had a little bit of faith. And so, I didn't give up.

Instead, I had the attitude, "If this takes me out, I'm going out swinging."

Then, I hit the six-month mark, then a year. I started to gain some weight and regain my energy. Doctors told me not to get my hopes up, as the cancer was still in my body. But I kept going, and at 15, my blood work came back normal. A year later, I turned 16. It was the most emotional birthday I've ever had because the doctor initially told me it would be a miracle if I made it to 16.

I was a walking miracle.

Not only did I make it, but I was back to playing sports, applying for my first job, and trying to get my Driver's License.

While I never felt like I was entirely in the clear with cancer, getting regular checkups, I was able to return to a normal life.

I went to a health, science, and engineering school before studying biology at Fort Valley State. At first, I wanted to go into sports medicine or orthopedic surgery. But after scoring well on my exit exams, a recruiter reached out to me and asked me if I had ever thought about being a chiropractor. It never crossed my mind.

I told the recruiter I had surgery on my right hand and lost some of my sense of touch. After all, "chiro" means hands, and "practic" means the use of.

Chiropractor literally means the use of hands.

The recruiter told me I'd be fine and to come check out the school. So, I did, and I decided to attend. The technical classes came so naturally to me, and I excelled in school. I knew I was exactly where I was supposed to be. I knew this path was meant for me. One of my professors even taught me how to regain most of my sense of touch.

A few years after school, I moved to Cleveland to work for a large practice, where I hit another roadblock. Doctors found and removed a benign tumor from my brain. It reminded me of that mustard seed, the importance of faith, and that nothing in life is guaranteed.

After getting better and starting my new job, I began to feel unfulfilled. There were times I wouldn't be able to help people because they didn't have an insurance policy that the practice accepted. So, with a partner, we created our own practice offering affordable health care. No matter your income status or insurance, we provide quality care for everyone.

For the first three years, I went from making guaranteed money to not knowing exactly where I would get my next meal. But as the years went on, we grew, and it has all been worth it.

When I meet with patients, I try to speak and listen with compassion, learning not just about their ailment but paying attention to what's going on in their lives. I want to know how your son's football game went or whether or not you accepted that job offer. My goal is to provide patients with the grace and compassion that many doctors failed to give me.

I have helped a pro athlete with a dislocated shoulder get back in the game. I've helped patients who had severe migraines, to the point where they couldn't work or play with their children, restore their quality of life. A couple brought in their four-month-old baby because the baby was suffering from constipation. Before they even got home from our appointment, the mother called and said they had to change their baby's diaper twice. Another patient had severe scoliosis. He used a wheelchair. I worked on him repeatedly, and while he will never be 100%, I did get him out of that chair.

The Kleenex on my desk gets a lot of use, as many people come to me after nothing else has worked.

I am truly making a difference in people's lives, and I am using my hands, including the one I wasn't supposed to have still, to do so.

So, for anyone who has been told they don't have a chance to live or reach a goal, I want you to know there is always a chance. Don't settle for what people tell you. Follow your gut and your heart because nothing is final. And always have faith, even if it's only as much faith as the size of a mustard seed.

When I was a child, I didn't know why I got to live and keep my hand or why I had to battle cancer in the first place.

I didn't know the purpose of my journey or my life. But now, I do.

It is to not just be a miracle but also to have a hand in creating them as well. Don't give up.

With faith and gratitude,
Dr. James Alberty

If Chemo Can't Cure Me, I Believe This Will

To my wife, Elizabeth, and my son, Braden,

Three months after I got the most shocking news of our lives, we were on a family vacation in Hilton Head, South Carolina. On our last day, Elizabeth, you and I decided to wake up early and take a walk on the beach at sunrise. During that walk, I broke down. I hugged you, and for about 10 minutes, you hugged me back. We didn't say a word. You just let me release all of my emotions.

However, we didn't stay in that moment for too long. That's because this circumstance has given me a new perspective on what matters in life.

It's a perspective that is hard to understand and even harder to put into practice unless you face a situation like mine. But as both of you go along this journey with me, I want to make sure you absorb the wisdom this situation has granted me.

I love you both so much.

Elizabeth, I still grin when people ask me how we met. When I first moved to Atlanta, I went to a local pub with one of my best friends, John Dowhy. Five girls walked into the bar, including you. John introduced me to all of you.

When I asked John about you, I realized you were the woman he told me he recently dated for a few months, but it didn't work out.

I told him I thought you were beautiful.

Then, we kept bumping into each other. We realized we had a lot in common and became best friends — walking our dogs together, going skydiving, and hanging out regularly. While I started to really like you, you resisted and wanted to stay friends. Then, I bought two tickets to South Africa and told you to come with me.

You said, "We are going as friends, right?"

I said, "Yeah, sure."

It was a 15-hour flight to Johannesburg, and we talked the entire time. It was amazing. During our two-week trip, our relationship changed. Within six months, we decided to get married and buy a house, and you got pregnant.

Twelve years later, I still love everything about you. And Braden, you are now 11 years old, and you have added so much love and joy to our family.

Together we've built a beautiful life and created so many memories. But in May of 2021, our lives came to a screeching halt. For two or three days, I had this gurgling in my stomach. I went to the doctor, who thought it was acid reflux. He gave me a couple of pills and sent me home. But the gurgling didn't stop. So, I went back to the doctor for an X-ray. After the X-ray, he told me it looked like I had a massive lump on my colon and liver and suggested I go to a Gastroenterologist right away. That was on a Wednesday. By Friday, my doctor confirmed that I had late-stage 4 colon cancer, which spread to six areas of my body.

Very active and health-conscious, the diagnosis felt surreal.

Then, on that walk in Hilton Head, it finally hit me. The reality sunk in of what the future could hold. But after that moment, my new perspective kicked in, and I started to live my life a little differently.

Before my diagnosis, I took life very seriously and had a lot of stress. I felt as though I was the man of the house and had to provide for my family. Work was very important to me. Keeping the house maintained also mattered to me. I was a very structured person. Now, work or chores don't stress me out one bit. I live a stress-free life because I realized most of what previously bothered me doesn't really matter.

Throughout this last year, my faith has grown a lot deeper as I began to notice all of these signs that God is giving me to show me he is with us and watching over us. For example, when we were on that trip in Hilton Head, we were waiting to go kayaking with this other family. When the mother told me they were from Houston, I told her I was going there the following week.

She said, "You have cancer."

I said, "How'd you know?"

And she said, "Nobody goes on vacation to Houston. They typically go to one of the cancer hospitals."

When I told her I had stage 4 colon cancer that spread to six areas of my body, she said her husband got colon cancer, and it spread to four places of his body.

He wasn't with them at that moment, so I asked, "Is he still around?"

She told me, "Oh yeah! Five years ago, they gave him two years to live, and now he is out playing golf."

It was so random and one of many moments that have led me to feel closer to God.

Also, I don't let obstacles stop us from doing what we love: travel. Traveling opens our minds and hearts and allows us to escape the stressors of everyday life. In our house, I have a map with little pins that represent everywhere we've been, and everywhere we want to go. Daily, I look at that map.

I told my doctor I would do whatever it took to ensure we travel every year. I was and am determined. When I started chemo, I told the doctors to throw everything at me.

They looked at me and said, "This is going to kick your ass. You're going to lose your hair. You will lose about 30 pounds. You're going to be throwing up every day. You won't want to get out of bed. Your bones are going to hurt."

I told them, "I don't care."

When I receive my chemo treatments, I arrive with a smile on my face. I bring my laptop, put my headset on, take conference calls, and plug away.

Every other Tuesday, I consult with my doctor, and one day he looked at me and said, 'Man, you are crushing this."

I still have my hair. I have never been sick a day on chemo, and I have actually gained a little weight.

After eight treatments, four of my six tumors shrank. From there, the doctors dropped me down to a lower dosage to maintain the tumors. They told us not to expect more shrinkage from the lower dose. Two months later, to the doctor's own surprise, all six tumors shrank.

Elizabeth, both of us were in tears. The doctor told us I was doing so well I could skip a treatment and go away for three weeks. Over Christmas break, we went to Tahiti, Bora Bora, and Mo'orea for 15 days.

It was so beautiful, and we had an incredible trip.

Elizabeth, this is not a challenge we planned to face, but you are my rock. Without you, I would be a mess. You help me with my schedule and keep me organized. Every day, you ask how I'm feeling, how I'm doing, and what I need. With all my heart, I know if there's one person on the planet I can count on, it is, without a doubt, you. You are my biggest cheerleader, soulmate, and the absolute love of my life. You have stood by me through everything. You sit with me in the doctor's office with your laptop open, pecking away at what seems like 100 words per minute. You ask questions that I don't think of or forget. You tell the doctors what you notice or pains I may not have remembered. You are my everything, and I couldn't do this without you. We pray together every night, laugh, watch TV, and talk for hours. God has put you on this earth for me.

Braden, throughout this year, you've become more of a jokester, trying to make me laugh. Also, our conversations have exploded. You used to be a kid with one-word answers.

I would ask you, "Hey, how's school?"

You'd respond, "Good."

Now, you will tell me this or that happened.

Also, this year you have been more attached, affectionate, and aware of my feelings.

Remember when I started kickboxing again? It's a sport that I have done for many years, and I missed doing it. It was a bold undertaking. My first class with you was an hour-long session, but I only lasted about 30 minutes.

My core hurt like hell. It was extremely tight, and I felt like I had a basketball in my stomach.

That evening, when you and I got home, you made fun of me for not finishing the class. I know it was innocent, but it hurt more than the class itself. During dinner, your comments weighed heavily on my mind. Just a year prior, when I was at my peak condition, I would have never let anyone outdo me.

That day I felt broken, and Braden, you saw the sadness on my face and realized you hurt my feelings. You stopped eating, came over to hug me, and apologized for what you said. Your hug was sincere, warm, and strong.

For just the second time since my diagnosis, I broke down into tears. I didn't want to do it in front of you or Mom, so I got up and went to the bathroom. So many emotions ran through my mind, but the one that hit me the hardest was the thought of never feeling your touch again. I want you to know that your sweetness, love, and enormous heart carry me through my journey and carry me as a father.

Elizabeth and Braden, I know this year has been incredibly difficult for us all, but both of you have been amazing.

Unfortunately, the doctors already told me that my body will likely one day build a resistance to the chemotherapy, and, eventually, the cancer will overtake the chemo. However, I try not to give too much thought to that negativity.

With both of you by my side, I am not giving up, and I am using the power of positivity to my advantage. But no matter what, I hope we all always remember the perspective I have right now — how I live right now as a 49-year-old husband and father fighting for his life.

I want both of you to always remember that there will be ups and downs in life. There is going to be loss of life, jobs, and relationships. But whatever obstacle you are facing, my wish is that this past year I have shown you that you can take a moment to grieve, just like I did that day on the beach in Hilton Head, but then you must move on. You must always pick yourself back up, stay positive and pursue happiness.

Every day, I wake up thanking God for my life as I visualize my tumors getting smaller and smaller. I wake up excited for the day to come.

If chemo can't cure my cancer, I firmly believe my happiness will because happiness is what I have learned life is all about. It is all that matters. And luckily for me, my happiness is time with both of you.

I love you.

We got this.

Kris (Dad)

I Was Excited To Be Pregnant But Scared To Fight Cancer

To my four-month-old son, Ethan,

I am sure you have seen that sign in your nursery, or maybe you noticed the necklace I often wear. You can't read yet, but both say, "Warrior." That's the nickname you earned on your way here.

Last September, your father and I were over the moon when we found out I was pregnant with you. We couldn't wait to expand our family and give your big sister, Emmy, a sibling.

A few short weeks later, I was in the shower and felt a bump. When I showed the doctor, she said it was probably nothing. However, after expediting the necessary tests, she called me and told me I had breast cancer.

I was just 11 weeks pregnant, and I didn't know what stage of cancer I had, if it had spread, or the size of the two tumors.

While a million thoughts ran through my head, my very first thought was you. I had no idea if I could get treated and keep you. The following week, I met with several specialists. It took a few days, but finally, my doctor told me they could keep you safe. When I found out, I was so relieved that I fell into your father's arms and broke down into tears.

That's when our fight together officially started. We went through surgery and chemotherapy. Every step of the way, I was concerned for your well-being. I had a fetal heartbeat test before and after every chemo session. I would do stress tests. You just kept fighting along beside me.

We found out I had the BRCA gene, which is a gene that increases the chance of breast cancer, among other cancers. Even through that news, on top of all the procedures and drugs, you motivated me to stay positive. I didn't feel like I had any other choice except positivity because I knew that you would be stressed if I felt stressed. You pushed me each and every day, helping me put one foot in front of the other.

It wasn't easy.

I was fighting cancer. I was pregnant. I was holding a full-time job while also being a mom to your two-year-old sister. I didn't take one step back, but I also wasn't alone. Thankfully we have an amazing and supportive family, especially your dad. He came with us to doctors' appointments. When I would wake up in the middle of the night crying, he was right there to comfort me and keep me upbeat. Your dad went through cancer with us, bringing love and light to a dark situation.

Together, as a family, we made it to nine months.

It all hit me the first time I held you right after you were born. I cried hysterically. It was the most beautiful moment to see you and to know that I brought you into this world healthy. I was so happy. Ethan, you are the most amazing miracle.

You're four months old now, and I am in remission. I beat cancer with grace and a good attitude. For that, I am so proud of myself, but I am also so proud of you.

There is a mantra I have lived by this past year which is "You never know how strong you are until strong is the only choice you have."

While cancer revealed my strength, it also showed me yours.

Most children don't go through what you went through. And I don't want you to ignore that.

Instead, as you grow, embody the strength that both you and I exhibited throughout this last year. Go through life standing a little taller and a little prouder, knowing what you had to withstand. Whatever dreams you develop and whatever goals you set, always keep pushing, recognizing that you can accomplish whatever you want in life. That is because you endured your first fight before you even took your first breath. Before you stepped foot in the world, you already proved you have the spirit to conquer it.

Ethan, getting you here may have been a battle for us all, but I want you to make your life our winning celebration.

I love you always my little warrior.

Mommy (Jordana Beck)

How Nearly Losing My Life Led Me To My Passion

To those who are dealing with an unexpected challenge,

Six years ago, I was working in a spa as an assistant manager. It wasn't my passion. It wasn't my dream. I was like a zombie — wake up, go to work, and come home.

I started to think to myself, "What is my life?"

So, I put in my two weeks' notice and quit. I didn't want to live my life working a nine-to-five, making zero money, and struggling. Instead, I wanted to have more freedom and find a career I enjoyed. And then, in the weirdest way possible, it actually happened for me.

I remember being on a golf cart. Then, all of a sudden, I woke up in a hospital bed. First, I made sure I had all of my body parts. I looked down at my feet and wiggled them. Then, I moved my arms. When I tried to turn my neck, I realized I had a neck brace. And before I could touch my head, a doctor walked in and pulled my hand down.

First, I asked, "Why am I here?"

He said, "You just had brain surgery."

Then, I asked, "How long have I been here?"

He said, "Three days."

Apparently, while riding on the back of the golf cart, I fell off and hit my head on pavement. There was a lot of blood, and I needed emergency brain surgery. They told my parents they didn't know if I would make it. And if I did survive, they had no idea if I would be able to walk or talk again. Thankfully, I am not paralyzed, and I can speak. But after spending a total of seven days in the hospital, I went home with several frustrating and debilitating symptoms often associated with traumatic brain injuries.

I had major headaches, the worst headaches you could imagine. I had aphasia, which is where you jumble up your sentences. For example, when I would try to say, "I want to go for a walk," it would come out as "Walk now go I."

That's not all, I couldn't walk in a straight line, and sometimes I'd lose my balance to the point people had to hold me up. Bright lights and loud noises bothered me. And I got physically exhausted just from thinking. My sense of taste was gone, and the muscle in my jaw wouldn't open wide. Everything just felt screwed up. One day I was completely fine; the next day, it seemed like everything had been taken away from me.

My neurologist told me, for six months, I couldn't do anything. I couldn't read, look at my phone, watch TV, drive, drink, or work. Also, I had to eliminate all sugar and salt from my diet. My brain needed to rest and heal.

I moved back in with my parents, so they could help take care of me.

After three months, I decided to try neuro rehab. We did a lot of color therapy, computer games, and art. But I didn't have insurance, and the bills started to pile up. I began researching ways to retrain your brain after a traumatic brain injury. The same suggestions kept coming up: art, color therapy, and smells because they stimulate your memory.

I started to think about what I could do that combines art, smells, and colors. And then it clicked — FLOWERS!

When I was able to leave my parents' house and return to Portland, Maine, I got a job answering phones at a flower shop. Right away, I became bananas over it, asking everyone so many different questions, smelling the flowers, and wanting to know the names of everything.

After spending a year there, I started to feel a lot better and decided I wanted to pursue my dream of being an entrepreneur. I really liked flowers. However, I didn't think I could be a florist in Portland, so I officially moved back to Fryeburg, Maine, where my parents lived and where I grew up.

I planned to freelance, but there was a local flower shop in Fryeburg called Papa's Floral. My mom asked me if Papa's Floral was for sale, would I want to buy it.

I asked her, "Is it for sale?"

My mom, who is a realtor, said, "Everything is for sale."

She then went to Papa's Floral and asked the owner if he ever thought about selling the place.

He told her, "Every single day."

So about five months later, we signed the papers, and it was all mine.

Every day I wake up for work, I have a smile on my face, and I am excited to start the day. I love what I do. From weddings to daily orders, the responses I get from the pieces we create for people are incredible. But selfishly, I also love how creative and artistic I can be with flowers.

It's now six years since my accident. I no longer suffer from any symptoms of a traumatic brain injury. The flowers provide a zen environment for my mind, as they aren't too harsh, smell good, and make me feel refreshed.

I don't know if it wasn't for my accident if I would have ever found flowers or another path that would make me this happy. It's crazy to think that nearly losing my life led me to my passion. But now, as cliche as it sounds, I truly believe everything happens for a reason.

So if you are currently coping with the unexpected, try not to worry too much. Take each day one step at a time and trust that the pieces will naturally fall into place.

I went to flowers to heal my brain, but they did so much more. They gave my life the color it needed to finally blossom.

Whatever you are going through, I promise there is hope.

Alexandria Regan (Owner of Lemon and Tulips)

Mental Health

To The Little Girl Who Wants To Be Beautiful

To the eight-year-old girl who wants to be beautiful,

I know exactly how you feel. When I was eight years old, I didn't feel good enough. I did not think I was cute. My best friend was skinnier than me, and it was no secret. "Bigger boned" is what my parents would say about me when they jokingly compared me to my friend.

As a result, I, like you, just wanted to be beautiful. But for a long time, I looked in all the wrong places.

Even though I wasn't super thin, at age 14, I begged my mom to take me to a modeling agency. The agent told me to lose 10 pounds. That 10 pounds quickly turned into 20 pounds. That's when my extreme dieting began. I would wake up and not eat breakfast. At lunch, I would have an apple and a Diet Coke. Then, I would go to the gym and do two hours on the StairMaster. For a snack, I would eat raw broccoli with fat-free dressing. At dinner,

I would pick at the meal my mom made just to make it look like I ate some food.

It wasn't just about dieting and being thin. With a controlling mom, my behavior with food made me feel like I had control of one aspect of my life. Yet, I simply steered myself in a downward direction.

During my senior year of high school, I started taking laxatives and began trying to make myself throw up. I went from being a star cross-country runner to my athletic career completely tanking. Not to mention I became so dehydrated I was hospitalized. That wasn't even my rock bottom. I just blamed my symptoms on the laxatives and returned to not eating.

It wasn't until college that I started to get healthier. I was not able to starve myself or throw up anymore. Someone from the modeling agency I went to recognized me. From a distance, I overheard him comment on how I had gained weight since my super skinny days.

At that point, I started to admire strong and athletic women that I saw in fitness magazines. Instead of being stick skinny, I wanted to be athletic. I went from doing mostly cardio to lifting weights. As my tricep muscles grew and my body changed, I became amazed by my transformation.

Strong and fit, many people started to take notice. I was photographed for magazines. I became a WWE star, even though pro wrestling was never really on my radar. With blond hair, big boobs, a confident walk, and skimpy clothes, I strutted across the ring, playing the part of a sex symbol. Over and over again, people told me I was sexy and beautiful. Playboy, a magazine that consists of what society considers very attractive women, even called and offered me the chance to be on the cover. Yes, the cover.

However, the positive affirmation I received from the world around me didn't resonate within me. Even though I felt excited and honored about the cover of Playboy, a part of me felt ashamed in fear of the judgment of others. The self-assured and sexy aura I presented to the world did not accurately reflect how I looked at myself, as I still, believe it or not, lacked self-confidence.

On top of it all, I have experienced a lot of heartbreak when it comes to love. There were times I just wanted to end it all. Thankfully, every single time I fell into the pits of despair, I picked myself up again. While the heartbreak hurt me, it is also what healed me.

See, I had a boyfriend who was verbally and emotionally abusive. While the rest of the world showered me with attention because of my sex appeal, he never complimented me at all. At first, I accepted it, but then the relationship made me realize that I deserve to be treated better. Now, I no longer accept people and partners who do not show and express true care for me.

When I retired from wrestling, I continued to grow. I recognized society misguided me, preventing me from seeing my value beyond my appearance. So I decided to stop seeking approval from the outside world. It did not happen overnight, but ultimately, I knew this mentality was necessary for my life. I have so much more to offer other than the shape of my body or the color of my hair. I have a really big heart. I am extremely compassionate. I get along well with almost everyone, and I am very smart.

At 44 years old, I can say that I have learned to love myself. As I teach people about fitness, I try to help others feel good about their entire being as well. On social media, I share struggles while making it clear that there is so much beauty beyond someone's body in a bikini.

What I have finally learned is that beauty is not defined by what others say. It's marked by the boundaries you create. Beauty is not reflected by weight on a scale. It shines through the kindness in your heart. Beauty can't be seen. It can only be felt. And most importantly, beauty doesn't stem from the way you look on the outside but rather from the qualities you possess on the inside.

So before you, a young eight-year-old girl who is so similar to the little girl I once was, begin your long quest to find your beauty, I just want you to look inside yourself and realize it's already there.

With insight and encouragement,
Torrie Wilson

This Is How Making Mistakes Made Me Happy

To young athletes who feel the pressure to be perfect,

It took me years to realize that life doesn't end when you lose a game or make a mistake.

I grew up in Fairborn, Ohio, between Cincinnati and Columbus. I'm the second to the youngest of five boys. With three older brothers, I started playing sports very young.

As a kid, my older brother's friends would always say, "Yo, your little brother is really talented. He's going to be special when he gets to high school."

During my freshman year of high school, I played varsity baseball and basketball. Soon after, I emerged as a standout football player. It wasn't long before I became well-known around town for my athletic ability. People would come up to me to tell me they saw me make a play or wish me luck on our next game.

Everything I did, I felt as though it was bigger than just me. I was one of the very few people in my school's entire history to have a shot at getting a scholarship to play Division I football. It felt like everyone was counting on me to win and go on and do big things with my life. Looking back, I now can see how unhealthy it was to try and live up to other people's expectations.

In Ohio, football was a big deal, and my high school never made the playoffs. My senior year, we started the season 5-1. I played quarterback and safety, and people expected me to lead us to the postseason. All we had to do was win two of the next four games.

In one game, I threw a pick-six right before halftime, and we lost by seven. The next game, we were driving down the field to win. I fumbled, they recovered the football, and we lost that game by five.

We didn't make the playoffs, and I felt like it was all on me. I didn't shake it off. I wasn't just disappointed. I was devastated. After the game, I stood on the sideline, hugging my mother as I cried uncontrollably.

I felt like the biggest failure because I thought I had let everyone down. For years, I did everything I could to avoid moments like that one — to prevent mistakes on or off the field.

I didn't go out with my friends or go to parties. I didn't try new activities outside of sports. Paralyzed by this idea that I had to live up to the expectations of others, I really didn't explore a lot of my interests.

In college, I received a football scholarship to play at the University at Buffalo. But I continued on the same path, trying to do everything the way people told me to, so I could make it to the NFL — just like everyone hoped. It was as though my whole high school and college career, I walked on eggshells, trying so hard not to slip up or let people down.

When I graduated college and the NFL was no longer an option, I realized I had no idea who I was or what I liked outside of sports. That's when I went back home and hit rock bottom.

I couldn't find a job or keep a job. For the first time, I didn't feel wanted for anything. And I no longer had sports, the one thing I had always used to bring people joy.

After never drinking in high school or college, I started to go to the bars four, five, six times a week. I stopped working out, gained weight, and I got a DUI.

I ended up getting a job as a busboy at a restaurant a few miles from my house. Because of my DUI, I couldn't drive, so I traveled by bike. When I rode my bike, whether it was summer or winter, I wore a hoodie all the way up because I didn't want anyone to see me. Anytime I walked the streets or went to a store, people recognized me. They were still talking about the hail mary I threw my senior year or a dunk I made in basketball. I was supposed to "be somebody." Instead, I was just another kid that went away for school and came back.

I was depressed.

One night, I got drunk and high at a friend's house, and I had a very bad trip on edibles. After watching the movie The Matrix, I thought a creature from the movie was coming after me, and I started running. No socks, I just started running down the street to my house.

In a full-blown panic attack, I remember thinking, "What am I doing?"

When I woke up at my house the next day, I was in the fetal position, and that's when I realized I needed to get it together.

Around that same time, a girl who worked with me at the restaurant, Amanda, asked me out a few times. I repeatedly said no because I didn't think I had anything to offer her.

Finally, one day I said to her, "I have no money. I can't take you anywhere, and I can't drive you anywhere."

She told me to come get drinks with some friends and that she'd pick me up and she'd also pay.

Amanda wasn't from my hometown and knew nothing about me, which was amazing. There were no expectations, and right away, I felt comfortable and safe with her. After our first date, we spent every single day together. And with her by my side, I started to explore and discover my identity.

I realized I love music, particularly old music. So, I started listening to Frank Sinatra and buying old records. Also, I enjoy cooking. Sometimes, I will just sit around and watch cooking shows like Bobby Flay and Chopped.

Three months after my first date with Amanda, we moved in together, and I ended up getting a good job at a nearby college, working for a program called Upward Bound. The program provides academic services and resources to underprivileged high school students, giving them a better opportunity to attend college.

With Amanda, I wasn't afraid to be myself or try new things, and above all else, she made me feel like it was OK to make mistakes. I remember one day, I made lamb, and I burnt the mess out of it, and we laughed about it. It was OK.

In 2018, I married Amanda, and a year later, we had our daughter. Now, I run my own business called Learning 2 Cope, talking to young athletes about mental health.

I want you all to know that you don't need to live up to anyone's expectations. You decide what defines success, and you decide where your life takes you. Don't be afraid to explore interests outside of sports.

Your identity should never be wrapped up in a sport or an activity because everything you do in life has a season. Maybe you'll play sports for 10 years or 15 years or 20-plus years like Tom Brady, but at some point, it will come to an end. The only thing in life that's with you forever is yourself.

That's why it's so important to figure out what makes you happy. To do so, you have to be willing to make mistakes. If you never try oysters, you'll never know if you like them. If I had never burnt that lamb, I would have never taken the time to learn how to get it just right.

The less I am afraid of making a mistake, the more I have come to love myself.

So, whether it's fumbling on the football field or losing a job, or not reaching a goal, please understand that mistakes allow you the freedom to experiment, learn and grow.

Life does not end when you make a mistake. Mistakes are actually where life truly begins.

So, don't worry so much and enjoy your life!

Josh Copeland

Depressed And Stressed, This Is What Helped Me Transition To Life After Football

To my fellow athletes,

Like many of you, after I stopped playing football, I felt lost. For a long time, football was everything to me.

In middle school, I began to recognize that I had a lot of challenges learning. Reading, writing, and comprehension were hard for me. Diagnosed with several learning disabilities, my school placed me in a special education program, which hurt me. I was 14 years old and already dealing with a lot of insecurities. So, I wouldn't go to class. A lot of the time, I would roam the hallways and get in trouble.

However, in eighth grade, I also tried out for football. While I made the team, I barely played because I didn't know how to make contact. But during my junior year of high school, I earned a starting spot at defensive end and led the state in sacks. That's when I realized I had the talent to play in college.

Coaches from big-time programs started coming to my games: Clemson and the University of Wisconsin. It was a real slap in the face when they told me that I was good enough to play, but I wouldn't qualify for a scholarship because of my grades.

Football motivated me to accept that I learn differently, and I started going to class and grinding. Ultimately, Washington State University offered me a grayshirt scholarship. Before heading to WSU, I had to go to junior college first and improve my grade point average. When I finally got to WSU, I couldn't believe I was there. I couldn't believe I made it happen.

In college, my whole life was football and school. I never had a chance to explore my passions and interests outside of football. All I cared about was football. At school, I used to get up in the morning, eat, work out, go to class, eat, practice, eat, watch film, and go to sleep. That was it, every day. After my junior year, I declared for the draft.

The draft was exciting but stressful. I was predicted to go in the second round, but that didn't happen. After the third round started, my cousin, who was incarcerated, called and told me not to get discouraged. He told me whatever happens to recognize my blessings. In the middle of my conversation with him, I got a call from Ohio. It was the Browns, telling me that they drafted me with the 96th overall pick.

My mom and everybody cried. I didn't cry until that night. I was about to sleep and just started bawling. It was a huge moment for my whole family. We didn't have a lot of money. My parents were blue-collar people, and there were times we struggled. To me, it was crazy that I worked hard and made it that far.

Once I got to the league, it was once again football non-stop. People think we only work six months out of the year, but most of us work every day. While you are only in season for six months, the rest of the time you are working out, watching film, and trying to figure out how you get better for the upcoming season.

Ultimately, I played two years for the Cleveland Browns, half a season for the San Francisco 49ers, and half a season with the New York Jets.

When I got cut by the Jets, I remember sitting in my hotel room thinking, "What am I going to do next?"

At the time, I wasn't feeling right mentally or spiritually. So, I went back home to Tacoma, Washington, to reassess my life. While I got a few calls from teams, I decided not to return to football. I wasn't happy, and mentally, I wasn't healthy.

Transitioning to life after football has been incredibly difficult. Depression and stress, at times, have overwhelmed me. At first, I really didn't know much about who I was or what I liked outside of football. Not myself — I lost a relationship. Simultaneously, I also started to see people's true colors. When I was in the league, I would get a hundred texts a day. Suddenly, I was only getting five texts, mostly from my mom, dad, sister, and a couple of friends.

The depression and stress were only getting worse.

Then, my best friend encouraged me to start writing. On January 22, 2020, I started putting pen to paper, writing about my depression, memories, and past experiences. I write about 1,300 words every day. Through writing, I can declutter my mind and find more clarity in my life.

Writing has helped me realize that I am interested in business and finance. I enjoy philanthropy and helping the community. Also, I love sharing stories, especially my own. Throughout the past year, I have been able to put many of my newfound interests to work.

I have a scholarship for teens called Everyone Learns Differently. The goal is to provide financial assistance for higher education for teens with learning disabilities as well as teens who've been in the juvenile justice system. Also, I went back to my old high school and asked them to take my jersey out of the Hall of Fame, explaining to the principal that our high school, Woodrow Wilson High School, was named after a racist. I wanted to take a stand and start a conversation.

Ultimately, we drew enough attention to the issue that the Tacoma Public Schools' Board of Directors recently voted to change the name. My alma mater is going to be named after a heroic and trailblazing Black woman, Deloris Silas. It will be the first school in Tacoma to be named after a Black woman.

I still deal with mental health challenges as far as depression and stress. It is up and down, but thanks to writing, I'm able to manage it more.

Writing is magical. It's the key to our soul.

But ironically, who knows if I would have ever had the discipline, the patience, or the courage to learn to write if I had never had football to motivate me to accept my learning disabilities and find ways to get through school.

There is absolutely a dark side to football, with concussions and the psychological effects of playing such a brutal sport in extremely competitive and high-pressured environments.

Still, there is so much we can take from football as we enter this new phase of our lives. As athletes, who made it to the very top of our sport, we know structure and discipline. We have opportunities, resources, and notoriety. Unlike most, we also have the time to learn ourselves.

If you are struggling, wake up every morning and create a new routine that allows you to explore new interests.

When I first left the game, I may have felt lost. But it's the tools football gave me off the field that are now helping me to write the next chapter of my life.

While I still don't know how my story will unfold, I hope you find comfort in knowing I am now excited to turn the page.

It can get better.

Xavier Cooper

Addiction

How I Learned To Live In My Own Light Instead Of My Brother's Shadow

To those who feel like their living in their sibling's shadow,

I know how you feel, and I want you to know that your feelings are normal, as I certainly have had them.

I remember when Broadcast.com, the company my brother, Mark Cuban, founded with Todd Wagner, went public. After the Initial Public Offering, Mark hosted a big dinner for all of his friends. I was ecstatic when he invited me. As everyone drank and enjoyed themselves, I realized for the first time that Mark was at a level that most people would never reach, and he was going to keep growing, which was a good thing.

Sitting at that table toasting and laughing, I also thought to myself, "Where's my place in my world?"

With no answer to that question, I felt an emptiness inside of me. That, of course, is not my brother's fault. It came from long-standing feelings of inadequacy that many kids go through.

In my family, Mark is the oldest, I am the middle child, and my brother Jeff is the youngest. Growing up in Pittsburgh, Mark and I were always very different, as he was very outgoing and charismatic (at least as I perceived him). Even as a teen, he was out making money. I was shy and trended toward isolation. My bedroom was my haven.

In the early 1970s, our local newspapers went on strike. Mark and his buddies drove the 134 miles to Cleveland, Ohio, bought copies of the Plain Dealer, and brought them back to Pittsburgh. They sold them on a street corner in downtown Pittsburgh for multiple times what they paid for them.

He was also buying and selling stamps and making money doing it. So much so that my dad's friend gave him $5,000 to go to a stamp convention in New York City. He was only 16 years old.

Meanwhile, I was working at Hardees, a burger place. I was very shy, and I would look at what Mark was doing and feel unworthy. Again, that is not his fault. He was living his best life, and I love him dearly for the person he was and now is.

I, however, felt like a spectator, self-imposing my existence into my brother's shadow. On top of that, I was severely bullied at school, even physically assaulted over a pair of shiny bold, bell-bottomed disco pants Mark had given me.

The kids thought they were too tight on my obese body frame and decided to rid me of them. They ripped them off me, tore them into shreds, and left them in the middle of a busy street. They left me in nothing but my white Sears brand underwear, Keds tennis shoes, tube socks, and a Pittsburgh Pirates T-shirt.

As time went on, those feelings of worthlessness became more apparent and more destructive. In January of 2000, when I was 39 years old, Mark purchased a majority stake in the Dallas Mavericks. All of a sudden, my last name had an impact nationally and, more importantly to me, around the Dallas club scene. It was also at a time when I was filling the holes in my heart and soul with alcohol, cocaine, and anabolic steroids.

I had no self-identity, so the path of least resistance to obtaining one was to capitalize on my last name and live off the fact that I am Mark Cuban's brother. It got me into nightclubs. People gave me free drinks and free drugs. I dated girls substantially younger than me, indulging in narcissistic object choice. Those relationships, more often than not, revolved around alcohol and drugs. But none of that made me feel any better about myself. It was all about gratification in the moment.

When you spend your entire life hating yourself, you value any moment you can get that allows you to look in the mirror and think you are someone — to love yourself, even if artificial and temporary. None of it was real.

Over time, I dealt with two different eating disorders, drinking problems, a cocaine addiction, major depression, and multiple failed marriages. I had no identity. I didn't know what it meant to walk in my own shoes.

In July 2005, a friend alerted my brothers that I was suicidal. I had a 45 automatic on my nightstand. That led to my first of two trips to a psychiatric hospital here in Dallas. My second trip to the psychiatric hospital was on Easter weekend, 2007, which ended up being my recovery turning point. My girlfriend, who is now my wife, came home and found me passed out in bed. There were drugs everywhere. We went back to that same hospital. Standing there in that parking lot, I decided that there wouldn't be a third trip back. I realized that I was destroying my life.

Getting healthy was a process that included self-exploration, partially through reading and writing.

I began public speaking about my experiences at Rotary Clubs. One time, I walked into a Rotary Club and it was a group of middle-aged men and women. Here I am, a guy going to talk about body image — talk about a tough audience. I thought I did horribly because I saw people with drool coming out of their mouths. But after the talk, I received a tweet from a young girl.

She tweeted, "Mr. Cuban, you don't know me, but my father is a lawyer and was at your talk. We are having dinner together for the first time in a year. Thank you."

While the speech was about body image, I discussed the role of my family in my recovery process. That's the part that resonated with her father.

That tweet was a pivotal moment for me. It made me passionate as a storyteller, and it made me recognize that everyone views a story through their lens and will incorporate it into the context of their lives. Someone doesn't have to share your struggle to be inspired by it.

I have since done hundreds of talks, and I am working on my third book. I have found my purpose, which is to live each day doing the next right thing.

Every day, I talk to people and try to give them the benefit of my lived experiences in hopes of helping them.

Finally, I built my own identity and my own life.

I have come to peace with being my own person, motivated by different things than my siblings. We all should embrace ourselves and our uniqueness at the earliest opportunity in our lives.

Finally, I am comfortable with the man I am and the man I have become. And that can happen for you too. I say that to you with a full understanding of the nature of privilege. Not everyone gets the same opportunities in life.

But regardless, living in someone's shadow, whatever your situation, can make it very difficult to find your purpose. Living someone else's life is living THEIR purpose.

Focus on learning what you love, which you can only do by searching within yourself.

Be happy, be you,
Brian Cuban

How I Went From A Janitor To The Founder Of A Multimillion-Dollar Business

To those who want to change their life,

I hugged the toilet hundreds of times and cried to God, "Stop this, and I'll quit."

But this one night was different. I cleaned out my bank account, buying an eight ball of coke and paying for drinks for everyone at the bar — like I was a big shot. Out all night, I came home at sunrise. When I walked into my house, my then-wife was across the kitchen buttoning her blouse and getting ready for work.

Expecting to get my ass chewed out, she just looked at me with tears running down her cheeks and said, "Thank God you're alive."

Then, she turned around and walked away. It was the lowest moment of my life. But I am grateful for that moment.

See, in all of my drinking and drugging days, I blamed everybody else for my problems. I grew up fast and hard. My parents got divorced when I was eight years old, leaving my mom to raise three boys on her own. She barely had time to sleep. I hung out in the alleys with older kids, drinking and getting high off of anything. I sniffed glue, popped pills, and smoked weed. At 12 years old, a woman raped me and gave me an STD. A year later, I got someone pregnant. Our parents arranged a back-alley abortion. Shortly after, I was labeled incorrigible and sent to a juvenile detention facility. Upon my release, my behavior only got worse. I stole, cheated, and lied and got sent away to a tougher place. When I got out, I started doing harder drugs, and I quit school.

As a kid, I watched the show "Leave It to Beaver." It was about a family that consisted of a mom, a dad, and two boys. They lived in a house with a white picket fence. The father had a good job, and the mom stayed home and cleaned. Their home life had everything mine was missing. Deep down, I wanted that life. I wanted to be a good person, but I had no idea how to do it.

Early on, I had many jobs, including installing kitchen cabinets, driving a truck, and landscaping. I even worked for a garage company picking up garbage. I was always a good worker, which I learned from my mother.

After I got married and we had our first child, I got a big job in the steel mill. But the mill eventually closed, and I lost my job. During Thanksgiving of that year, I remember standing in a food bank line in McKeesport, Pennsylvania, where I broke down in tears.

I thought to myself, "I will never, ever, ever, under any circumstances, allow me or my family to be put in this position again."

So, I took two jobs as a janitor and discovered that I loved that type of work. I was good at it, as I'm a very organized and neat person. Ultimately, I got approached by a chemical company that sold cleaning products. I was kicking ass, as I had this "nobody can beat me" type of attitude. To be successful, I read every book. I went to every seminar, and I listened to every success-driven person I could find.

But my addictions continued to get in the way of the "Leave It to Beaver" life that I subconsciously always wanted.

That morning after I was out until sunrise and spent all of our money, I went into the living room, got on my knees, and cried out to God, "Help me, please!"

From that moment until now, 33 years later, I've never had the desire to take another drug or drink. The power addiction held over me was lifted.

Looking back, I finally understand why that day and that instant was different from all the other times I prayed and pleaded to God for help.

This time, after seeing I could achieve some success, I finally realized that no one was holding me back in life. Everyone else was not the problem. Instead, my failures and my sickness were on me.

So, after that day, I went to Alcoholics Anonymous. They read the 12 steps, and it was like a light bulb went off in my head.

I'll never forget sitting there thinking to myself, "This is what I've been looking for — directions on how to do life."

After that, my career in sales took off. I am the only person in the history of that company to be the Salesman of the Year two years in a row. Money didn't drive me. Winning motivated me. And for a moment in time, I had the wife, the kids, and the house — just like the show "Leave it to Beaver."

I worked for that company for about 20 years. As my kids got older, I started to want more. That's when I decided to start my own business. Thanks to my work ethic, relationships in the industry, and knowledge, it quickly became a multimillion-dollar distribution company.

Today, I am retired and enjoying my life in Florida. However, since starting my company, I have faced many more challenges, including getting divorced, battling illnesses, and selling my company. But no matter what I face, I never give up.

That's because my lowest moment taught me that regardless of the hand you're dealt, if you want to change your life, you first have to take responsibility for it.

Larry Fagan

I No Longer Need To Be Lucky To Survive Addiction, I Just Need You

Karson,

The day you were born was by far the craziest, scariest, and most exciting day of my life. Seeing you and hearing you cry for the very first time, I immediately fell in love.

I felt lucky that I never gave up on myself or life and was able to be your dad. While I still have struggles, I no longer need luck to survive. I just need you.

See, when I was in middle school, I started to doubt myself. I felt an intense amount of self-inflicted pressure to be perfect. Throughout high school, my football career took off, and I ended up playing college ball at the University at Buffalo. As my stats on the field grew, so did my anxiety.

By 20 years old, I had lost all control. I didn't know who I was anymore. There were days I did not want to get out of bed. Crazy thoughts went through my mind.

I remember times when I would drive to practice and think to myself, "If I get into a car accident, I would have an excuse not to play football anymore."

At night, I would go to sleep wondering if I would feel this miserable for the rest of my life. Then, I broke my wrist in my junior year, and my doctor prescribed me painkillers. Almost immediately, I began taking the pills to heal all of my pain except the pain in my wrist. The pills took away my stress, my anxiety, and my depression. It made me feel numb and happy.

I never got so much as detention a day in my life. I was a perfect golden boy who, in an instant, became a drug addict.

You would need to show me a highlight film from my senior year of football for me to remember anything I did on the field that season because there wasn't a day that I was sober. Still, I graduated as UB's all-time leader in touchdown receptions with 31, but my life beyond football was destroyed by the pills. It took away all of my money. It took away all of my friends. Most of all, it took away who I was as a person.

All I cared about was buying pills and consuming pills. I owed a whole slew of people money. The amounts would range anywhere from $100 to $1,000. I sold everything and anything in my house. Every single dime I got went straight to pills.

My health began to deteriorate quickly. After college, my once 6'3", 205-pound stature dropped down to 165 pounds. If that wasn't bad enough, I was even robbed and held at gunpoint. Then, one day I was driving looking for drugs. I got pulled over, and the cops found pills in my car. They arrested me for criminal possession of a controlled substance. You'd think that would have been my rock bottom moment, but it wasn't. I didn't hit an all-time low until a few months later, when I realized I would rather die than be addicted to painkillers.

The problem was I didn't know how to tell my parents that after all I had accomplished, I needed to go to rehab. Society made me feel ashamed and embarrassed, even in front of my own family. A friend recognized my desperation and thankfully told my mom and dad, who responded with love and grace.

I went to rehab and was reminded of how much I enjoyed life. I educated myself on addiction and worked with a cognitive-behavioral therapist. I started meditation as an alternative coping mechanism. But the most important component of my recovery was opening up, talking about how I felt and why I needed the pills to numb my pain in the first place.

We live in a society where there is a cast of shame over mental health issues, especially in football. If you talk about your problems or struggles, some will say you are weak or aren't cut out for the gridiron.

I no longer fear people's judgment. I wear my story like a badge of honor instead of hiding it like a shameful secret. It's not about who I was or what I did, but I am proud of what I have overcome and how the lessons I have learned prepared me to be your dad. Plus, every time I share my story, I heal myself while also possibly helping someone else.

Even though I have come so far, I will be honest, Karson, it's still not easy. I am three years sober, but I battle with anxiety daily. It's you, Karson, that stops me from succumbing to any temptations.

Karson, you are only one year old, but one day you will realize that the world is not fair. At some point, you will struggle. Life will be tough. You will have some rough days. But I want you to know if you have a bad day, it does not make you weak. If you are stressed, depressed, or anxious about life, it is OK to talk about it. I want you to talk about it. I want you to feel free and safe to express yourself.

I never want you to feel alone in life. I never want you to feel judged or lost. I don't want you to carry the burden of your struggles all on your own. We all need people to help us get through rocky times, and I want to make sure there is always someone you are comfortable going to with all of your problems. I want to promise you that you will always have a person by your side through every rough moment or disappointment.

Karson, you keep me healthy each and every day because the only way for me to guarantee you will have that person in your life, that person who will listen to you and love you unconditionally, is if that person is me.

So, I may have given you life, but since the day you were born, it's you who's been saving mine.

I love you, Karson.

Dad (Alex Newtz)

Dad, I Want You To Know This Is How My Life Turned Out After Going To Rehab 38 Years Ago

Dear Dad,

Two months before you died, which was 38 years ago, I called you up, and you told me, "Dee, you did the right thing."

It's only now, looking back, that I realize what you meant. At that moment, you knew I had an opportunity that you never got in life. Alcohol was always in your way. And until age 29, it was in my way as well.

My earliest memory in life is of a babysitter holding me and saying with a thick New York accent, "You poor, poor kid."

I must have been only three years old.

She kept saying it over and over: "You poor, poor kid."

In the next room, you and Mom were drunk and screaming at each other. Mom hit you in the face. Both of you were alcoholics, and alcohol fueled many arguments between you. While there were some good moments in my childhood, most were overlaid with this constant feeling of dread. I never knew when you'd start to throw the dishes or hit each other or toss aside the kitchen table. Many nights, I'd go to bed holding my pillow over my head to try to block out the screaming so I could fall asleep.

Growing up, I didn't invite any kids to our house because I worried you two would start going off at each other. Instead, I kept to myself. I always felt alone, like I didn't quite fit in. Uncomfortable in my own skin, I developed this nagging feeling that something wasn't right about me. Every day, I would get that feeling. It was terrible, and I so badly wanted it to go away.

Then, one day, like magic, it did go away.

I didn't expect it to happen this way — especially since my experiences in high school with drugs and alcohol were not good. In high school, I accidentally ate strawberries that contained alcohol. I got drunk, and it was terrible. Then, I started smoking pot, and I loved it. But after getting caught by the police and spending a night in jail, I became paranoid and couldn't enjoy it anymore.

Truly, I never wanted to drink because I saw how miserable it made you. However, one day when I was in college, I was walking past the student center at The University of New Haven, and there was a sign asking for volunteers to help build the radio station at the school. I have always loved music, so I decided to help. I walked in, and they handed me a hammer. After that day, I continued to come back, and one night these guys who were also building the radio station invited me out for pizza.

Introverted and quiet, I didn't have much of a social life, so I said, "Yeah, sure. Why not?"

They all ordered a round of beer. I wanted to fit in, so I ordered a Miller.

I thought, "Hey, that's pretty good. I think I'll have another one."

So, I drank a second Miller, and that was even better.

I said, "Give me a third one."

About halfway through that third Miller, the magic happened. All of a sudden, I felt free. That terrible nagging feeling was gone. I felt great — like I was good-looking, intelligent, and capable of talking to anybody, which I did. That night I talked and talked and talked as I drank more beers. It was one of the best nights of my life.

For the next 10 years, all I wanted to do was get that third Miller feeling again and again and again. From that third Miller, I became an active alcoholic.

Once we finished the radio station, I became a disc jockey, and after college, I became a professional musician. Our band became pretty successful. The lifestyle of a musician allowed me to drink and snort all I wanted. I lived in a world of sex, drugs, and rock and roll.

The problem was I kept chasing that third Miller — to the point that I would go so far beyond it. I would get sloppy drunk, and I started getting sloppy on stage and missing practices. After five years, they kicked me out of the band. I was devastated. As far as I was concerned, my life was over. I was done.

The guy who promoted our band was the head of advertising for a local startup company in the fast food industry. It was a small company. He offered me a job doing public relations and sales, among other tasks.

This wasn't supposed to be my life. I was going to be a rock star.

All I could think was, "This sucks."

Not to mention, in the band, I didn't have to hide my drinking. At a nine-to-five job, I couldn't exactly keep my beer on my desk.

Two years later, while still working for that startup company, I reached my rock bottom. I was 29 years old and went to the 10-year reunion for the radio station I helped build. To get to the reunion, I needed a few drinks. I was supposed to be famous. Instead, I was this guy sitting at a desk just like you.

Miserable and embarrassed, I drank a lot at that reunion. My last memory from that night is going into the bathroom, snorting a line of coke off the back of the toilet, and throwing up while thinking, "Oh God, I better go back and get another drink."

Someone told me years later he fought with me for my keys. When I wouldn't give them to him, he tried to follow me home, but I was going 70 mph down Route 1 in New Haven, a street with a lot of traffic lights.

I don't remember any of that. The day after the reunion, I woke up and went through my usual morning routine. I went down the hallway to the kitchen, poured orange juice, brought it back to my room, and filled the rest of the glass with vodka. After I got it down, I brushed my teeth and went to work.

When I left for work, I was hungover and had this terrible feeling of impending doom.

At work, a secretary left jelly donuts for everyone. Just looking at the donut made me nauseous. Then, according to everyone in the room, my boss, the one who got me the job, walked over to me and asked me a question — just a simple question. But in my mind, I thought he screamed at me. So, I stood up and threw the jelly donut against the wall.

In front of everyone, I screamed, "You're right. I am a fuck up."

And I turned around and walked out.

That was my rock bottom. And that vodka I had that morning of June 6, 1983, was my last drink.

I finally admitted that I drank about a quart and a half of Scotch vodka every day and snorted cocaine whenever I could afford it. That day, I decided to go to rehab.

In rehab, I was so hopeless that I was willing to listen. And as I am sure you know, willingness is not willpower. Willpower doesn't work. I needed the willingness to listen and learn.

It was in rehab that I made that call to you, and you told me, "You did the right thing."

I began going to Alcoholics Anonymous (AA) meetings. I still remember the first time I said, "My name is Don, and I am an alcoholic."

As soon as I said it out loud, that feeling of impending doom went away, and it truly opened the door for my recovery. I followed the 12 steps, and spirituality helped me feel comfortable in my own skin.

Meanwhile, I assumed I had lost my job. But while I was in rehab, I got a call from human resources. They told me to come back whenever I was ready. The head of the company wanted to give me a second chance.

Two months later, you passed away from esophageal cancer because of the years and years of drinking. You died an active alcoholic, eating a diet of chickpeas and vodka and wasting away to practically nothing.

While you knew that I went to rehab and got sober, you never got to see how my life turned out. Dad, I spent 38 years at that small startup called Subway, which ended up not being so small. When I started, we had 166 franchises, and when I retired, we had more than 40,000 locations around the globe. I had a tremendous career, holding many positions, including chief development officer. For many years, I was one of the top executives at the company.

In my personal life, I married a great woman, and we have two wonderful children. Your grandson, my son, just graduated from college, and your granddaughter, my daughter, is away at a university now.

For 10 long years, alcohol came between me and life. But since the day I said, "My name is Don, and I am an alcoholic," I have been able to experience and appreciate life's precious moments — moments of joy and moments of sadness. The day my son was born, I held him in my arms and felt the joy of being a dad. When my wife was pregnant with my daughter, we were hoping for a girl and had only chosen a girl's name, but we didn't know.

When she emerged, I said to my wife, "It's Caroline!"

Your addiction and alcoholism showed me just how bad it could get. As a result, I stopped before it got any worse.

Dad, I love you, and I knew you loved me as best you could.

You never got sober. You never "did the right thing." So, you never got the opportunity to feel the true joy of living. Not only did I get the chance, but I want you to know that I made the most of it.

I am living a very blessed life. I miss and love you, Dad.

Your son,
Dee Gee (Don Fertman)

Trauma

> PLEASE BE AWARE THIS LETTER CONTAINS GRAPHIC CONTENT

After Spending Five Years In Prison, Here Is Why I Believe In Second Chances

To those who feel like they don't deserve a second chance in life,

In life, there will be many people who won't want to give you a second chance, but that doesn't mean you can't have one. Your mistakes, your past, and your pain don't have to dictate all of who you are or all of what you can become.

In 2007, I was convicted of manslaughter.

My father, whose name was Eric, physically, emotionally, and sexually abused me throughout my life.

Three years old.

That's how old I was the first time I remember him abusing me. I was wearing a daisy-print underwear/top set, which he took off before getting on top of me. I wasn't aware of what he was doing to me. I only recall that it hurt.

At about four or five years old, he once told me to "Suck it like a bottle."

Through the years, sexual abuse became another form of punishment. He would also physically abuse me, using the belt or locking me in the room all day without giving me any food.

The physical and sexual abuse persisted on and off for years, only stopping when I lived with other family members for periods of time, both in the U.S. and in Liberia. At one point, my sister told my stepmother what he was doing to us, and my stepmother told the police. But Eric denied it, and that was that. He said we imagined it all.

The abuse continued until I was 18 and able to leave home. At that point, I was in Liberia and took out a loan to come back to the United States. But as a young adult, I suffered from severe depression and suicidal tendencies. The emotional pain was overwhelming, and I did not have the resources to get the help I needed. I didn't even understand why I was hurting so much or how to help myself feel better. And then, one day, I found out Eric was back in New York, where I lived.

At that point, I was 26 years old. He was no longer abusing me, but I was angry, depressed, and worried about him hurting other young women in my family.

I thought about going to the police, but I had no proof of what he did to me. There was nothing they could or would do. In my 26-year-old mind, I thought the only way to protect other young girls would be to take away his weapon, which was his penis. He came over to talk, and that's when I cut it off. In the process, he started screaming. I put a towel in his mouth. Unfortunately, he choked on it, and that's how he died.

My intent was not to kill him, but I did want him to suffer — just like he made so many others suffer, myself included.

After spending some time in a psychiatric hospital, the police arrested me. My sister testified that Eric also abused her. Everyone seemed to believe us. The jury convicted me of manslaughter instead of murder, and many of the jurors wrote letters to the judge saying they hoped I would only receive probation. Politicians like Eric Adams and Chuck Schumer also advocated for me. Even so, the judge gave me the maximum sentence, five to 15 years.

While I didn't want to go to prison, my five years in prison helped me build a foundation for my second chance at life. It was where I started to see a future and a reflection that extended beyond the trauma and pain I endured.

I found excellent therapists in prison and began to work through my past. To this day, I still see one of my therapists that I met in prison. Therapy has helped me realize why I was so depressed. Also, it gave me the vocabulary to express myself. It's where I learned how to build a new relationship with myself and others.

In prison, I also started to dream. I baked for people in prison. People liked my baking so much that my peers told me to open a bakery. Now, I am working on opening a Liberian food truck before I establish a Liberian restaurant on Staten Island. And it's not just an idea. I completed a business plan. There is a nonprofit called Kiva that provides interest-free loans to people in situations like mine, and I plan to apply. In preparation, I have worked with several programs, including Leap for Ladies, SCORE, and Defy Ventures. They are all organizations aimed at helping me achieve my entrepreneurial goals.

Since I have been out of jail, I have also been able to give back to others. During this pandemic, I worked for DoorDash, delivering food on my bike. While working, I noticed restaurants throwing out so much leftover food at the end of the night. One of my younger brothers died of starvation, and I remember often being so hungry as a child. I hate seeing food wasted. When I found out about an organization called Rescuing Leftover Cuisine (RLC), I was excited to get involved. In between working for DoorDash, I picked up leftover food from restaurants and bakeries and delivered it to homeless shelters and food pantries around the city.

While I enjoyed the work I was doing, unfortunately, several months ago, while making a delivery for DoorDash on a rainy day, my back tire slipped, and I fell, dislocating my shoulder.

Now, I am out of work and on workers comp. But I have come too far to give up now. Instead, I am still pursuing my second chance at life. I am currently saving money to begin the process of acquiring my licenses and permits for the food truck. Also, I am focusing on my physical health and preparing to start work again.

I know second chances don't come easy. And not everyone thinks I should have one. There are family members and friends that no longer speak to me. There are strangers that are scared of me. And in our society, there is a lot of rejection. I tried to get my coast guard license, but I was denied admission into SUNY Maritime College. I went back and forth with a large employer for a month, applying for a job delivering groceries. After I provided recommendations and told them my side of the story, they sent me a letter telling me they could not hire me. New York City wouldn't even give me a job picking up garbage and cleaning graffiti during the pandemic.

All the rejection is frustrating and discouraging. It feels as though even after I paid my debt to society and did my time, the world continues to punish me.

But even if the same happens to you, keep pushing forward. That's what I am going to do.

I am going to make it happen. I will get my second chance at life — my second chance at happiness. And you can too. If someone abused you, let go of the guilt. As a child, abuse is so hard to process and understand. But I want you to know it is not your fault.

And whatever mistakes you've made or however people may perceive you, always know who you are and what is in your heart.

My past is painful and complicated, but when I think about everything that has happened to me, I am proud of myself and how far I have come. I know I am a good person, and I love and care about people.

So regardless of the negative comments tossed your way or how much rejection you receive from society or the people around you, keep finding ways to grow and heal. Seek help. Go discover your passion and chase your dreams. Please, let yourself feel joy.

You deserve a second chance, and if no one wants to give one to you, I hope you do the same as me and you give one to yourself.

2022 is going to be my year. The best is yet to come for me, and the same can be true for you!

With love and hope for the future,
Brigitte Harris

How Playing Football At Michigan Led To A Life Filled With Pain And Trauma

To those who want to keep young people safe,

Growing up in Florissant, Missouri, a suburb of St. Louis, my passion was soccer, and I dreamed about going to Europe to play. But during my senior year of high school, my mother was battling breast cancer.

She said to me, "If I die through this, I've achieved all my goals in life because I got my boys to college."

That was when I knew I had to get serious about college. And thankfully, I was already highly recruited to play Division I football.

Les Miles recruited me to go to Michigan. Unlike other coaches, he didn't offer me any illegal benefits. He told my family and me that I'd get an education, the program would watch out for me, and I would become a Michigan man.

I thought he valued me as a person, so I chose Michigan.

My childhood was filled with trauma and violence. So, when I arrived in Ann Arbor in the fall of 1988, I felt like I had escaped all the horrors of my youth. Finally, at Michigan, I thought I was free.

But I wasn't.

After orientation, I had my first physical with the late Dr. Robert Anderson, the physician that worked for Michigan's athletic department. He went through some standard tests: blood pressure, height, and weight.

However, after revealing that my mother was battling breast cancer, he told me I needed an exam for testicular cancer and requested I drop my shorts. That's when the abuse happened — disguised as a medical examination.

I saw Dr. Anderson, who died in 2008, approximately 50 times throughout my next three years at Michigan. And whether I had a cold, strep, or any other ailment, he always asked me to drop my pants. After that very first appointment, I don't remember him ever using gloves again.

For years, I didn't realize I was again the victim of abuse. I trusted Dr. Anderson. I trusted Michigan.

On March 26, 2020, two weeks after my 50th birthday, my former teammate called me asking if I had seen his email. The email revealed that all those exams — all those times he asked me to drop my draws — weren't for my health. It was for Dr. Anderson's pleasure.

Dr. Anderson was a predator.

Like many victims, the experience took a toll on my physical and mental health — sometimes without realizing the source. For years, I truly didn't care if I lived or died. I'd ride my motorcycle recklessly and walk through life numb — not wanting to feel pain or even acknowledge the pain existed. Some other players avoided going to doctors for all these years. Now, at least one is struggling with a fatal illness that could have been avoided if he had gone for his checkups.[1] When all the pieces started coming together, I felt so many emotions, including anger, confusion, and betrayal.

I had so many questions: What did Michigan know? Why didn't they protect us? How many people did he abuse? And what now?

An independent report commissioned by the university answered some of those questions.

According to the report, Dr. Anderson worked for the university from 1966 to 2003.[2] In 1975, a wrestler, Tad DeLuca, complained about Dr. Anderson, but his concerns fell on deaf ears. A senior university administrator was told about Dr. Anderson's misconduct several times between 1978 or 1979 and 1981, but he did not take appropriate action. And in 1981, the school transferred him into the athletic department. Through the years, there were many warnings and many people aware of wrongdoing, yet Dr. Anderson was able to abuse students repeatedly for 37 years.

In a lawsuit against Michigan, there were 1,050 plaintiffs, but the number of victims likely well exceeds that.

The school settled our lawsuit for $490 million, roughly $466,000 per plaintiff.[3] The school's insurance will pay

---

[1] McLaughlin, Eliott C. "Alleged Sex Abuse Kept a Michigan Football Player Away from Doctors for Decades. He Now Has Stage 4 Cancer." CNN, 4 May 2020, www.cnn.com/2020/05/04/us/michigan-university-alleged-doctor-abuse-chuck-christian/index.html. Accessed 22 Aug. 2023.

[2] "Report of Independent Investigation: Allegations of Sexual Misconduct Against Robert E. Anderson." University of Michigan Board of Regents, 11 May 2021, regents.umich.edu/files/meetings/01-01/WH_Anderson_Report.pdf. Accessed 22 Aug. 2023.

[3] Jesse, David. "University of Michigan Reaches $490M Settlement with Dr. Anderson Sexual Assault Survivors." Detroit Free Press, 19 Jan. 2022. https://eu.freep.com/story/news/education/2022/01/19/university-michigan-robert-anderson-settlement-sexual-assault/6553333001/

us, and the school will move on nearly unscathed. Brands will continue to pay the school. TV rights will continue to pour in income for the school. Reporters will still hustle for interviews and press passes.

Sexual assault, in general, continues to be a massive problem on college campuses, including Michigan. In 2021, Michigan reported 530 total complaints of possible sexual and gender-based misconduct on campus.[4]

The problem is that Michigan and many other universities do not prioritize students' safety on campus over making money.

Instead of coming together to help victims, schools are joining forces to protect each other. Ohio State, Michigan State, USC, and Minnesota are among the schools with sexual abuse scandals involving adults in power positions. And after a judge ruled that victims could sue Ohio State for abuse by Dr. Richard Strauss, seven universities, including Michigan, signed a letter supporting Ohio State's mission to try and prevent victims from filing lawsuits.[5]

Even when lawsuits, like the one at Michigan, are settled, cutting a check doesn't equate to accountability.[6] The previous or current university president at Michigan wouldn't talk to me one-on-one. How can you change if leaders don't listen and speak to the people who have been harmed?

---

4 "Annual Security and Fire Safety Report." Adobe InDesign/University of Michigan, indd.adobe.com/view/56572e9d-45da-45b9-9ba3-907059e4da37. Accessed 23 Aug. 2023.

5 "Midwestern Universities Support Ohio State's Appeal Against Court's Ruling That Helps Strauss Victims." The Lantern, 6 Oct. 2022, www.thelantern.com/2022/10/midwestern-universities-support-ohio-states-appeal-against-courts-ruling-that-helps-strauss-victims/. Accessed 23 Aug. 2023.

6 Jesse, David. "University of Michigan Reaches $490M Settlement with Dr. Anderson Sexual Assault Survivors." Detroit Free Press, 19 Jan. 2022. https://eu.freep.com/story/news/education/2022/01/19/university-michigan-robert-anderson-settlement-sexual-assault/6553333001/

If we want to create a safer campus, anyone who had any awareness of Dr. Anderson's abuse should be fired. More protocols need to be in place. The school has apologized for Dr. Anderson's behavior but not for their role in allowing it to continue for so long.

Many of the late Dr. Anderson's victims were young Black men. Society often doesn't accept that men could be raped, especially big strong men. At Michigan State, where Dr. Larry Nassar abused young, primarily white, females, the school settled for 500 million with 332 plaintiffs.[7] We settled for $10 million less, with more than triple the number of plaintiffs.

There is often this "shut up and dribble" mentality toward us. People don't want to talk about our abuse, and often, people don't sympathize with us, which makes it easier for it to keep happening. Sexual abuse against us is real and shouldn't be ignored, dismissed, or viewed as any less traumatic.

Victims, students, and future students need your support. We need all of your voices. We need our stories to be more than a two-minute news clip but rather an ongoing movement influencing change.

Recently, I launched One Solidarity, a global movement to fight sexual assault predators, promote institutional accountability, and unite survivors.

It's up to us to fight back — to join in solidarity — to make universities and their staff more accountable and put more protocols in place for student safety:

1. Write letters
2. Sign petitions.
3. Share your story, my story, and this letter.

---

7 "MSU Makes $500 Million Settlement Payment to Survivor Fund." MSU Today, 4 Feb. 2018, msutoday.msu.edu/news/2018/msu-makes-500-million-settlement-payment-to-survivor-fund. Accessed 23 Aug. 2023.

4. Don't buy tickets to games until schools stop covering up and enabling sexual assaults on campus.
5. Stop purchasing goods from brands in business with schools that have enabled sexual abuse.

Michigan should have been where I found freedom from abuse and violence.

I can't change my past, but together we can stop Michigan, or any other university, from becoming someone else's prison.

Sincerely,
Jon Vaughn

I Thought It Was Love — It Was Abuse

To the person who hurt me,

I am now seven years removed from the last time you put your hands on me. Seven years ago, my words to you would have been a lot different than they are now because I was really broken. I trusted you, and I really cared about you. I didn't realize at the time how much the way you treated me negatively impacted me and my self-image.

So if I was younger, I think I would say to you, "I hope karma bites you and blah blah blah."

But now my words are different because I have grown and matured and been educated. Though, I will admit it's been quite the journey.

In the beginning, it was young love for us, a high school relationship that went over into college. You were very charming, good-looking, and athletic. I was athletic, too. So we had that in common.

Early on, the good part of our relationship was just being there for each other, hanging out, being best friends, and growing up together. However, it wasn't long before our romance started to turn toxic.

After just three months, there was a lot of jealousy displayed. At prom, you got really upset that I walked across the dance floor to get a drink of water. On my way over, I was chatting with people, being really outgoing and charismatic. You accused me of wanting to go to the dance with somebody else's date. You were so angry, and it became such a big deal.

When I got to college, the abuse became physical. We would have arguments. In the beginning, it was just getting in my face, yelling at me, swearing, and calling me names. Then it evolved into ripping the jewelry off me, pulling my hair, and shoving me to the ground. One time at a party, a guy said that my mole above my lip was sexy. Immediately, you took me to the next room and yelled at me. Your anger quickly escalated as you shoved me to the ground.

Our relationship was exhausting. I was anemic. We were constantly arguing into the late hours of the night. If I turned off my phone, you would call my roommate. If I asked my roommate to turn off her phone, you would drive to school and throw rocks at the window until we answered. It impacted me in so many ways. My hair was falling out. I was really skinny, and I was just tired all the time. In track, I didn't win any races. Running wasn't that fun. I wasn't good, and I wasn't fast.

Our rock bottom moment was when we were arguing at my school all night, and you got so mad that you were on and off choking me. You pinned me down, and you were shaking me and choking me.

As messed up as it sounds, that was just when someone else called the police. After that, I had to leave you because that is when my family and friends found out the extent of the abuse.

I didn't press charges because I didn't know how everything worked, and I didn't want all that attention. Also, I knew I would die if I couldn't prove something and you denied it.

I was scared I would just look like a big dummy, and people would say, "Oh, she must have made it up."

That would have killed me at the time.

After we broke up after nearly three years of dating, there was a lot of unwiring that happened in my brain. You really convinced me that I was the problem. You had me convinced I was the one making you behave this way.

All the time, you told me if I were a good girlfriend, I would call you back on time. If I were a good girlfriend, I wouldn't talk to the people on my team you told me not to talk to because you thought they had a crush on me. Or if I were a respectful girlfriend, I would not be so social, trying to get everyone's attention all the time. You really hated that I was outgoing.

As time went on, after we broke up, I started to focus on me more. I got to sleep, and I wasn't so emotionally drained all the time. I didn't have to play the game of covering up all of your actions. I was living honestly. But the real turning point came when I started going to a support group at the Domestic Violence and Child Advocacy Center. They made me feel empowered. That was the first place that I heard that it wasn't my fault. The way that you behaved was your fault. You have to take accountability for your actions. And just because I am outgoing or I stayed at lunch for an hour longer than I said I would and didn't call back until later, I am not a bad person or a disrespectful girlfriend.

I came to accept that even if I was the most perfect person in the world, you were always going to find a way to blame your behavior on me.

Ironically, the further I got from our relationship, the faster I ran. In my senior year, I broke nine records in indoor and outdoor track in different events, ranging from the 4×4 to the 10k. I became an All-American in cross country, and I went to nationals. I was literally so much lighter emotionally and physically, and I started to enjoy my life. That was really great.

In fact, I was so thrilled about my success running and how I felt about myself personally that I created Love Doesn't Shove. Initially, it was more of a fundraiser/awareness campaign. We sold wristbands and donated the proceeds to the Domestic Violence and Child Advocacy Center. Then it evolved. I made it its own entity, my own nonprofit organization. I developed a presentation I give in high schools and even middle schools.

To this day, you have never apologized to me. I have come to terms with it. But do you know what really upset me? Do you know what really motivated me to start Love Doesn't Shove? I didn't read the police report until my senior year. I was devastated when I read that you said you didn't put your hands on me. That was a real blow to the gut. I couldn't believe you did not take any accountability. I couldn't believe people could get away with abuse so easily. I feel like my "apology" or "justice" could and did come from educating other people about dating violence.

I tell students to believe people's actions, not their words. When someone tells you everything you want to hear, like, "You are so beautiful, and you are the only one for me," it is so romanticized. You can fall right into that trap, especially as a young teenager. It is important to understand that people's behavior will tell you who they are as a person. In our case, you would say sorry. You would say it would never happen again. The reality is I was being mistreated, and it was a pattern of behavior. I needed to trust that the cycle was going to continue and only get worse.

Now that I am a little bit older, I have more empathy for how your upbringing shaped who you are. I feel sorry you had to develop in an environment where you didn't experience a healthy dynamic. As unfortunate as it is, a lot of abusive behavior is learned, and it's not exclusive to either gender. It's unlikely you were born this way.

Today, seven years since we have been together, I don't wish any harm against you. Instead, I encourage you to recognize the past, take ownership of your actions, and mature and grow in a positive way without any excuses. I completely forgive you for what you did to me. I have been educated. I have been loved. I am OK now. I have moved on, and I will never be with you again. But what I really want to say to you is that I truly want you to know unconditional love because even though you can't harm me ever again, I don't want you to hurt anyone else.

With a better future in mind,
Gab Kreuz

LAUREN'S THOUGHTS

Your Body Can Only Be As Strong **As Your Mind**

It was a sunny day in June 2003. I woke up earlier than usual because I was excited about the day ahead. My parents were throwing me a huge high school graduation party at our house in Suffern, New York, a suburb of New York City. Before getting dressed, brushing my teeth, or washing my face, I went straight to my parents' bathroom, as I had done for the previous 10 months. My mom kept a scale in there so she could track her weight. I stepped on the scale, and the red handle ticked to just 113 pounds. I was 5'7, a size zero, and 113 pounds. That was more than

30 pounds less than I weighed one year prior. It is the lowest I have ever weighed in my adult life.

I was sick. Very sick.

Growing up, I had a sensitive stomach. But this was something else. At the time, I couldn't see the whole picture of what was happening.

After those two teenage boys sexually assaulted me in June 2002, I didn't talk about it. Instead, I tried to push it down and completely forget about it. I lost about five pounds, without trying, at the start of the following school year. My stomach hurt, and I was constantly throwing up from discomfort. When people noticed that I had dropped a few pounds, they complimented me on how great I looked, motivating me to lose more weight intentionally. Quickly, I became obsessed with counting calories and restricting my diet. But the pounds were falling off at an unhealthy pace because everything I ate made me feel an uncomfortable sense of pressure.

When my mother asked me if I was bulimic, I answered her honestly and said, "I don't know."

I didn't want to throw up or starve myself. My stomach hurt. I didn't know what was wrong with me. Doctor after doctor, and test after test, no one could figure out what was happening to me.

My friends and family watched me slowly waste away, losing all my muscle mass and athletic ability. One day, at soccer practice, I went to kick the ball, and I was so dizzy that I completely missed it. My mom's friend called and said her daughter was concerned that I might be experimenting with cocaine since I lost so much weight so rapidly (I absolutely was NOT). My old teammate warned me that I was dying slowly as my body spiraled out of control, and my mind couldn't fully understand it.

When I went to college, I got progressively better each year. But at about 25 years old, a few years after college graduation, I still had stomachaches and was still a bit underweight. Then, one night, I was arguing with a friend in a spacious hallway just outside his apartment. He kept asking me over and over and over:

"Why don't you drink?"

"What happened?"

"Why don't you drink?"

"What happened?"

"Why don't you drink?"

"What happened?"

After years of burying it, the memory of my sexual assault slipped into the forefront of my brain, and I had to get out of there. Without responding to him, I went straight for the elevator and back to my apartment. When I got home, I told him what happened to me via text. And the next day, I called my mother and told her about the attack for the first time.

About a year later, I shared with my mom a horrifying detail that haunted me in ways I did not and still do not fully understand.

See, when those boys assaulted me, my body reacted in a way that expressed pleasure, NOT pain. My body was turned on.

In the years following my assault, I was confused and angry at myself and my body, wondering, "Did my body want this? Did I cause this?"

I hated myself and my body's physical reaction. It was a hefty burden for a young woman to carry.

My mom told me, and scientific research confirms, that that is a normal response for women during an assault. She told me it was simply a physical reaction. And it was OK. It wasn't my fault. The day I had this conversation with my mom was the last day that I had chronic stomachaches. In a matter of months, I returned to a healthy weight, and I have stayed that way ever since.

After that, I realized all those years, my stomach was reacting to what my mind couldn't process. The more I faced, healed, and coped with my past, the stronger and healthier I became. Of all the goals I have accomplished in life, getting healthy is the one for which I am most proud. There is an undeniable connection between our brains and our bodies Whether it is a disease, disability, addiction, or trauma, how you manage your mind matters.

In this chapter, you read letters from cancer patients, sexual and domestic violence survivors, addicts, and people with spinal cord injuries. You read about people with autism, traumatic brain injuries, depression, and Down syndrome. Each one of them, in one way or another, used the power of positivity or perspective to heal, beat the odds, or make the absolute most of their circumstances.

So if you or someone you love is suffering, I want these letters to remind you that no matter how grave a situation appears, you must acknowledge your pain while keeping hope in your heart. And that's because a positive and powerful mindset is the most magical medicine.

Lauren

- chapter 5

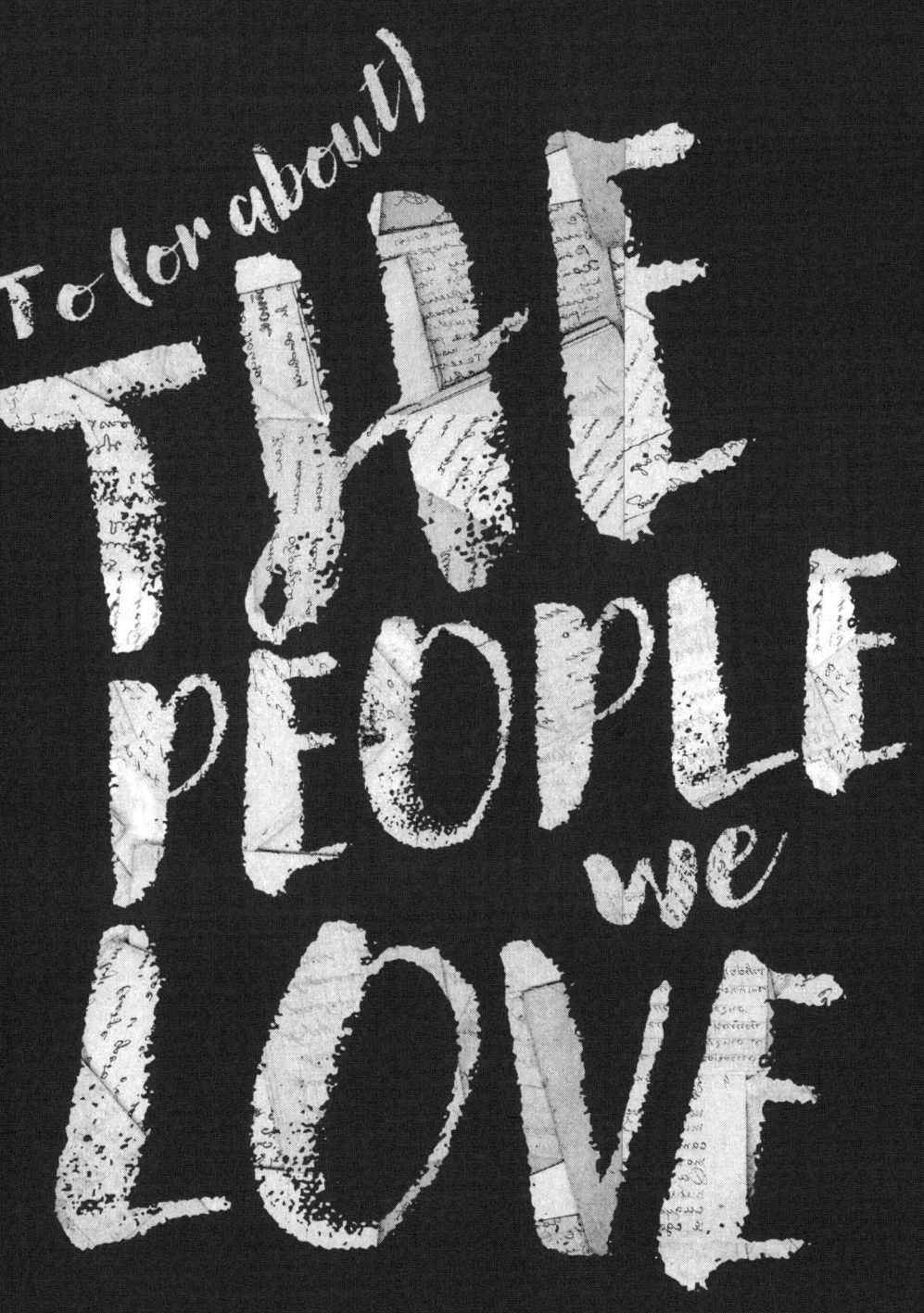

"My parents have made the hard days of my life a lot easier and have made the best moments of my life more fulfilling, as I know my happiness is their peace."

-Lauren

To One Person
Who Changed
My Life

Oprah, I Have Written You Many Times, But Here Is Why This Letter Is Different

Dear Oprah,

It's been about 15 years since I last wrote to you. As a teenager, I probably sent you about 10–20 letters. But this one is different.

I grew up in the foster care system, living in seven different homes throughout my childhood. My life was filled with abuse and suffering. It was tough, real tough.

With no self-esteem, at 13 years old, I was lonely, sad, and confused.

I used to wonder, "Why didn't I have a home with nice parents like most other kids?"

Then, one day my younger brother and I watched "The Color Purple," and we absolutely loved it. I remember your character was a strong Black woman who stood up for herself. While I already knew who you were, after watching that movie, I became a huge fan.

That same week, I was flipping through the channels and happened to come across your show for the very first time. It was an episode about child abuse and molestation. As I watched the show, I began to cry. The stories shared so closely resembled my own experiences. That's when I finally was able to put a name to the abuse I endured. That's when I realized what I experienced was wrong.

Then, you also began to share your story. You grew up in Mississippi, where you were molested as a child and gave birth to a premature boy who died soon after. Like me, you endured racism and hate. Learning about your childhood and seeing what you achieved inspired me.

You made me start thinking about my future. It was you who made me believe a future was even possible.

And I loved the way you treated people.

On your show, everyone was welcome: Black, white, gay, and transgender.

It was amazing to me how much you genuinely wanted to change the world. You were so aware of all the bad happenings in our society, and you went through bad situations yourself. You wanted to help people get their stories out. When people would talk, you would look them in the eye. It was clear you cared. If they cried, you would touch their hand as a sign of support. You had a softness about you, but you were also very tough.

As time went on, I started to lean into you and your show even more. See, at 15, I climbed up a tree. I had a rope in my hand and began to tie it around my neck. Out of nowhere, one of my brothers appeared and convinced me not to hurt myself.

I was unhappy, and I was hurting.

Shortly after, I went to juvie. I spoke up, but no one would listen to me about what really happened. So, I became very closed.

Oprah, I didn't open up to my therapist, foster families, teachers, or social workers anymore. I felt like I had no one except you. And you led me to books and writing.

I began writing about my good days, my bad days, and my goals for the future. The books you shared with me pulled me out of a deep depression. These books gave me an escape from my reality and hope for my future.

You introduced me to Maya Angelou, and I read "I Know Why the Caged Bird Sings." I also read "A Child Called It" by Dave Pelzer. These books made me feel less alone. They made me feel seen.

Without knowing me or speaking to me, you gave me the love I needed in my life. I never got in trouble again, and I never tried to hurt myself again. I even fantasized about one day writing a memoir and making it into your book club.

After high school, instead of going to college, I worked for a publishing company. But when I got laid off after five years, I didn't know what to do. In school, I learned the basics of cooking, and I always enjoyed it. So, I decided to try working in a restaurant.

At first, I hated it. I started on a salad station, and I think I cried almost every single day when my girlfriend dropped me off. But then I realized the kitchen is a community. It is a bunch of misfits — each with their own stories — coming together for a common goal. The kitchen gave me a sense of family. I fell in love with it and realized I had a passion for cooking.

I have worked in restaurants in Massachusetts, California, and New York. Now I am in New Orleans. From Mexican to Indian to Japanese to seafood, I've worked with a variety of cuisines. After growing up on cereal, pop tarts, bagels, and frozen pizza, I now can cook myself a fresh, healthy meal.

While many say I should be proud of myself, I grew up with you as my example. And your career was not just about what you could achieve, but rather what you could do for others. Now, at 31 years old, I feel a deep hole in my life because I have yet to help the next generation of foster children.

So, just recently, I have begun to dream bigger than ever before. I have decided I want to try to create a kitchen that is like your show. Instead of cooking for patrons, I want to cook for at-risk youth and foster children. I want to teach them how to make healthy meals, and I want to make meals for them. After we cook, I want to enjoy the food with them and allow them the chance to share their stories. I want to be that person that touches their hand and looks them in the eye when they speak. In my kitchen, their voices won't be ignored, and their stories won't go untold.

I don't know precisely what to do or how to start, but I believe in myself. And that's because of you.

Oprah, as a teenager, I wrote to you over and over and over again, and I never heard back. I realize now that you receive so many letters, and it's unrealistic to read all of them. But even if this one ends up unanswered like all the rest, it still feels good to write to you — to see my own evolution.

When I was a teenager, I wrote to you because I desperately wanted you to listen to my story. Now, I am writing to you to let you know that you inspired me to make sure more children are heard.

If you ever want to do dinner, I will cook.

Thank you.

Briana Lee

This Is How Our Friendship Made Me Feel

To my old friend,

As you know, through the years, it hasn't always been easy for me to make friends. I have been bullied. In group settings, it is hard for me to engage. When talking to people, sometimes, I struggle to find the right words to say. Most kids don't take the time to get to know me — the real me.

I have Asperger's, a form of autism characterized by difficulties socializing.

I am different from most people. But I want you to know you are also different even though you don't have a condition like me.

Our parents say we met in first grade, but I remember you from second grade when we were in the same class. Even back then, you were so sweet to me. However, it wasn't until middle school that we started to hang out. It was right before my family and I moved to Texas.

One time, toward the end of seventh grade, we spent the whole day together. We saw the movie "Maleficent," walked around the shopping area, and got some frozen yogurt. It felt so good to have someone my age spend time with me. I felt appreciated. I realized that you do care about me and understand me.

When we moved from New York to Texas, it was hard. Honestly, I still miss New York, and it's mostly because of you. I have never made another friend who treated me with the same kindness and compassion. That's why even though it's tough to maintain a long-distance friendship, I have made sure to stay connected to you through text and Facetime.

One day, during my senior year of high school, I called you on Facetime. Simultaneously, a family friend brought a tray of cookies to your house. The cookies spelled out "prom" with a question mark.

You said, "Yes!"

And on the inside, I screamed, "Yes! Yes! Yes!"

I was so relieved. I would not have gone to prom if I could not go with you. You flew to Texas and wore a blue dress. You looked beautiful.

As always, we had a great time together.

We are both in college now — you in New York and me in Texas. Our friendship is special. Because of you, I am more confident and comfortable with myself than I would have been otherwise. You were never afraid to talk to me — someone who gets lost in the crowd or doesn't always fit in as well with others.

Growing up, you were one of the very few kids my age who accepted me and got to know me for who I am, which is a person who values intelligence, works hard, and wants to be there for others.

The reason you are also different from other people is because you were one of very few willing to give me a chance.

Thank you!

I am forever grateful for your friendship.

Michael

From A Follower To A Friend: How One Instagram Message Changed My Life

Larry,

Nearly four years ago, I was just a fan and one of your 500,000 Instagram followers. Nonetheless, I decided to sit down and write you a very long message. When I pressed send, I didn't expect you to respond at all. My parents warned me not to get my hopes up. They explained to me that as an NBA player, you probably receive hundreds of messages a day, and my note would most likely get lost in the mix.

They didn't want me to get disappointed, but I thought to myself, "Why not? It's worth a shot."

I wanted to thank you for publicly sharing your diagnosis of Crohn's disease, giving the disease a face, and showing kids like me that athletic success is still possible.

A year and a half before reaching out to you, at 11 years old, I received my Crohn's diagnosis. My parents noticed my shoe size didn't change for an entire year. I was losing weight. I wasn't growing, and I was very fatigued. There were a few days I couldn't even make it through my AAU basketball game, which upset me.

When we finally figured out it was Crohn's disease, my family and I were somewhat relieved because we at least felt we now knew how I needed to be treated. But I was still frustrated at times. I would see my friends being able to play sports, and I would watch them grow while I plateaued. Then, there were many days I had to leave school or sit out from sports as doctors adjusted my medication. I wanted to be a regular kid, and my illness was getting in the way.

The summer I reached out to you, I was supposed to be at sleepaway camp with my friends. Instead, I was at home sick, watching the summer Olympics on TV. That's when I saw a swimmer, Kathleen Baker, hop out of the pool and thank her doctors for helping her overcome Crohn's disease. That was the first time I saw a professional athlete with Crohn's succeeding. It inspired me to search the internet for more athletes living with Crohn's. That is when I found you and your story. And that is when I decided to reach out to you.

As I mentioned, after pressing send, I kept my expectations low and continued with my life. One day my mother told me to keep my phone nearby. She said my orthodontist was calling to confirm my appointment. The phone rang. It was a Wyoming area code; my orthodontist is in New York. Without giving it too much thought, I answered the phone, expecting to be talking about braces, not basketball. When I said hello, it was you, Larry Nance Jr., on the other end. I was in shock, completely star-struck.

As thrilled as I was to hear from you, at that moment, I had no idea that you would be better for me than any solution modern medicine could offer.

You invited me to a game in Brooklyn a few months later. That's when we first met, and you told me and my family you wanted to get more involved with the Crohn's and colitis community. So, the next time you were in New York, I asked if you wanted to grab lunch. That's where I pitched you the idea of starting a foundation together, Athletes vs. Crohn's & Colitis.

You agreed! Can you believe it's been about three years since that day? So far, we've raised $300,000, which goes to research, mentorship programs, and scholarships for graduating high school athletes who have achieved their goals in sports despite being diagnosed with Crohn's or colitis. We also established a program called Larry's Leaders, where families affected by Crohn's get to meet you at a Cavs game. For your games in New York, we created Noah's Crohnies. I take about 10 kids impacted by Crohn's or Colitis to meet you. We all get to spend time together and share our stories.

Larry, the entire experience with our foundation has been incredible, and I can't wait to see how we expand our reach and our impact as time goes on.

That's not all, Larry. As our foundation has grown, so have I! Since my diagnosis, especially in the last two years, I have skyrocketed eight inches — still not quite as tall as you, but I am taller than both my parents. And Larry, thanks to you, I haven't just grown in inches. I have matured as a young person living with this chronic illness. Throughout these last few years, you've become more than a basketball star who shows up at a charity event, takes a few pictures, signs some autographs, and leaves. You have become more than my friend. You are like a big brother to me. We play video games and shoot around a basketball. During the NBA season, we text and stay in contact.

You showed me that my illness doesn't define my life. I can still achieve my goals. You told me that Crohn's is like having brown hair or brown eyes. It's a part of me, but it won't hold me back. Your encouragement changed my mindset. Now, I am happier and hopeful, which has allowed me to feel more energetic and live a more normal childhood.

Of course, I still have my bad days, where I don't feel well, but you taught me to focus on the good days and to make sure I make them count, which I believe I do. For my high school, I play volleyball and baseball. I also love playing spike ball with my friends or basketball in the neighborhood. Once again, I am able to fully experience the joy I get from playing sports. Larry, I truly believe it's because of you and your influence on my life.

Nearly four years ago, I wrote to you to thank you for showing kids like me what is possible. Now, I am still writing to thank you, but this time for giving me the confidence and courage to become an example for someone else.

While I was once just an Instagram follower and a fan, these last few years, you've made me feel like family.

Thank you for changing my life by showing me the way.

Noah

Here Is What Happens When A Dad Believes In His Daughter

Dear Dad,

"Hi! I can't give you my name, number, or address because my father is a killer, and he will continue to kill."

I am sure you remember that line as well as I do. You made me recite it every time I left the house. As my father, growing up, you had a strong instinct to protect me from the dangers of the world.

We had a fancy alarm system. Your phone was never off. And if anyone messed with me, you turned on the intimidation. While you consciously focused on my safety, unknowingly, you also guarded me against an invisible danger hurting young women, a lack of self-esteem.

According to Dove Self-Esteem Fund, seven in 10 girls believe they are not good enough or do not measure up in some way, including their looks, performance in school, and relationships with family and friends.[1]

Dad, I was the three in 10. I have and had high self-esteem, and I know exactly why.

Every single day of my childhood, you repeatedly told me I was the best. But you offered more than just compliments.

We have had a special relationship for as long as I can remember. According to you, it started on day one. One of your favorite stories to tell is about the day I was born. You claim that I wasn't crying and screaming like most babies. Instead, when I entered the world, I looked up at you and smiled. That's the moment you say you knew you were in trouble.

As a toddler, instead of calling me your princess, you told everyone I was your pit bull. That's because I would bite if I didn't get my way.

When I was six years old, you bought my brother season tickets to New York Rangers games. I got so mad.

I said to you, "Just because I am a girl, that doesn't mean I don't want to go."

The very next game, I was front and center in my oversized Messier jersey, screaming at the top of my lungs, "Fight! Fight! Fight!" the entire game.

Charming. I know.

I wasn't the quiet and graceful little girl you and Mom probably once pictured. Instead, I was outspoken, opinionated, and aggressive. You often teased me about my toughness.

However, I knew it gave you tremendous pride because you would have this smirk on your face when you would tell everyone, "In my career as a lawyer, I have stood

---

[1] "11 Facts About Teens and Self Esteem." DoSomething.Org, www.dosomething.org/us/facts/11-facts-about-teens-and-self-esteem. Accessed 23 Aug. 2023.

in front of some of the meanest judges, but the only person that scares me is my daughter."

You encouraged me to continue to advocate for myself, except, of course, when I disagreed with you. Without realizing it at the time, you were the first and most important feminist in my life, giving me the resources, support, and opportunities needed to chase my dreams.

However, as I got older, I was exposed to more influences, messages, and people. There is a long list of social pressures and standards for women — some more troubling than others.

We are told to be skinny without losing our curves.

We are told our appeal is in our appearance.

We are told if we are outspoken, we are bossy.

We are told if we are smart, we are know-it-alls.

We are told if we aren't perfect, we aren't worthy.

We are told we are better as followers than leaders.

We are told to become wives, not businesswomen.

Dad, there is a whole bunch of BS out there that you couldn't and can't stop me from hearing, witnessing, or experiencing. While boasting about my boldness made me smile as a child, what has made me tough in life is your time.

There is no dramatic story or life-changing moment that illustrates your impact on my life or the significance of our relationship. It has always been the little moments, or maybe simply the fact that we have so many moments, that's mattered most.

You never missed a soccer game, as you screamed on the sidelines at the refs even though I was always the dirtiest player on the field. When I needed new clothes, or even when I didn't need new clothes, you took me shopping. You didn't just pay the bill; you helped me choose my outfits.

When I was a TV sportscaster, my shows were often embargoed, but you would tune in to every single one, even if all you could hear me say was, "And that's a look at sports tonight."

After my shows, you would immediately text me, "Great job."

To this day, you always answer my calls, even when you can't talk. The attention you have given me has made me feel important, loved, valued, competent, and worthy.

From my sexual assault, which I once thought would kill you if you ever found out, to the naysayers who focused on my body and dismissed my brain, life has tried to rattle me more times than I can count. But I have remained resistant to other people's opinions of me and resilient against all the roadblocks aimed to hold me back.

You convinced me that my abilities have no limitations.

Now, as I embark on this new journey of entrepreneurship as the founder of The Unsealed, I am met with puzzles that need to be solved and a future with no guarantees. But instead of being fearful, I am optimistic and excited.

I believe in myself, Dad. And that is all because of you.

See, your goal as my father may have been to protect me from the world, but by making me a priority in your life, you did one better. You instilled in me the confidence to conquer it.

Thank you for always telling me that I am the best, but the truth is you are.

I love you more,
Lauren

Here Is What You Did For A Little Boy Who Loved Baseball

Dear Dave Bristol,

I see a lot of people walk into a clubhouse: politicians and movie stars. They come in, and they're nervous. Not me. Not even close. When I walk into the clubhouse, I'm so comfortable. I walk around in my underwear when it may not be politically correct to do so.

That comfort level in a clubhouse evolved from what I consider the best 10 days of my life, the 10 days you allowed me to join you and your team on a road trip.

It was the summer of 1970. My dad, Tito Francona, was in his 15th and final year of his Major League Baseball career. You were his manager on the Milwaukee Brewers. Back then, kids didn't hang out in the clubhouse, and you were kind of a crusty old-school baseball guy. So, I don't know if my dad asked you if I could come on this 10-day road trip or if he just told you I would be there.

Either way, I was so excited. At age 11, I knew I was lucky to have this opportunity. My mom bought me a sport coat, got me a haircut, and cleaned me up. The trip was to Kansas City, Chicago, and Minneapolis.

When we got on the plane for the first leg of the trip, Al Downing, who was traded with my dad to Milwaukee, said to my father, "Hey! Is it OK if I borrow him?"

Downing added, "He's sitting with me."

I felt like I was 10 feet tall. There I was on a charter plane with the Milwaukee Brewers, sitting with Al Downing.

At the hotels, I didn't want to miss a moment. I would get up in the morning and sit in the lobbies. If a player came down and needed a newspaper or a coffee or a Coke, I'd get it for him.

In Chicago, they wouldn't let me on the field. But you couldn't just leave me behind. Instead, the players got together, and they put me in Tommy Harper's uniform because he was the smallest guy on the team.

They taped the uniform around my ankles and my waist. I went out and shagged in the outfield, and I probably looked like a clown. The players had fun with it, and I, of course, had a ball.

In our final city, Minneapolis, my understanding of the nuances of baseball became very apparent to the players, including my dad. Bert Blyleven pitched against us.

After the game, I said, "Dad, I have never seen a curveball that good in my life."

He looked at me and knew I wasn't like any other 11-year-old kid. I was locked in on the game.

When I got back from our road trip, it looked like I'd been gone for a year. My hair was a mess. My sport coat was gone, as the trip was quite an adventure for me.

Dave, even today, when I think of those 10 days, I smile. My dad made me thank you back then. You didn't say a whole heck of a lot, but I think deep down you knew you made this 11-year-old boy's life.

But at the time, I had no idea that those 10 days would have a subtle but profound impact on the way I'd conduct myself throughout my baseball career.

When I became a major league player years later, I wanted to be rich. I wanted to win a batting title, and I wanted to retire on my own terms. But my plans changed when I tore my ACL early on in my career. After my knee injury, I harbored that same energy as that little kid trying to do whatever he could to help the players in a hotel lobby, as I tried to find any and every way to help my teammates and bring value to an organization.

After my playing career was cut short, I went into coaching. When I was 37, I was hired as the manager for Philadelphia. I spent four tough years there. After I lost my job, I didn't know if I wanted to manage again.

I spent some time in the Cleveland Indians' front office.

In 2002, I got a staph infection and was at risk of losing my legs and my life.

I kept telling all the doctors, "Hey man, spring training starts February 15th."

They'd look at me like, "I'm just trying to keep you alive."

Because of our trip, I already knew for a long time that baseball is where I feel most alive, regardless if I am the star of the team, a manager, or a kid dressed in an oversized uniform.

And Dave, to this day, I still light up when I see Al Downing. In fact, as a manager, I have tried my best to replicate his warmth in my clubhouses.

When I was a manager in Boston, we had one rule, which was when a kid came into the clubhouse, they had to stop in and say hello to me.

On Sundays here in Cleveland, we have girls days. We wait until everyone gets dressed, and then players go and get their daughters so they, too, can hang out with their dads.

Win, lose, or draw; I'll end up grabbing some kid and holding them or bouncing them around.

Every so often, we get letters from the league to keep the kids off the field. But I'd rather pay a fine from the league than have our players and their families unhappy.

While creating positive atmospheres and family-friendly clubhouses, we won two World Series in Boston. In 2016, with the Indians, we lost to the Chicago Cubs in Game 7 of the World Series.

On those teams, the ride was even more incredible than the outcome. Each day, I did not know how my plan would play out, but I felt confident that we would figure out a way to win. Just like I locked into the Bert Blyleven's curveball in Minneapolis, throughout my career, I have locked into games, almost craving the intensity and the challenge of baseball.

At 60 years old, the demands of the travel are getting harder for me. Brad Mills is my bench coach. We've been together since 1977. He takes a ton off of my plate, but there is going to come a time when I don't want to shortchange people, and I am going to step away. Even then, I can see myself going back to the minors. That's because, at heart, I am still that little boy excited to be around baseball and all the people involved.

Regardless of whether or not my dad gave you a choice, I wanted to thank you one more time.

From opening my clubhouses to children to leaving a sickbed to go to spring training camp to wearing my underwear at the wrong time, the clubhouse is where I feel most comfortable, and much of that comfort started with you.

That's because 49 years ago, you and your team opened the door for me to professional baseball, and in doing so, you welcomed me to a place I still consider home.

Thanks again,
Little Tito (Terry Francona)

Why My Dad Is My Hero

Dear Dad,

I know all you want in life is for me, Mom, and my brother, Sam, to be OK and succeed in our chosen paths. You were always an involved parent. As a kid, you coached my soccer team and came to Boy Scouts with me, which included hiking and camping.

Around my sophomore year of high school, you could no longer do many of the activities we once did together. Physically, it was impossible for you.

So, instead of using sports to teach me lessons, you used your experiences, telling me stories about your life and the hurdles you have overcome.

My favorite story is about the start of your career. You have dyslexia. Your school placed you in a special education class, mostly offering life skills. People didn't think you could be successful. Because you were different, it was hard for them to see your ability or potential. Frustrated with the situation, you only graduated high school because your parents begged the school.

Then, you went to BOCES, a technical school, where you received your electrical and plumbing licenses. From there, you went to work for Lockheed Martin, an aerospace and defense company. That's where you and 14 others got together to try and find a way to play music through a satellite in space and hit cars at a moving rate.

An investor gave $100 million in today's money to the project. It was a gamble. No one knew if you all could make it work. But after several years, you did it. You were among the creators of the technology for Sirius Radio. Not bad for a guy who barely graduated high school.

You made me realize that even though I am different, I can still achieve in life. I, too, am dyslexic and was placed in special education. The state exams in New York were hard for me, and I barely got through them.

When it was time for my Bar Mitzvah, I got very frustrated. Reading Hebrew with dyslexia was extremely difficult. I started to read Hebrew with English letters. When people told me that that wasn't a real Bar Mitzvah, I felt discouraged. However, you encouraged me to continue, and I am glad I did. It showed me how to adapt to situations with confidence, regardless of criticism.

Ultimately, I became an advocate for dyslexia, speaking on Capitol Hill, interviewing President Obama, and helping experts develop a test to more easily diagnose children with dyslexia.

I went to Curry College in Milton, Massachusetts. After school, I worked in media. However, I decided to start a cleaning business, Windows By Jared LLC, and a nonprofit, Simon Research Foundation, which raises money for research for multiple sclerosis. I created the Simon Research Foundation in honor of you.

In my sophomore year, when you stopped being able to play sports and go camping, it was because you were sick. You had back pain and started tripping over your own feet, and finally, your doctors diagnosed you with multiple sclerosis. Over time, the disease became more and more debilitating, but you never let it stop you from continuing your job as a VP for Sirius Radio.

When you couldn't take the bus to Manhattan because it made you dizzy, you got a car service. When it was too much to work in an office, you started working from home, which significantly increased your productivity. You now use a walker to walk and a motorized scooter for long distances. Also, you wear a brace on your left leg, which keeps you from tripping over yourself.

Working is not easy for you. It takes its toll. By 5:00 p.m., you are tired; by 7:00 p.m., you are in bed because your body shuts down. You have made enough money, and you don't need to work. But you keep pushing because you want to be able to give every bit that you can to me, Mom, and Sam.

Dad, I would not choose anybody else other than you to be my father. You have had some huge roadblocks, but you have faced them like a champion, going right through them. Yes, it has been scary. Yes, you have cried, but you never sat on the couch and said, "I'm done." Even if the doctors and nurses told you it's not possible to work, even when you have gotten terrible news, such as more lesions on your brain, you have always figured out a way to make your goals happen. You do it for us, your family, because you want to make sure we will be OK after you are gone.

That's why I am writing you this letter. I want you to know that whatever challenges I face in life, I know that I will always be OK. You showed me what it looks like to never give up, even in the most difficult of circumstances. And because you have continuously persevered, I promise to always find a way to do the same.

You are my hero then, now, and always.

I love you, Dad.

Jared

To My First Boyfriend, After 20 Years, I Want You To Know This

To my very first boyfriend,

When we were in high school, our principal told me to stay away from you. He, along with others, worried that you would have a negative influence on me.

I was a straight-A student en route to a top college. Meanwhile, you were already on probation for gun possession.

Growing up, people saw you as a "bad kid." But I didn't see you that way.

Our friendship developed somewhat unexpectedly. According to you, a few of your friends thought I was pretty, but no one had gone out with me. So, you wanted to be the first. Even though you were probably the most charming 15-year-old boy to walk the planet, I didn't make life easy for you. I was innocent but very strong-minded, unafraid to tell you no or put you in your place when I thought necessary.

My stubbornness, coupled with your love for a good challenge, led to us spending more and more time together before ultimately developing a genuine friendship.

Every night, before you went to sleep, no matter how late, you would call me to say goodnight. I pushed you to pay more attention in school. I remember how excited you would get to tell me you got a good grade. When we met up on the weekends, you would always let me know how pretty you thought I was by saying "Wow" or "Damn girl." I tried to play it cool, but I'd crack a slight smile.

You taught me dancing at a club was not the same as dancing in a tap or jazz class. When you moved to South Carolina for a few months, you sang the lyrics to the song "Angel" by Shaggy when you hugged me goodbye. And whether it was on the phone or in person, if you ever noticed that I was stressed, you would remind me that there was nothing I couldn't accomplish. You were sweet, supportive, and very protective of me.

Even when you messed up, I could never stay mad at you for long. In 10th grade, you forgot Valentine's Day. The next day at school, you gave me candy and a rose. I looked at you and rolled my eyes.

Then, you said, "Lauren, you are too special to get your Valentine's Day gift when everyone else does."

It was complete bullshit, but it worked.

Since I met you, I have always been lucky enough to see a different side of you than some other people, but I certainly am not the only one.

During our sophomore year, our lockers were across from each other. Every once in a while, I noticed this very quiet girl walking beside you in the hallway. She wasn't friends with any of your friends. It struck me as odd, but I didn't bother to ask you what was up.

One day, you were over at my house, and you left your email open on my computer. When I went to close it, I saw she sent you a message. Curiosity got the best of me, and I read it.

A few boys from our grade were continually making fun of her. One day, they bullied her in front of you, and you made it very clear that they should stop. She wrote a heartfelt message thanking you, explaining that those boys never bothered her again.

To me, that's who you are, and that's who you have always been.

Even so, as we got older, you continued to make poor choices. After we both switched schools junior year, our paths diverged. When I began college, you became a father. When I started my career, you went to jail.

From drugs to gangs to guns to I don't want to know what else, you spent much of our 20s in and out of prison.

I don't dismiss or condone any of your transgressions — but they also don't change my opinion of you.

While I have not seen you in almost 20 years, now and then, we catch up over the phone. Each time, you talk about how much you love your kids. You tell me how proud you are of me, and you let me know if anyone gives me any trouble, you always got my back — and I know you mean it.

Since ninth grade, you've been a caring, fun, protective, and loyal friend who has always built me up and cheered me on.

The same qualities I liked about you as a kid are the same qualities I like about you now. But for a long time, the contrast between the person I know and the criminal record you have acquired confused me. About six years ago, I started to ask questions:

"Why did you make such bad decisions?"

"What could you have done differently?"

"How come you were never scared to get in trouble?"

You explained to me that while I was busy with my schoolwork and extracurricular activities, you had plenty of time to spend with the wrong people. Also, you shared how you were exposed to experiences that normalized violence or illegal activity. The more honest you were with me, the more I understood that life wasn't as simple for everyone as it may have been for me.

For that reason, I have learned not to judge anyone, which has not only made me a better journalist but a more compassionate human.

But unfortunately, as you move through life, most people won't be like me. Most people will google your name or see your history and pass judgment, the same way our principal did when we were kids.

Even so, I want you to know that I will never see you as a bad person because I know you have a good heart.

I just pray that with every decision you make going forward, you always choose to use it.

I still believe in you.

Your old friend,
Lauren

When I Tell You "Good Game," This Is What I Actually Mean

Zoe,

You know me. I am not the kind of dad to express my feelings. It's not my style. But thankfully, we have basketball.

It all started when you were four, and your brother was nine. I trained your brother in the backyard. We had cones, parachutes, and all sorts of stuff. You'd come outside to watch and sometimes beg to join. At first, I thought it was cute, but it didn't take long for you to prove you had some serious athletic talent, which definitely did not come from me.

You started coming to your brother's basketball games and practices. So, I signed you up for the local boys' recreational league. You were one of the only girls, and you were better than the boys your age. Even when you went one-on-one with your older brother, he couldn't take it easy on you.

Now, you're only 14 years old and in eighth grade. Already, you are one of the best players in the country. Eight Division I schools have offered you scholarships. You have played in higher age brackets against top competition. At 13, you tried out for the under-16 U.S. National Team. Trophies overwhelm our basement, as letters from colleges continue to fill up our mailbox.

This is a journey we are on together. We spend hours alone in cars and on plane rides. Trips allow us the opportunity to go shopping and eat meals — just you and me. Sometimes we talk basketball. Sometimes we do not.

I try to go to every single game, but on occasion, I have to miss one because of your brother's football schedule. You know, as soon as the game is over, you have to call me and give me a play-by-play of what happened. We have similar builds, so I try to teach you tricks I used to do growing up.

At games, I notice every detail. If the last person on the bench scores, you are usually the loudest one cheering. I tell you to be more selfish sometimes, but you like to pass to your teammates and get everyone involved. You get more joy from watching your teammates score than you do yourself. Tournament and MVP trophies usually end up in my hands because you are that humble. You are growing into a leader. You are a good teammate and a good person.

During a game, you hear my coaching tips from the stands. I know you pay attention and don't mind the feedback. That is good because I can't help myself, Zoe. I live and die with each made or missed shot. When you play well, I am in a good mood. If you play poorly or just don't give your best effort, I am in a bad mood. It probably shouldn't be that way, but I know firsthand all the work you put in, and I want to see you be successful.

And I am putting in the work with you.

Whether it is a Saturday or a Tuesday, if you ask me to go to the park to practice, I am always willing to go. You shoot, and I chase your rebounds.

Before a big game or a top opponent, I do research and show you film. I just want to make sure you always feel prepared. There are times that I have been hard on you. I am working on making sure I highlight your good plays as opposed to only criticizing your mistakes. Either way, you seem to respect and appreciate my honesty. That's probably because you are so competitive and open to learning how to better your game.

You still have so much ahead of you, and while you are putting in the time in the gym, I hope you are also enjoying the journey. And just so you know, if your journey takes you to California for college or Oregon for a tournament, I am coming, too.

Zoe, I do love that you play basketball because it provides me with a familiar way to show you what I struggle to say.

When I drive for hours on end to a tournament, I am cherishing the time I spend with you. When I come to your games, I am giving you my support. When I get moody over a loss, I am feeling your disappointment even more than you do. When I make you give me a play-by-play reenactment of your game, I am trying to avoid missing a moment of your life. When I post your highlights on my social media, I am showing the world how proud I am to be your dad. And Zoe, every single time I tell you, "good game," it is my way of saying I love you.

Love,
Dad, aka your biggest fan (Mo Brooks)

To A Community That Means So Much To Me

Many Of You Don't Even Know Me, But I Would Risk My Life For You

To the Sixth District of Washington D.C.,

Throughout the last four years, I have seen someone get shot in the head. I have answered the call for stabbings and rapes. I recently responded to a call about an 11-year-old boy who was beaten up and killed. I have walked into a scene where a lady slashed her boyfriend's stomach from the top all the way down to the bottom. It is hard to witness such crimes, but I still want to be here. In fact, when I graduated from the police academy in 2015, I chose to be here. I believe my purpose in life is to help the hopeless find hope.

Most people don't understand the pain and darkness that permeates these inner-city communities. But I want you to know that not only do I know your struggle, I have lived it. I grew up in Fort Myers, Florida, an area similar to the Sixth District. At about 12 years old, I remember waking up at about 5:00 a.m., walking outside, and seeing a SWAT team three doors down. They were breaking down the door to a drug house. I played with the kids who lived there. They were my friends.

I grew up with two moms at a time when it wasn't cool to have homosexual parents. I got taunted and picked on by my peers. So I fought. I fought a lot — so much so that I turned to boxing. The sport became an outlet for me. At 13, I began fighting for the Police Athletic League, a boxing program run by the police department.

However, I was still not immune to the struggles of the streets. I was faced with this reality in 2010 when I got a call that my brother had been murdered.

At the time, I was on the cusp of graduating with a degree in criminal justice at Columbus State in Georgia. My brother's death really took me by surprise because he had stopped hanging out with the wrong crowd. He was having his first baby. I was sad and depressed. And it was at that moment where it all came together. I knew that I wanted to help people. I wanted to save lives.

When I started working here in the Sixth District four years ago, there was a lot of tension between the officers and the residents. There was a lack of trust in the officers, and I can't say that that was without reason. And even though I am a Black woman, I was just another badge. I was not to be trusted, and I was not respected. I have tried to show you that no officer is the same. My job is to protect and serve the entire community, not to exert power over you or lock people up for petty crimes. Many of you don't even know me, but I would risk my life for you.

When I am off the clock, I volunteer in this community, going to events to feed the homeless or provide them with clothing and shoes. I volunteer with the Humane Rescue Alliance, which helps homeless pets, and I spend time with Martha's Table, an organization that provides bags of healthy foods for the less fortunate. I do it because I care.

As a result of my efforts, I was named D.C. Officer of the Year. Even more importantly, I seem to be helping to bridge the gap between the officers and the community we serve.

Many of you call me Officer Friendly. You tell me that you view officers differently now that you know me. It makes me smile when you walk up to me, shake my hand, say thank you, and tell me you appreciate me.

But we still have so much more work to do. I am writing you to ask you to continue to come together as Black people and to continue to let us, the police, earn your trust. The violence, the crime, and the hurt in this community need to come to an end. To do so, we all need to take responsibility for each other's pain. We need to place ourselves in other people's positions and learn to support and love each other. We need to love ourselves. There is so much talent here. I want you to believe and encourage each other and, most importantly, believe in yourselves.

Effective change can only happen if everyone within this community works together and then, as a united group, works with the police. For that to happen, you need to have hope that together we, police and civilians, can stop the violence, hunger, and desperation in this community. Because it's when the hopeless find hope that we will be able to give this community what we all really want. Only then will we be able to give each other what my brother and so many others from here already lost — a future.

With endless hope,
Officer Tiara Brown (aka Officer Friendly)

I Could Be On The Path To Make Millions — I Choose To Be Here With You

To the community that raised me,

I often interchange the words community and family. Communities should watch out for each other. Families should watch out for each other. Communities should help each other out. Families should help each other out.

I remember during a kickball game in our community on August 9, 2016, a 65-year-old grandma was up to bat. We had these high schoolers that played on the basketball and football teams in the outfield because they had the best hands. When Grandma was up to bat, all of them took 10–20 steps forward, and Grandma kicked it over their heads.

They were running to get the ball, and we were like, "Ahh! Granny got legs."

She walked to first base like, "I still got it."

It was at that moment I knew we were onto something special. But it took me years to not only get to that moment but to help create it.

I grew up in the Glenville neighborhood near the first of 99th and St. Clair. It is on the east side of Cleveland. Glenville has a bad rep right now. It is highly segregated. But I want people to know our community isn't how it's often portrayed in the media. I brag that Bone Thugs-n-Harmony, one of Cleveland's most famous hip-hop groups, attended my second birthday party.

In fifth grade, I got straight A's at St. Aloysius. When school finished that year, my mom told me I had to go to summer school. I qualified for The Reach Program, which is for gifted African-American students in the Cleveland area. University School, a private school on 250 acres with a 50-million-dollar building, hosted the program. I did very well in the program, and University School offered me a scholarship to attend as a full-time student.

University School was very different from our community. St. Aloysius was 98 percent African-American. University School was six percent Black.

I remember my first day at University School. While we were in The Reach Program, my mom got into three car accidents. My aunt let her borrow a car that had been stolen. It had some dents and scratches, but it drove fine.

When we pulled up to the circle, I saw Lexuses, Beemers, and Audis, which were all brand new. The cars cost more than $50,000–$60,000

I was like, "Oh my goodness. What is going on?"

I asked my mom to park around the corner, and she did.

Once I walked up to the school, I was super intimidated. Nobody looked like me. It took me about three to four months to really get comfortable. Eventually, I realized it's not where you come from; it is what you can do. I could still open up a book, memorize material, calculate, and problem-solve.

I did well at University School and applied early decision to Columbia University's engineering school.

One day in December, after basketball practice, I called my grandma. She said you got a letter from Columbia.

I was like, "Is it a big letter or a little letter?"

She said, "I do not know."

I told her to open it, and it said I was accepted. It was one of the happiest days of my life.

I made 80k right out of college at UBS investment bank. By night I was just a party animal, making up for the partying I missed in college because I worked so hard. I had zero cares in the world. I had no sense of community or what it meant to donate to a charity.

I ended up leaving UBS when the housing market crashed, and I started my own marketing company and did various startups.

Randomly one day, while I happened to be visiting Cleveland, someone from our community development corporation knocked on my door.

They said, "Hey! We are starting this youth landscaping program. Would you like to be a part of it?"

At the time, I had this big boot on because I tore my Achilles playing basketball at Euclid Creek Park. I couldn't even walk.

He said, "It will pay 12 bucks an hour, and you can ride your bike. You don't have to do much but be a mentor to the kids."

I took that offer. I wasn't doing anything else. And I got to meet some of the youth that grew up in our neighborhood, the neighborhood I grew up in 10 years prior.

One particular kid changed my outlook on life. I forgot his real name, but his nickname is Bricks. He wanted to be an interior designer. He said he didn't want me to tell any of his peers because he was afraid of how they would treat him. They wanted to be musicians, rappers, or professional athletes.

I am like, "Dude, that's awesome. You can do anything you want from this neighborhood. Hey! Look at me."

And then something happened. I felt like I could make an impact. I felt like I had a moral obligation to support this community because I do have the power to create change.

I took over Cleveland's Youth Landscaping. We provided free landscaping services while helping at-risk youth acquire job skills and learn about financial literacy and entrepreneurship. In the three years I was there, I interviewed over 400 kids. We ended up hiring 25–50 kids each year, so 100–150 kids got paid nine bucks an hour, which is pretty good for a 14-year-old kid.

Recess Cleveland, my own nonprofit organization, actually started during that program.

See, at University School, we had a field day that we called Founder's Day. We played large-scale games of dodgeball, soccer, tug of war, and sports like that. I was really, really good at dodgeball in high school, so I wanted to relive those days. I asked five of my employees when was the last time they played dodgeball, and four of them said they never played.

I said, "Woah, you haven't played dodgeball? Woah, this is an injustice."

That's the moment I decided to start Recess Cleveland. We provide safe places to play in multiple communities throughout the summers, and then we move into schools during the school year.

We call it recess because it is unstructured. The people who attend decide what games we play. It is a way to get together.

I threw our first event on my birthday, August 9, 2016. That was the day the grandma showed everyone that "she's got legs." But it was so much more than just that moment.

We played 30-on-30 dodgeball. We played soccer. There was a hula-hoop contest. We gave away prizes. We ate together. It was a big kickback. We chilled and got to know our neighbors.

We ended up throwing 10 events that first year and averaged about 65 attendees. Recess events include food, music, dancing, and concerts.

Recently, one woman said at an event, "I lived in this neighborhood for 10 years, and I met one of my neighbors who also has lived in this neighborhood for 10 years for the first time today."

The number one outcome we want is relationship building and community engagement. Hopefully, that leads to other benefits, such as crime reduction.

Also, we recently just started adding wraparound services to some of our events. If you come to a Recess event, you might see The Greater Cleveland Food Bank giving away food. You might see a caravan making healthy smoothies. You might see a nonprofit organization giving away free books for children. It's all about enjoying the people in the neighborhood and taking advantage of the resources available to us.

Back in the day, Glenville was known as the gold coast. There are a ton of young and old Black entrepreneurs that own businesses up and down 105th Street. There are a bunch of athletes and well-accomplished writers who have ties to Glenville. Superman was created in Glenville. Olympian Jesse Owens stayed in Glenville for a bit. These are names that are internationally known.

What I want people to know, which I didn't necessarily realize when I pulled up to University School on my first day of school, is there are a lot of reasons to be proud of our community. I try to promote the fact that you can do anything you want to do from Glenville. Look at me!

I could have stayed in New York. I see all these major donors, with their names on buildings, who went off and made millions and decided to make a large donation. I could have been on that same path, and I still can, but I choose to be here, on the front lines with you. It gives me a sense of purpose. It gives me a sense of accomplishment when I see a smile on a kid's face.

I want to play kickball, give kids the experience of playing new games, and help children build relationships with other children in their neighborhood. I want to help our youth practice the skills needed to get a job and retain a job. I sleep a lot better at night, not only being a part of this community but helping us all realize the greatness that lies within it.

It doesn't matter what walk of life you are from or your socioeconomic status. At Recess, we are all playing kickball together. We are doing yoga, arts and crafts, or bouncing in the bounce house. We are helping shape our community. We are bonding together as we create not just any family but one big HAPPY family.

Your fellow Glenville native,
Alex Robertson, Founder of Recess Cleveland

What Matters Most Are Not the Memories We Are Missing

To my senior class,

We started the year off so strong. After losing to our crosstown rivals, Clarkstown South, in football four years in a row, during the playoffs this year, we finally did it. In the opening round of the postseason, we beat South 20-0. From the parents to the students, everyone was excited. It was an unforgettable moment that we all celebrated together.

It was supposed to be just the beginning of our senior-year celebrations. But those other significant events we have seen our older brothers, sisters, and friends attend, like prom and graduation, might not happen for us.

I remember when I first heard of the Coronavirus. It was across the world in China and spreading. At the time, it wasn't close to home. So, it was hard for me to be worried or mindful of a disease I didn't see or deal with personally. Then, it spread quickly.

In March, they canceled school for a few days but then switched it to a few weeks. When Governor Cuomo extended school closures a second time, I knew we weren't going back to normal so quickly. While our prom and graduation have yet to be canceled, there is a good chance that we won't go back to school this year.

We are all upset. For me, even more than possibly missing graduation or prom, I am most disappointed about the little moments. Senior Skip Day, where seniors head to the beach for a day, is probably not going to happen. Right now, we should be having our school-wide volleyball tournament. We won't get to share College Decision Day, taking pictures with our friends, as we reveal what's next for us. I miss even the day-to-day interactions, walking through halls and joking around with all of you.

However, what's been cool to see is that we seem to understand that this is bigger than us. I've seen from all of you a lot more advocacy, positive vibes, and optimism than I have seen complaints or pessimism. Some of you that I thought couldn't care less are advocating for your friends to stay at home. Others are trying to raise money for charities and GoFundMe accounts for those who need help right now. I have even seen some of you making masks and assisting first responders in any way that you can to help stop the spread of the virus.

I feel a real sense of community. No matter your group of friends, everybody wants to make sure everybody is OK. The other day, I posted a video basically saying wash your damn hands. People I haven't connected with in years have swiped up on it and told me it was great.

Instead of trying to find ways to meet up with our friends, we are listening to health officials and doing our best to adapt and make the most of the situation. I still talk to many of you every day on Zoom and group Facetime. Our amazing student council created an Instagram account and a Facebook group, posting our college decisions, so people can still share and celebrate their college choices together.

All of this is very hard, but we are doing our best and supporting our community, which has made me realize that, as a class, we genuinely do all care about each other.

So, even if we miss out on our final moments of high school, what I will remember most about this time is not the memories we lost but the character we showed.

I am proud to be a member of Clarkstown North's 2020 Senior Class.

Hopefully, I will see you all soon.

Go Rams!

Daniel Kantrowitz

Dear Buffalo, This Is How Our "Mafia" Backs More Than Just Our Bills

Dear Buffalo,

Many believe we created the Bills Mafia in 2010, but I've always been a part of the Bills Mafia, and so have you.

I grew up around Bills fandom. Many Catholic families have a picture of the pope in their house, but we had a picture of former star running back O.J. Simpson (which came down in 1994).

Every Sunday, my mother would invite friends over to watch the game. She'd make the same dip with pumpernickel bread. When I began high school, my friends started to come over as well. I watched every Bills game in our living room until the late '90s, when I moved out. For me, football has always been as much about the community surrounding the game as it is about the action on the field.

However, in 2010, thanks to former Bills receiver Stevie Johnson and ESPN reporter Adam Schefter, I began to realize the real power and meaning of our community — the Buffalo community.

It was late November. The Bills were 2-8 when they faced the Pittsburgh Steelers. Tied at 16 at the end of regulation, the game went into overtime, where Johnson dropped what would have been the game-winning touchdown. Disappointed and upset, he took out his frustrations on Twitter, where he blamed God for the dropped ball. The tweet went viral. As Bills fans, we rallied around him. You could see he was hurting. We made sure he knew the City of Good Neighbors was there for him.

The next day, around 4:00 p.m., Schefter retweeted Johnson. We teased Schefter with the hashtag #schefterbreakingnews since he shared the tweet 24 hours later. He ended up blocking a bunch of us. Fast forward to April 2011, I sent a tweet featuring those of us who got blocked by Schefter and referenced us as the #BillsMafia.

It was supposed to be a joke between me and some other Bills fans, but the players ended up discovering the hashtag. All of a sudden, the players are tweeting at us, and people think our opinions are valid.

Around the same time, my youngest daughter had a seizure just before her fifth birthday.

I remember being at the doctor and thinking, "Just fix her. Just bring her back to where she was. Please, make this go away."

The experience made me more aware and compassionate about the struggles of families with sick children. In August of 2011, I, along with two other Bills fans, decided we should do something positive with our growing Bills Mafia popularity. So, we started selling "Mafia" shirts and raising money for charities and people in need in Western New York. A lot of you bought our shirts. Within a couple of years, I created a business, 26

Shirts. Eventually, I left my career as a web developer. We now give about a third of our gross to different charities or people in the Buffalo community.

Early on, we made a shirt for a young man named Nathan. He was in high school and battling brain cancer. With medical bills and other unexpected expenses piling up, as they do for all families with sick children, we were able to sell several hundred shirts. Unfortunately, he passed away. But a few years later, his mother said in an interview that our help meant so much to her that she considers me a de facto member of her family.

We've helped hundreds of Buffalo families, raising more than $900,000 through the years.

It means so much to me to give back to Western New Yorkers, and I genuinely believe this is what I am supposed to be doing with my life.

While our beloved Bills have had their ups and downs through the years, it's exciting to see them doing well right now. They are 4-0 and in first place in the division. We can feel the city's positive energy with flags in front of people's houses and signs in the windows. But regardless of how this season or any season pans out, Bills Mafia isn't just a hashtag on Twitter we created in 2010. It's so much more. It is a name for our longstanding Buffalo family.

And what these last 10 years have shown me is that our family doesn't just love and support our teams. We truly care and watch out for each other.

Whoever you are, if you're connected to Western New York, Buffalo has got your back.

Go Bills!

Del Reid

To My Students, I Trained In The Ring, But This Is What I Fight For

To the kids who ask me why I still teach,

Often, many of you ask me, "Why are you a teacher if you are a professional boxer?"

The truth is, growing up, I didn't know that I wanted to be either. I just knew I wanted to be successful.

Adopted from Greece as a baby, I grew up in a small town in Massachusetts with wonderful Greek parents. They owned a restaurant, liquor store, and convenience store. My parents asked me if I wanted to take over the businesses, and I told them no. Instead, I liked the idea of helping people.

While I was always athletic, playing three sports in high school, including softball, which I played in college, I never thought about becoming a professional athlete. So, the focus was always on my education. At first, I became a speech therapist. I wanted to work in a hospital, but I got an internship working in a school. Quickly, I fell in love with being in the school and seeing how I made kids so happy every day. So, I went back to school to get a degree in teaching.

After I received my degree, I taught fourth grade in Springfield, Massachusetts. During that time, I went to an ATM late one night, and two people jumped in the back of my car, put a knife to my neck, and robbed me. I went home, and I cried the entire night.

About a week later, I went to the gym and told my friends what had happened.

They told me, "You should learn boxing. You should learn self-defense."

So, I went down to the South End Community Center in Springfield and met my first boxing coach, Victor James. Three months later, I fought a woman who had 24 fights and won the first Gold Medal for the Pan Ams in America. She whipped my butt. But even though I lost, I knew boxing was meant to be a part of my journey. From being in the ring to jumping rope and learning to fight, I loved it all. And a year later, I came back and fought that same opponent and won.

Ultimately, I moved to New York City, turned pro, and started teaching in New York City public schools. Boxing gave me instant credibility with all of you.

Students have shown up to class with my stats, or they have said stuff like, "My teacher will knock you out."

But more than credibility, boxing has given me more confidence.

When I first started boxing, I was always insecure about my weight. I grew up with filo dough dipped in butter, stuffed in my mouth, and every Greek meal you can imagine, so weight has always been an issue for me. As a child, I was bullied.

Around 2011, I remember reading a horribly insulting comment on the internet — something to the effect that I shouldn't be boxing and heavyweights are slow. In the comments, everyone started defending me.

A little bit down, there was one comment that said, "She really doesn't care what you think."

I took that to heart, and at that moment, I never flinched again about anything I saw online. It was the last time I was insulted or cried, or had my feelings hurt.

And I continued to box by night and teach by day.

As a teacher, I care more about your well-being than you memorizing Pythagorean theorems or something that's not going to really matter. I care about your emotional state and that you are safe when you are not in school.

Through the years, a lot of students have come back and thanked me. They thanked me for buying them clothes and food, not snitching on them, and giving them opportunities. I helped one of my kids get a YouTube contract because he was making little videos. Now, he's excelling in music.

I have always tried to be there for all of you, and you certainly have been there for me.

In 2014, I traveled to St. Martin to face a world champion. She was a little bit older, a tough girl, and had already won a world title. After the fight, in my heart, I knew I won, but I didn't know if the judges would give it to me.

I was waiting for the decision when they said, "And the new..."

Before he finished the sentence, I dropped to my knees, hitting the floor.

Then, I started screaming, "Mom!"

That's when my mom came running to the ring, and I gave her a big hug. The referee took my hand, and I stood up as he declared me a world champion. It was at that moment I knew I could do anything I set my mind to do.

That Monday, I went back to school with my new belt. It was like John Cena just showed up. All of the students there at the time were so excited and so proud of me. All the hard work and long days led me to a world title, one of my proudest accomplishments, only to be met recently by something we achieved together in school.

A few years ago, I noticed all these schools around our school, P.S. 183 in Rockaway Beach, Queens, got new playgrounds. So, I took my seventh graders outside one day and asked them to measure the yard. I wrote a letter to Donovan Richards, who was the district rep, and I started attending town meetings. I just kept pushing and pushing, and I wasn't going away until all of you also got a new playground. One day, he finally responded. He came to our school, and I showed him the plans. He was so happy that we created the initial ideas for the playground together. After three years of meetings, phone calls, and picking out materials, they are going to start building in just a few weeks.

When we got approved for a $1.3 million grant, I remember I went outside my condo right behind our school and stared at the spot where they are going to build the playground for a good five minutes. Then, I began to cry. I couldn't believe I was going to be able to do this for all of you. It was like winning a world title all over again.

These last two years, I tore both my rotator cuffs and had two surgeries. I am on the up and up and back in the gym training. If I get to fight again, cool. If I don't, I am alright with that. There are so many ways I am still involved with the sport. I am the vice president and registration chair of USA Boxing Metro, which creates opportunities for kids in New York City. Also, I am a part of the Give A Kid A Dream charity out of Gleason's Gym, which helps disadvantaged youth become champions in life through boxing.

The sport of boxing has given me so much. I have shadowboxed in the ring with Usher, and traveled the world. The sport has shown me I can beat the odds. It has given me a level of self-confidence and empowerment, allowing me to achieve more success than I ever imagined as a child.

But success isn't about the money I make or the titles I have won. It's about being a good person and giving to others.

So, I am thankful for the sport because even though I initially stepped in the ring for myself, boxing trained me to fight for all of you.

Boxing is my hobby, but I teach because all of you are my purpose.

Mrs. Lamonakis

This Is What I Want To Say To Those Who Helped Me Make It To the Big Leagues

To all the people who helped me reach my dream,

When I was a young boy, my dad, Pedro Borbón Sr., played in the big leagues for the Cincinnati Reds. I lived with my mother and my brother in the Dominican Republic, but I would visit my dad in the summer. He would take me over to a fountain near the field and give me some quarters.

He would say, "Think of a dream. Then, make a wish and throw the quarters in the fountain."

At that time, I didn't have much of a dream. While growing up in the Dominican Republic, my dad was rarely around. When I went to play baseball in the field with other kids, everyone expected me to be great because of my dad. It was big shoes to fill. And while I had good aim and could throw the ball, I had no confidence. Truthfully, I always thought that I would one day run one of my father's businesses — never did I think I, too, could or would play professional baseball.

My life completely changed when my dad abandoned us and started a new family in the United States. I went from being a rich kid to having nothing — not even essentials like food and clothing. I told my mom I couldn't live like that and wanted to move to the United States, where I thought I would have more opportunities to help my family. That's when some of you began to come into my life.

At 14 years old, I moved to the Bronx in New York City. It was not an easy place to live in the '80s. There were times when I thought I was stepping on glass and it was crack bottles. I saw people get shot right in front of me. There were nights where a husband was beating his wife next door. There was nothing I could do because if I had called the cops, I would have been a snitch, and I would have been in trouble. I never knew if I would make it at home at night. The city was filled with so much drugs and violence.

I attended DeWitt Clinton High School. One day, I was walking to the lunchroom, and the security guard asked to see my ID to make sure it was my time to have lunch. I showed him my ID, and he saw my name, Pedro Borbón.

He goes, "Pedro Borbón, are you related to the baseball player?"

I said, "Yeah, that's my dad."

He said, "What the hell are you doing in the Bronx?"

I explained that I lived with an uncle and was there for school.

He said, "You don't play baseball?"

I told him, "No."

He asked me to try out, and I said no. So, he waited for me after school and took me over to the field. He asked me to throw a few pitches. So, I probably threw about 15, and 14 of them were strikes.

That's when he said, "You're pitching for me Friday."

He was the junior varsity coach and wasn't taking no for an answer.

That first game, I went seven innings, and I think I gave up one hit and struck out 14 or 15. At that moment, a dream was born, and all of a sudden, I had some confidence. My JV coach is among you — the people who helped me realize my dream — and I want to say thank you.

After winning Rookie of the Year on JV, I met Steve Nathanson, my varsity coach, the following season. He took me under his wing and taught me the game — everything from the rules to how to throw a changeup. He helped me fall in love with the game and stay focused. More and more, I started to believe I could make it, which made me want to put in the work. My uncle was a Vietnam vet. He used to go jogging every morning, and I started to join him. In high school, I never drank or did drugs because I never wanted to do anything that could affect my game. My work ethic was second to none and remained that way for years. Coach Nathanson is among all of you, and I want to say thank you.

During high school, a big-time sports agent named Jerry Davis gave me a job paying $150 a week. All I did was pick up newspapers and talk baseball. When I finished high school, the Milwaukee Brewers drafted me in the 35th round. I knew people who got drafted in the sixth or seventh rounds, and I was better than them. But Milwaukee told me they thought I needed more experience and suggested I go to college. They told me if I wanted to sign, all they could offer me was a glove and a plane ticket.

I wanted to quit right there. I didn't want to do anything. But thank God Jerry Davis wouldn't let me give up. He called Ranger Junior College in Texas and got me an opportunity there. Jerry is among all of you, and I want to say thank you.

In Texas, my coach, Don Flowers, turned me from a boy to a man. He was the first person to be really tough on me and yell at me. I was not into school, so he signed me up for welding and auto mechanics to get me enough credits to play. But I used to fall asleep in the cars during my auto mechanic class. One day, the professor called Coach Flowers while I was sleeping, and he came to my class, pulled me out of the car, and nearly killed me. That day at practice, he made me go on a five-and-a-half-mile run in 100-degree weather. If I didn't make a certain time, I would have had to run it all over. Coach Flowers taught me discipline. He was among all of you, and I want to say thank you.

After my time at junior college, I got drafted by the White Sox. I had a great rookie ball. They took me to instructional ball the year after, but one of the coaches didn't like me.

I asked him a simple question.

I said, "How come I am going back to rookie ball after spring training?"

He looked at me and said, "Are you better than those guys?

I said, "I don't think I'm better, but I have better numbers."

He responded, "Those guys got drafted high. They are going to play. We don't have room for you."

I said, "So, what am I doing here?"

The White Sox released me the next day, and I went back to Texas. By this time, I was married, and I needed a job. So, I worked in an oil field as a fire watcher, sitting around all night with a fire extinguisher, waiting for somebody or something to light up on fire.

For a while, I was lost. I didn't talk to my mom for a year and a half because I was too embarrassed.

While realistically, I thought my baseball career was over, I didn't stop running or training. At times, I used to play catch with my then-wife's grandfather.

One day he said to me, "Man, you are throwing harder than usual. You need to go try out for a team."

He didn't let me stop believing in myself. That is why he is also among you, and I want to say thank you.

I ended up playing for a summer league team. That's when I realized my fastball went from 87–88 mph to 93–94 mph. The Atlanta Braves signed me, which turned out to be my big opportunity.

Immediately, I had success in the minors as a starter, but they threw me into the bullpen.

I told them, "OK, you throw me in the bullpen, then I am going to be the best reliever you have ever had."

After our team won the championship, I was packing to go home when my manager from Double-A told me I needed to go to Florida because they might call me up.

I went for two weeks and didn't get a call-up.

Finally, I'm running in the outfield, and one of the coaches comes over and says, "Hey now, you've been bitching about going home. Well, it's time for you to go."

So, I'm pissed off and ask, "Where's my plane ticket?"

He said, "Go get it from the office. And by the way, say hi to the guys for me."

I was like, "What guys? Who do you know in Texas?"

He said, "You're not going to Texas. You're going to the big leagues."

I thought to myself, "Holy shit!"

I didn't believe it and was almost late for my flight. I didn't even have proper clothes. This guy, who was way smaller than me, lent me his clothes, and I looked like a freaking ballerina wearing his shirt.

After 1992 I started making a little more money, and I was able to help my mom and my brothers a bit more, which was my goal all along.

I had some incredible moments throughout my major league career, including striking out Barry Bonds, Ken Griffey Jr., and Tony Gwynn. In 1995, I pitched in and won a World Series. But of all the moments I had in my nine-year Major League Baseball career, which included five different teams, my absolute favorite memory was when I went to Cincinnati for the first time as a major league player. The hotel was in front of the fountain I threw quarters in with my dad as a child.

I went down there and threw a bunch of change in the fountain, only to realize that I was finally living the dream that that little boy couldn't even see until he met all of you.

From the many uncles who took me in and treated me like their son to my teammates, friends, and coaches who supported me and listened to me through the years, there are so many of you that contributed to me making it.

To each one of you, I just want to say THANK YOU.

Pedro Borbón Jr.

Thank You, Astros, By Giving My Dad Baseball In October, You Gave My Dad So Much More

To the Houston Astros,

I want to thank you for giving my dad October baseball.

As a season ticket holder and lifetime fan, I am attending the World Series with my 87-year-old father.

In my family, the love for the game was passed down from one generation to the next. My grandfather used to play barnstorming leagues around South Texas, going from little town to little town to play baseball. He was a heck of a pitcher, and a scout wanted to sign him, but my great-grandfather didn't understand the idea of playing a kid's game to make a living. So, he wouldn't let him sign. But he continued to play in barnstorming leagues way into his 40s.

My father watched him play, and that's where his love for the sport began. As a child, my dad would ride his bike in town to hear the World Series on the radio from the barbershop window.

In 1959, my father was serving in the Army in Germany when rumors surfaced of indoor baseball being played in Houston, Texas. While still serving in 1960, the league announced that Houston would get a National League franchise. In 1965, when the Astrodome opened, he went with his father.

My dad was a huge Astros fan by the time I came along, and I have pictures of me as an infant dressed in overalls and a jersey. When I was seven, my dad became my T-ball coach, and on September 6, 1986, when I was 10 years old, he took me to my first Astros game.

It was a Saturday afternoon, and it was raining hard. We drove two hours from my hometown of Victoria, Texas. I remember walking into the dome and seeing all the colors: the green turf, the gray wall with the orange stripe on top, and then those rainbow-colored jerseys. It was amazing to me.

Jose Cruz, a Houston legend, hit a two-out, two-run walk-off home run in that game. The Astros won 7-6, and the big scoreboard lit up, and "Crruuuuuuuuzzz" was written across it. I knew at that moment that, like my dad, I, too, loved the game.

As the years went on, sports remained the way I connected to my father, and he nurtured my love and passion for baseball. We talked about baseball at dinner time. We went to games together. When he picked me up from school, he'd tell me that I needed to finish my homework by 7:00 p.m. so we could watch the game or listen on the radio together. Storytime, for me, meant Astros history. He told me how in 1980, the Astros and the Phillies played an epic playoff series — four extra-inning games. He said the Astros came so close to getting their first World Series. Every story he told, I just gobbled it up.

At a young age, while watching an Astros game with my dad, I decided I wanted to be an announcer. By age 16, I was calling Little League games and working at a radio station. My dad always encouraged me.

As I grew up, left the house, and started my career, my father and I continued to go to games and travel the country, watching the Astros play. But 10 years ago, in 2011, our lives changed forever.

My dad was visiting me in Houston to go to an Astros game. It was around lunchtime, and I was going to get us some food. He was using a walker because of back surgery when he almost fell, and I grabbed him.

Then, I noticed he was limping and said, "Dad, raise your hand like a baseball pitcher."

He couldn't, and I noticed his lip started to droop. Immediately, I called 911. My dad had a massive stroke. He is now paralyzed and confined to a wheelchair. To this day, he still has cognitive issues, and speaking is difficult for him.

There are so many aspects of everyday life that my dad loved that he can't do anymore. He is very much a people person, and he loved talking with people, hearing their stories, and then regurgitating their stories to other people. His favorite food is Mexican, but his throat has become weak over the years, so now we have to feed him through a tube.

He spends much of his days sleeping and lying down, as he has lost so much of his freedom. But, thankfully, he has not lost baseball. And it means so much to me because I am still able to share baseball with him. I am now an announcer for the Sugar Land Skeeters, the Triple-A affiliate of the Astros.

My mom will pop on one of my games when he's lying in bed, and she'll say, "Do you know who that is?"

And he'll light up and say, "Gerald."

All my life until 2017, my dad would tell me, "The Astros are going to win the World Series, and we're going to be there."

We had heartbreak after heartbreak. But in 2017, we were at a watch party at Minute Maid Park when you all clinched the series. The tears were flowing as I hugged my father.

All offseason, my dad was so happy.

He'd tell his nurses, "Hey, you know, the Astros won the World Series."

This year, you made it back to the World Series, and my dad and I have been there along the way.

When I wheeled him in for Game 1 against the Chicago White Sox, he said, "I missed this place."

And when you turned a 6-4-3 double play in the series against the Boston Red Sox, my dad looked at me with a massive smile on his face and said, "Here you go."

I cherish every single moment that I get to watch you play with my dad. As much as I can, I try to hold on to every second because I know this won't last forever. I know you will have some bad years, and I know my father won't be around forever.

If my dad gets to witness you guys win another World Series, it would bring him so much joy.

But even if you don't, I am grateful for this season. I am thankful for each game you play. I am thankful for every inning and every at-bat. I am thankful to all of you for giving my dad baseball in October because when you give my father baseball, you give him life.

Good luck!

A lifetime fan and broadcaster,
Gerald Sanchez

LAUREN'S THOUGHTS

The Life We Live Is **Determined** By The Love We Feel

When I was a little girl, I had a small bedroom that overlooked our front yard. My wallpaper was white with pastel pink and gray hearts, and many decorative pillows in various shapes and sizes filled my bed. Every night, I would crawl under my covers, and my mother would come in soon after.

She would sit on my matching bed set, read me a book or tell me a story, and then say, "Give me some sugar."

That's when I would lean over and hug and kiss her. One kiss was never enough.

After the first embrace, she would purse her lips and say, "More sugar, please."

Throughout my life, my parents have given me a whole lot of sugar; they've been loving, supportive, and affectionate.

As I got older, our bedtime rituals changed from storytime and kisses to opening up about my worry of the week or the disaster of the day. In fourth grade, I walked through my school's hallway with four or five girls. As we headed toward the bathroom, one of the girls asked me to tell her which boy I liked in our grade. She promised to keep it a secret. So, I told her. Before we reached our destination, she rushed back to the classroom to tell the boy, who then pretended to throw up in front of the whole class, implying that I was gross. While I remained stoic in class and at dinner that night, when my mother came to say goodnight, she knew something was off. So, I told her what happened.

She told me to look in the mirror.

As I made eye contact with my reflection, she said, "You are beautiful."

Then she said, "Every day, you are going to get more and more beautiful. No matter what any boy says or does, I want you to know that, and I want you to always believe that."

And just like that, I didn't just feel better; I felt hopeful.

My dad was less interested in talking about boys and teased me about dating and relationships throughout my childhood and teen years. But since I was a young child, I had a lot of ambition. Whether it was sports or school, my father fueled my passions. Every day, he told me I was the best and capable of anything and everything I wanted. And he didn't only provide me with the resources to chase my dreams, such as an expensive education and travel soccer, but he was there guiding me every step of the way.

He came to every soccer game I played, and what I remember most is not so much him yelling from the sidelines (which he did plenty) but the car rides home, where he would go over each play, good and bad, and give his feedback. The man had never played soccer a day in his life. Who knows if he had a clue what he was talking about, but that wasn't important to me. The time he spent with me and the level of attention he gave me mattered most.

To this day, my parents are my best friends and support system. When I started The Unsealed, I was terrified and stressed, and I wouldn't take so much as a break to eat a full meal with my family.

My dad stopped me one day and said, "What is going on here? Why are you so scared?"

I told him, "If I don't succeed — if this company doesn't succeed, there is no one to blame, no fingers to point. It's on me. If I fail, it will be hard proof that I am not all you believe I am, and I don't want to disappoint you."

Without hesitation, my father said, "If you wake up every day with a positive attitude, you can never disappoint me. I will always be proud of you."

While my father keeps me mentally on track, my mother actively writes for The Unsealed, partakes in every show and workshop, and even sends emails for me. My mom is also still my first phone call when I have a problem of any kind: a relationship, a life transition, or a headache.

My parents have made the hard days of my life a lot easier and have made the best moments of my life more fulfilling, as I know my happiness is their peace.

What I hope you took from this chapter is that more than a job, an award, financial success, travel, a Chanel bag, or an Armani suit, it is the people in your life that give you sugar, aka love, affection, attention, and support, that truly make life so very sweet.

Lauren

Conclusion

CONCLUSION

It's The Spirit Within You That Unseals Your Superpowers

My dad always loves telling the story of the day I was born. Most children come into this world screaming and kicking, fighting for their lives. But apparently, that wasn't the case for me. According to my father, as I mentioned earlier in a letter to my dad, I didn't scream or cry after entering this world. Instead, I looked him straight in the eye and smiled. That's when he says he knew he was in trouble.

I never knew why he thought he was in trouble until I asked him when I sat down to write this piece. For years, I thought maybe he knew I would be tough. Perhaps he knew I would have boundless energy excited to experience each day and all it has to offer. Maybe he knew I would be fearless and independent, unafraid to go after everything I wanted. It turns out none of those are true.

He said, I had a look in my eyes that screamed, "I am going to have a whole lot of fun in this life, and it's going to cause some trouble."

However, at that moment in the hospital, neither of us knew what challenges I would face, what barriers would get in the way of my dreams, or what trauma I would endure that would attempt to threaten my spirit. The spirit that he saw the moment I was born.

There is so much in life we can't control. Christopher Rivero did not choose to be homeless as a child. Eric LeGrand did not intend to get paralyzed playing the sport he loved, and I had no way of predicting that those boys I met at a high school party planned to drug and abuse me.

Struggles and unexpected hardships are part of life. And so often, they cause us to become jaded, lost, hurt, scared, and guarded.

A few years after my assault, a friend commented, without knowing my story, that rapists should be charged with murder because when you rape someone, you may not kill someone's body, but you do kill their spirit. A piece of them will be gone forever.

When she said that, it hit me hard. I didn't want any of me to be lost, especially not my spirit.

Eventually, I realized, like many others in this book, that while I couldn't control what happened to me, I could control how it impacted me and my life.

It took me time to heal, a long time. But the more I wrote, shared, and accepted my story, the better I felt.

I created The Unsealed, its mission, and its community, not as a product of my pain but as a reflection of my perseverance and the perseverance of others.

Your challenges don't have to kill your spirit. If you are honest about your struggles, stay determined, continue to dream, and have faith in the universe, your hardships can fuel your soul.

And I hope this book teaches you that no matter how your story unfolds or what life throws at you, your superpowers lie in your will not to allow the hurt you endure to change who you are or how you live. Instead, let it inspire you to become the best version of who you have been since the day you entered this world.

With love, hope, and faith,
A woman who likes to have a lot of fun and cause just a little bit of trouble — Lauren Brill

If you would like
the chance to be
featured in our
next book or if you
simply would like
to use your truth
to help others, tell
your story on

TheUnsealed.com

Acknowledgements

Acknowledgements

Starting an online company with a big idea and very little money is incredibly difficult. But thanks to the people around me, The Unsealed has achieved what many told me would be impossible.

A very special thank you to my parents, Shelley and Alan Brill. The words "thank you" will never be enough to express my gratitude for both of you. Throughout my childhood and adulthood, you've never told me that my dreams were too big or unrealistic. Instead, you have tried to help me however you could so I could achieve everything I want in life. I am forever grateful for your love and dedication to my happiness.

My drive to succeed began at a young age. I was a competitive child, and my older brother, who is brilliant, set a high bar. To my brother, thank you for showing me an extraordinary work ethic and pushing me to challenge myself, especially when I experienced self-doubt. I possessed the confidence to start my company and write this book because you told me you believed in me and my ideas.

To the members of The Unsealed Community, my dreams would not be possible without you. You have shared your stories and shown up for our weekly shows. Because of you, my vision to create change in the world through open letters is coming to life.

To everyone featured in this book, thank you for trusting me with your truth and continuing to support the growth of The Unsealed by allowing me to share your stories in this book.

Lastly, a very special thank you to my friends, mentors and teachers, who have provided me with daily advice, knowledge, feedback, love, and encouragement: Delano Massey, Marty Shagrin, Varoon Sahgal, Willard Ogan, Willie Parker, Marcel Blythe, Rob King, Ron Insana, Liz Abzug, Hue Jackson, Kimberly Diemert, Tim Graham, Mike Hill, Alyson Cohen, Tonia Marra, Chip Mahaney, Lou DiBella, Gretchen Carlson, Jonathan Moser, Kevin Kaminski, Paul Mueller, Mike Lardner, Leandra Lardner, Vic Carucci, Joe Schlaerth, Ruth Wilson, Fred Daly, and Andrew Schonebaum.

I love you all.

Lauren

Made in the USA
Middletown, DE
14 July 2024

57241539R10267